For more than three decades, Paul Diel (1893-1972) has had an expanding influence on the post-Jungian generation of psychologists in France. The further expansion of that influence is attested by the fact that his complete works are currently being translated into German and by the additional fact of the appearance of the present book in English.

D1255601

SYMBOLISM IN THE BIBLE

OTHER BOOKS BY THE AUTHOR

Fear and Anguish: Primary Triggers of Survival and Evolution (Hunter House)

Psychological Healing: An Intimate Approach to Curing the Whole Person (Hunter House)

The Psychology of Motivation (Hunter House)

SYMBOLISM IN THE BIBLE

*The Universality of Symbolic Language
and its Psychological Significance*

Paul Diel

Introduction by Jane Diel

Translated from the French by Nelly Marans

1817

Harper & Row, Publishers, San Francisco

Cambridge, Hagerstown, New York, Philadelphia, Washington
London, Mexico City, São Paulo, Singapore, Sydney

Originally published in French by Payot, Paris, in 1975, under the title *Le symbolisme dans la bible*.

SYMBOLISM IN THE BIBLE: *The Universality of Symbolic Language and its Psychological Significance*. English translation copyright © 1986 by Harper & Row, Publishers.

Library of Congress Cataloging-in-Publication Data

Diel, Paul, 1893–
  Symbolism in the Bible.

  Translation of: Symbolisme dans la Bible.
  Includes bibliographical references.
  1. Symbolism in the Bible.   I. Title.
BS477.D5313   1986   ·   220.6′4   85-51106
ISBN 0-86683-475-3

FIRST EDITION

86 87 88 89 90 RRD 10 9 8 7 6 5 4 3 2 1

TABLE OF CONTENTS

SECOND PART

INTRODUCTION

Paul Diel was particularly attached to this book and when he was stricken by an illness that proved to be fatal, he realized that he would never be able to finish what meant so much to him. He then asked me to complete the work on the basis of the documentation he had prepared.

Since French was not his native tongue, I had always edited his books and I undertook this task with one concern only: absolute respect for his thought. Fortunately, he had been able to complete most of the work and I just had to edit the balance for which he had left a first draft, as well as set up a sequence for certain chapters he had not yet finalized.

This book does not claim to present a complete interpretation of symbolism in Scripture; though such a work is possible in principle, its very magnitude would require more than a lifetime of labor. The purpose of the author was quite different: he intended to apply to the Judeo-Christian texts his new method of translation of symbolic language previously used in his book on Greek mythology, a method stemming from his psychological theory, the constant basis for his research.

In order to present a clear overall picture, the application of the method has been limited to the texts of Genesis, the Prologue of John, and the Epistles of Paul (fall, incarnation, and resurrection). Restricting himself to this fundamental trilogy, the author had no other purpose than to show the possibility of a scientific translation of symbolism in Scripture. He left it to the mythologists and linguists to argue the merits of the various texts and their versions, trusting in the fruits of their labors as they appear in the best biblical translations. The quotations used throughout this book have been taken from The Jerusalem Bible and the Revised Standard Version Bible.

The theme of the present book is basically the same as that of a previous work entitled *La Divinité*. It carries on and enlarges upon the decisive epistemological contribution Paul Diel made to the sciences of man. To quote the words Albert Einstein used more than thirty years ago: "I read your book and was deeply impressed. It offers a new unitary conception of the meaning of life based on the contribution of Freud which it develops. Thus it is not only a remedy for the lack of ethical discipline prevailing in our time, but it also has the magnitude of a philosophical study which will have, I am sure, a permanent place in the history of ideas throughout the ages."

Jane Diel

FOREWORD

In previous works, the author of the present book undertook to analyze man's inner motivations, and to show their prevailing importance in meaningful or senseless behavior.

Motives—which must be distinguished from external aims of activity, environmental excitations (or stimuli)—are the products of a ceaseless inner deliberation leading to a reactive discharge. Even the slightest effort of self-observation makes us aware of such a psychic phenomenon, and there is a need to study this deliberation and its fruits, the inner motivations. This can only be achieved through a method adapted to the object of such a research—generally quite neglected—by scrutinizing the innermost depths of our psychic functioning.

One of the most important manifestations of human life—if not the most important—lies in the fact that the inner deliberation does not only bring about voluntary decisions aimed at a reactive mastery of the environment. It also creates guiding values and even systems of ideas, ideologies that are more or less right, and whose main purpose is not simply a utilitarian adjustment to the environment, but an adjustment to the meaning of life. The inner deliberation about what man ought to do with his life creates therefore a vision of guiding values, which are superior motives of action because they determine a will to self-mastery in the presence of external excitations.

Unfortunately, the valuating spirit that presides over the inner deliberation is not infallible. It is prone to error, and thus gives birth to contradictory guiding values, which in turn cause a disorienting anxiety,[1] and the latter is the ground of all the "illnesses of the mind."

Yet, there is a unifying ancestral guiding vision which is the foundation of all peoples' cultures: the mythical vision preserved in the various mythologies which are genuine historical documents. From this vision stem all contradictory ideologies (be they theological, historical, or even scientific), either through a credulous adherence or through doubt and criticism leading to a denial of the mythical vision seen only as vain fabulation.

The two approaches share one error: they take the narrative aspect of the myth at face value. The mythical vision is characterized by its enigmatic and symbolical expression which is irrational and illogical. The multiform symbolic tales of the various peoples' mythologies can also give the impression that they, too, are contradictory. However, the

---

[1] In French *angoisse* (German: Angst). A more satisfying term would be "anguish" but the term "anxiety" is commonly used in all English and American psychoanalytical writings.

fact is that there is only one mythical vision stemming from the human faculty to symbolize, even though it is expressed in the mythologies through the most variegated symbolic images. Nevertheless, all mythologies share typical symbols, even when historical interaction would have been impossible.

The most constant symbolism, the very foundation of the vision shared by all the myths, is the struggle between deities on the one hand and demons and monsters on the other hand, expressing the inner conflict between right and wrong motivations, a conflict which is nothing else than inner human deliberation.

If we posit that the mythical vision is an ancestral product of human deliberation (the elements being multiform motives, whether vitally right or wrong), should it not also be true that each symbol in itself, must have as a hidden meaning one or the other the positive or negative elements of human deliberation, one or the other motives which make up the essential factors of human activity? Mythical language would thus have an extremely precise vocabulary and even a grammar shared by all the mythologies, since it is based on the laws ruling the meaningful value or senseless nonvalue of the inner deliberation. The common meaning of all mythologies, no matter what their narrative facade happens to be, can only be unveiled through a preliminary study of motivations.

Such a unique method of accurate deciphering goes radically against all attempts at easy interpretations: against the interpretation that sees in the myths nothing but a vain fabulation as well as against the literal interpretation of the symbols. It also opposes the attempt to degrade deciphering into a literary game contented with a summary interpretation, based on vague and arbitrary feelings, of the so-called undecipherable enigma that myths bring forth in the human soul.

The author has endeavored to establish his method by analyzing the "God" symbol, and by translating in the present book the symbolic language of the Judeo-Christian myth into a conceptual language and a psychological terminology. His intention in extending the verification of the method to include the symbolic—and highly illogical—elements in the biblical texts is not to provoke vain polemics. The only goal is a quest for truth, a quest which is legitimate even if it does not agree with conventional beliefs.

FIRST PART

Chapter I

History of the God Image

A. Animism

All religions share a foundation of premythical and mythical fables. Whatever the latitude or the historical context of the peoples who created them, these fables or myths have a religious content of surprising conformity. They invariably deal with deities, monsters, the struggle of the man-hero against monsters and the help granted by gods to men. Imagined as residing on top of the mountains or above the clouds, the deities take on a human form and come down to earth to reveal their existence to mortals as well as to impose their will upon them. The deities are at the same time metaphysical images and ethical guides.

We are perfectly sure that the gods of the ancient world never really existed and thus that they were created by the—still purely imaginative—mind[1] of primitive man. But the gods of all the peoples and tribes—though they are not identical in their representations or visual images—always have the same function of moral protectors and guides: the formulations may be somewhat different, but the same ethical intentions are expressed. Since the latter are imaginatively personified by symbolic figures of real persons, would it not be right to acknowledge in the psychic functioning of man the existence of a certain innate inspiration, a sort of ethical conscience which is more than conscious—superconscious—proper to human nature? Man is superconsciously aware of the immutable ethical law that rules his life and he

---

[1] The French word *esprit* has been translated either by "mind" or "spirit" according to context. Diel defines it as the organizational aspect of matter. The concept is thus extended to the whole of nature instead of being restricted to man's thought. This definition is fundamental for the understanding of Diel's thought.

It would have been preferable to use "spirit" all the time for two reasons: (1) because the word "mind" is too extensive, covering at the same time psyche, spirit and intellect, which are concepts that Diel clearly distinguishes (see note 2 in chapter I, on intellect) and (2) "spirit" would link up better with "spiritualize," which, as defined by Diel, is the fundamental function of the human spirit.

However "spirit" has spiritual connotations that render it difficult to use in a scientific text such as this is.

projects it onto superhuman and supernatural figures which he calls "deities."

The common feature of all fabulations (religious or secular) is that they create characters—often animals speaking and acting like human beings or even magically animated objects—though there is no intention of passing them off as actual beings. What characterizes fabulating imagination is that it arouses our interest, moves us with the help of fables, and leads us to guess, to discover behind the events, the struggles, the peripeties of the narration, a secret significance which concerns us. In fact, it refers to our own intentions which are known to us even though we refuse to acknowledge them because they are often too painful for us to avow (intentions that are either too good or too evil). Without aiming at convincing through logics, the fable—if successful—acts on our emotivity and even on our repressed feelings of guiltiness. All artistic works have the cathartic function of creating fabulous characters. Here too, the metaphorical representation pointing to a hidden meaning, magnifies the emotional impact, providing however the symbolizing process is not artificial trickery. Mythologies are the highest of all artistic and ethical manifestations.

They are not individual creations but superindividual creative explosions, superconscious dreams expressing the meaning of life. Created by the primitive soul, mythologies exerted on primitive peoples and even on highly cultured ones a suggestive influence whose motivating power is difficult for us to perceive since we are overintellectualized.[2] In the primitive soul, premythical and mythical fabulations bred neither belief nor doubt but had an emotional impact enabling it to grasp the underlying meaning without any explanation.

On the other hand, religions and their explanatory theologies do impose a belief in the actual existence of the fabulous figures called deities. Their intention is to turn the imaginative fabulations which inspire true religiosity into a popular religion, based on a common belief dictating rules of behaviour, rites and taboos. Stemming from mythical fabulations, religions become social institutions. Such a conventional foundation is meant to strengthen the communal bond which was originally and essentially based on ethical superconsciousness and its fabulous creations, the true support of all cultures (animism, polytheism, monotheism). But on the other hand, conventionalization saps

---

[2]In the terminology of Diel's psychology of motivation, intellect means the capacity, proper to man, to act upon the outer world, to adapt it to his needs. It must be distinguished from the spirit which is the capacity to find essential orientation in the inner world and with respect to the meaning of life. Intellectualization is therefore an evolutionary stage bearing the seed of involution when man, dominated by his intellect, does not refer to the meaning of life. (This will be developed in the translation of chapters 2 and 3 of Genesis.)

the suggestive force of the underlying truth. Religions, wanting to impose a belief in the reality of the images, provoke skepticism which in turn destroys religious conventions.

In their widest and deepest significance, the premythical and mythical images deal with the ephemeral nature of temporal life and anxiety in the face of intemporal and eternal death. Images with an ethical meaning deal with temporal life and its sensible management. Metaphysical symbols deal with man's anxiety in the face of *death and its unfathomable mystery* and therefore with *the mystery of life* which leads unavoidably to death.

Thus metaphysical images do not express a tangible reality. They project the figurative personification of the deities (glorified ethical qualities) into a hereafter in accordance with the real fact of the immutability of ethical laws that cannot be changed with the passage of time. The soul (deep emotivity) and the spirit (the need for explanation, even of the unexplainable mystery) create the consoling vision of a divine providential intentionality. *Providence,* which is supposed to have intentionally created the universe—the latter being also subject to the ethical law of harmony—is represented as a person who watches over human intentions throughout life and with whom, in the framework of the metaphysical image, the man of good intentions will live after his death and for all eternity.

Even today, religious beliefs are far more deeply rooted in the somewhat naïve and touching image of the "good God" and his providential love than in the theoretical God of the theologies. Even in the atheist, when he is hopelessly confronted by the strokes of fate, there is a return to the ancestral magical belief in Providence. But the belief in Providence, though deeply rooted in the magical and animistic layer of man's personality, can stifle true religiosity which is awe in the face of the unfathomable depths of life and death. Who, among us, has not felt the emotion of mystery either when looking at the vastness of the starry sky or when confronted with the death of a loved one? Such an awakening of religiosity is too fleeting and disappears in the face of material conventions that occupy our attention so exclusively, but also in the face of religious conventions pretending to explain that which cannot be explained. A mystery which is explained is neither an explanation nor a mystery.

Sacred awe is aroused only by mystery, experienced as a feeling of the implacable solitude of man in the face of his destiny. Religiosity is intensified when man manages to detach himself—to the extent of actually uprooting the magical core of his attachment—from the idea of Providence, and begins to perceive, to sense, to know that nobody watches over him, certainly not God.

God is the image of mystery and man is only responsible for his own meaningful or senseless intentions; mystery is not a thing or a being existing outside the world and life itself. Mystery does not begin or end; it is before life, during life, and after death.

Human life has meaning and value only insofar as it is anchored in mystery, insofar as emotion in the presence of the mystery of life and death calms metaphysical anxiety instead of exalting it by speculation, insofar as man loves life in spite of death (and this is the only love that is not sentimental), knowing that mystery is everywhere around him and in him as well. Human life has meaning and value only insofar as man respects himself, others and all that is alive and existing—as mysterious phenomena meant to pass away—while feeling or knowing that in spite of the ephemeral nature of all things, nothing has being outside of mystery.

In comparison with this religious emotion which is the underlying meaning of all mythical images, whose facade only is fabulous, a belief in images mistaken for realities and all the correlative theologies are nothing but shallow flutter and social convention.

Religiosity is not a supernatural and metaphysical feeling. Its true and natural foundation is *ethical feeling: a certainty of self-responsibility. Man is his own Providence:* his essential destiny—his joys or anxieties in life, expressions of his vital value or nonvalue—depends on himself and no one else. *The immanence of ethos*—i.e., immanent justice—is not a fabulous imagination but a superconscious reality, creating all metaphysical images, all deities (who judge human behavior invented by the human spirit from animism to monotheism. In the soul of the primitive man (as in the soul of the child), the feeling of responsibility is still vague and open to all kinds of imaginative interpretations. It is experienced as a magical feeling of guilt and is felt all the more strongly that it is vague as to the actual fault, so that any natural happening often unexplainable in its cause, any human action often more or less ill-intended, can provoke a fear of providential punishment (just as a disobedient child lives in an ill-defined dread of his father). Primitive man, helpless in the face of all kinds of disasters (flood, drought, epidemics), interprets them as punishment for faults that were committed by the tribe or a member of the tribe. He creates "thanksgiving" rituals expressing his guilty regret and the promise to purify himself of his evil intentions, to "sacrifice" them to the Father-Providence in order to obtain his forgiveness and to feel once again that he is the beloved child. In primitive man, such an attitude is not infantile but natural since *the protective deities are his deceased ancestors* who are imagined as living in the hereafter and retaining their patriarchal powers.

These primitive beliefs have a deep suggestive and motivating influence on every member of the tribe and on the entire tribe. Providential intentions and the intentions of the tribe toward Providence are summed up in a kind of tribal law—the taboos—seen as expressing the will of the father-ancestor. Defined by taboo interdicts, guiltiness is no longer a vague feeling. Belief in the providential influence of the father-ancestor brings about ceremonies that are more and more ritualized. Ritual ceremonies—insofar as they are solemn promises of obedience—are supposed to have a magical influence on the good intentions of the father-ancestor toward the tribe. Man's intentions and those that he credits to Providence are mutually strengthened. A circuit of good intentions comes into being, supposedly through the magical procedures of the ceremonies.

In fact, the circuit of beneficial intentions works exclusively in the inner life of man through autosuggestive imagination. Religiosity, ancestrally based on the foreknowledge of death, is the most radical sign of Man's advent in the animal kingdom. Man was compelled to face the problem of his destiny. The answer he found, though it was only imaginative, already included the essential meaning underlying all religious imagination (magical and mythical), the meaning of responsibility, binding one generation to the next, sons to ancestors. Primitive man in the magical era does not yet feel that he is an individual, egocentrically detached from the common fate of the tribe. He experiences responsibility in the very depths of his inner intentions, wanting above all to be the worthy son of his ancestors so as to become in his turn a deified father-ancestor. The ancestral lineage and transmission of virtues overshadow the individual and lend to the life of every generation its meaning and significance.

The ethical demand to safekeep and transmit the virtues (inner strength) is not primarily a social one. It concerns the hope of being reunited after a courageous life with the deceased ancestor and it is biologically profound since it is the essential condition for the survival of the tribe, and therefore of the human species.

Among certain Oriental peoples, the son still bears today the sign of filiation: Ben among the Arabs, Poulos for the Greeks, etc. Of course, it is a way of identification, but it is above all an honorary sign. Thus nothing could be more insulting than calling a man: "son of a hyena" or "son of a jackal" and no greater honor can be bestowed than a title like "son of the lotus" or "son of a deity." In the mythologies following the animistic era, the defeated heroes are "sons of a demon or of a monster," the conquering heroes are "sons of a deity" who would have impregnated a mortal woman. The fable elaborates on these tales of symbolic filiations and unions which—due to lack of understanding of the underlying significance—brought upon the deities of the polytheistic peoples the reproach of adultery or incest. This most decisive error has led us to depreciate the polytheistic mythologies. Yet, our culture has retained the importance of spirtual filiation. The first name is inspired by the Patron, the Saint whose example should guide our life. It is in the framework of this age-old tradition that we can understand the meaning of the central symbol: "Son of the Father-Spirit, Son of

God." It is a historical fact: the many religions and their cults are all rooted in ancestor worship.

During the animistic era, the possible sacrifice of life which was a quasi daily demand in the struggles against wild animals and enemy tribes, was no more than an expression of physical courage. Yet, it already implied moral courage: *to die in the body rather than be subjected to the "death of the soul," the death of the valiant intentions animating man or that should animate him.* It is this essential aspect, the intrapsychic struggle against the danger of faltering inner intertions that—finally represented by symbolically exteriorized struggles against demons and monsters—will become during the mythical era, the central theme of symbolization.

In primitive man, the suggestive strength of the ancestors' courageous example is such that anxiety in the face of death and the wavering intentions resulting from it are almost totally overcome from the outset. His soul is imbued with the feeling that what matters is not to live long but courageously. He feels in the very depths of his being that life would have no more meaning if, at the decisive moment of struggle demanding the possible sacrifice of his life, he were, through fear of death, to allow himself to be led into retreat and cowardice. However, anxiety regarding the mortal danger surrounding him is certainly not alien to the primitive soul, which explains the various ceremonies of magically suggestive encouragement such as, for instance, frenetic dances prefiguring the battle. The dancers, wearing horrifying masks, personify mortal anxiety that must be overcome. One must also note here the ritual anthropophagy through which the victorious tribe wishes to magically absorb the physical strength and the moral virtues of the conquered enemy, thus regenerating by suggestion their own forces and virtues in preparation for future battles. Ultimate virtue being the sacrifice of life, primitive man does not ask for pity and does not grant it. Hence, among certain tribes, the custom of torturing prisoners in order to test their courage and to give them a last opportunity to redeem themselves since they have not been capable of dying and have been captured. However, autosuggestion has here, as always for primitive man, an essential role: each one of the warriors knows that were he to become a prisoner himself, he would be subjected to the same treatment and therefore he feels strengthened in his determination to die in battle rather than surrender.

Imposed by ancestor worship, the mores and customs of primitive peoples even to the least detail of their social life are based on religious rituals and the suggestive power they exert on the inner motivating intentionality. This suggestive power, which was meaningful in primitive man, remains manifest today in the degraded form of obsessive superstitions.

In the premythical mentality, the belief in a providential intentionality is not exclusively related to the deified ancestors. Belief in a magical circuit between man and the gods goes together with a belief in an animistic circuit between man and his natural environment.

Animism extends the belief in a protective or punitive intentionality to *Terra Mater,* the nurturing earth. The Providence of the Father-Spirit and the Providence of Mother-Nature complete each other. The circuit of intentional interactions includes the hereafter and the here and now.

The primitive soul projects its own intentionality (human motives) not only onto the transcendent image of the deities, but onto everything that actually exists: animals and plants and even inanimate objects insofar as they are desired or feared. Nature in its entirety is perceived by man as being animated by benevolent or malevolent intentions, depending on his merits or faults.

Primitive man is incapable of explaining to himself, by linking cause to effect, situations and events that—independently of his own intentionality—occur in his environment and yet trigger his own motivating intentionality, inciting him to active exteriorization. In his search for an explanation, he invents anthropomorphic deities; he anthropomorphizes nature. He animates it. He projects onto nature his own intentional spirit. In the primitive mentality, the ideas of "soul, spirit, will, intention, motive" are not—as is the case for us—abstract concepts with various shades of meaning. Primitive man does not know that he has—as we say—a spirit, a human spirit proper to him. For him, there are only "spirits" that are more or less personified and animate all that is alive and even all that is. What he vaguely feels in all his emotional being is *the mysterious intentionality of nature* (the evolutionary finalism linking man to the animal kingdom).

The core of animism is the brotherhood of man with the animals (Totemism). Being still very close to nature, primitive man sees himself, as it were, as an animal among animals. Each animal species seems to him to be animated by an intentionally self-organizing spirit, a spirit which characterizes it even in its behavior with regard to man, be it docility or aggressivity, which the primitive man understands as good or ill-will towards himself.

Animistic explanation extends magical intentionality to plants that are edible or poisonous (animated by a benevolent or malevolent spirit). This gives birth—through an astonishing knowledge of the plants' properties—to a medical lore which is quite effective, all the more so that the medicine man, using a suggestive ritual, manages to influence the psyche and to mobilize its defensive forces. Sickness can be influenced by magic because it is seen—in full agreement between the patient and the medicine man—as a struggle taking place in the deep-seated intentionality between courage to live and fear of death. A cure proves that the spirit of courage magically reinforced has managed to conquer the punitive spirit that had captured the failing body and had to be exorcised. Here too what is essential is the ethical axiom:

not to forget the life of the soul, the animating intentionality, and not to fear the accident of death.

The result of these two aspects of magical thought (the Providence of the deified ancestors and the Providence of magically animated nature) is a twofold significance in ethical observances. The taboo interdicts do not only concern hope for life after death but also the lifetime relationships with the environment. These taboo relationships with providential nature are an elementary hygiene of "earthly" desires (material and sexual desires). The egocentric exaltation of desires betrays impure individual intentions which are not only harmful for the prospects of afterlife with the ancestors, but dangerous for the healthy life of the collectivity. If the tribe tolerates transgressions, it will be subjected to *banalizing influence*. Banalization[3] of the mores as an uhealthy intention remains an offense against the example given by the ancestors; when it becomes actively manifested it is an offense against nature—itself magically deified and personified—since the desires have become unnatural and unhealthy. Natural cataclysms are interpreted as a punishment meted out to the whole guilty collectivity (on the mythical plane, punishment takes on a psychological significance: flood of perversions, aridity of souls).

Should exorcizing incantations and purification rites not obtain grace, it is because the guilty person or persons, instead of repenting, persist in their impure intentions or their perverted activities. Collective purification can therefore be obtained only through exemplary punishment: execution or banishment. (In mythical cultures, the underlying meaning of purification for the collectivity becomes quite clear; among others, in the symbol of the "scapegoat" on which the Hebrews loaded the sins of the community every year before banishing it into the desert to die of exposure. Such a symbol of collective purification would have remained totally ineffective if it had not represented the collective intention, the promise of a whole people to oppose the rule of banalization in order to placate divine anger, underlying theme of the entire Old Testament).

In premythical animism, the cult of deified ancestors and of magically intentionalized nature (since these cults address both the mystery of death and the mystery of life), are, thanks to their suggestive power, perfectly able to create a culture and sustain it for thousands of years. Animistic religions—primitive though they be—are founded on the

---

[3]Diel diagnoses banalization—a state generally considered as normal—as a form of mental illness never before diagnosed. Banalization attributes an excessive importance to material and sexual desires which are considered as the sole meaning of life.

Banalization is the ambivalent counterpart to the neurotic forms of mental illness characterized by the convulsion of spiritual desires and the inhibition of material and sexual desires.

guiding values sustaining human motivations which have a sublimating trend; yet, how prone they are to turn into superstitions!

As long as taboos remain imperatives of the ethical superconsciousness, tribal organization remains adapted to the demands of nature, even in its mores and customs.

Decadence occurs when taboos are arbitrarily multiplied. They no longer constitute a natural morality, but a dogmatic contrivance with a moralizing trend which is deemed indispensable in the struggle against the decline of ancestral mores. But taboo interdicts that are excessively multiplied and imposed from without, end up being felt as an unbearable weight, sooner or later arousing doubt. Motivating intentionality is disoriented. Its sublimating value is torn, in an ambivalent way, between half-submissive, half-rebellious inclinations.

The ensuing disintegration of the guiding imaginations and of their suggestive forces does not fail to affect the ancestral magical layer even in the ceremonies of the ritual institutions. *White magic*, superconsciously inspired, is finally overwhelmed by *black magic* whose ceremonial spells and superstitious conjurations appeal to the demonic forces of the subconscious. The believers, though they remain attached to the rites, see in them no more than a means to compel the conjured spirits to gratuitously grant protection and forgiveness. The medicine man no longer implores, he causes the fecundating rain, the end of the epidemics, etc. and finally, in a complete turnabout, implorations and rites retain only one purpose: the hope of providential fulfillment of the slightest material desires. The ritual institution remains but its suggestive magic, which is now misused, will in the long run destroy the primitive animistic culture.

Cultural decay has two aspects: it destroys the religious and social organizations which have lost their effectiveness and it prepares the advent of a new form of valid orientation. Renewal is not brought about by excessively good and moralizing intentions but is essentially due to the increasing suffering brought about by the desintegration of the guiding values of ethical superconsciousness. Consequently, superconscious imagination alone is able to achieve evolutionary renewal. The decadent animistic magic is thus replaced by the far more sublimely suggestive imagery of *mythical symbolization*.

Evolution of the cultural level (orientation toward the meaning of life) could not be achieved without the progressive appearance of a new stage in the progress of civilization (adaptation to the environment): *the advent of agriculture*.

Animism was, with a few exceptions, the religion of nomadic tribes. Hunters and shepherds lived in the simplicity of close contact with the animals. Their precarious situation shielded the primitive clans and tribes against the vital danger of excessive multiplication of desires. Thus the mythical era which starts with agriculture retains a nostalgic

memory of primitive animism whose quasi innocent naïveté is cele-
brated by mythical symbols: "golden age of mankind," "paradisiac life."
(The biblical myth clearly points to the advent of agriculture as the
cause for the loss of Paradise. "With suffering shall you get your food
from the soil.")

The historical fact is that agricultural peoples become sedentary out
of necessity, tribes converge and erect powerful cities, fighting for
hegemony. Material riches accumulate in the victorious cities and incite
individuals to debauchery while provoking envy among the neighbor-
ing peoples and leading to aggression and war. (These causes of "loss
of Paradise" and "breach of the Covenant" are the constant theme of
the Old Testament.)

But together with these complexities arousing the danger of wrong
motivation, the life of the farmer brings compensations of a sublimating order, apt to enlarge the animistic vision into mythical symbolization. The agricultural peoples of the ancient world have to discipline
themselves because of their work which, from sowing to harvesting, is
totally dependent on seasonal changes, the weather, and such disasters
as drought and flood. They get used, at the same time, to observing the
stars (astronomy in its infancy) and to wonder at the mysterious harmony in the celestial motions, a contemplation that is emotionally
enriched by a completely new dimension in worship.

The animistic belief in "intentional spirits" scattered throughout
nature is progressively condensed in the belief in a sole celestial intentionality favorable or not to the harvest without which survival is impossible. Ancestor-deities are replaced by the deification of the sky which
fecundates the nurturing earth. Rain which falls from the sky symbolically becomes sperm inpregnating the earth (for instance in the Greek
Theogony, Uranus or Heaven impregnates Gaea, the Earth). The image
is still half-allegorical, half-symbolic (for instance spring is personified by
a young man, winter by an old one). The sun is not yet the symbol of the
illuminating spirit; wheat and bread (products of agriculture) do not yet
have the symbolic significance of "food for the spirit"; the deities are not
yet symbols of the positive qualities of the psyche.

However, allegory already heralds symbolization whose most promi-
nent characteristic is a new vision of the relationship between man and
nature enlarged into a cosmic environment. Good and evil no longer
come from the countless "spirits" animating nature and magically pene-
trating the human soul according to its merits or faults. Due to total
helplessness in the face of cosmic events, a new threat of death appears
(famine). Magical implorations and rituals meant to exorcize evil having clearly proven themselves ineffective, the only way to overcome the
situation is recourse to the ethical force immanent to the psyche: *acceptance.* To be sure, primitive man did not lack it, but it did not yet have
in him the voluntary and reflective aspect which implies a more or less

conscious self-control, i.e., the elimination of self-pitying resentment and the planning of valid means to deal as best as possible with the threatening situation.

Acceptance is a sublimating force which is not possible without a spiritualizing elucidation of the malevolent motives leading to discouragement; it is—to use symbolic terms—"the bread of the spirit" and "the food of the soul." It is the "essential harvest," all the more indispensable to the farmer that it also shields him from the threat of the essential danger: temptation to forget the spirit and to give way to banal exaltation of material desires (riches of the earth, "treasures that rust"), the most constant theme of mythologies. *The advent of symbolization is due to man turning his attention inward* and voluntarily accepting responsibility for his own spirit and his own motivating intentions.

Motives being superconsciously clarified, mythologies will be able to symbolize the diversity of human motivations, be they sublimating and elucidating or monstrously perverse and blinding. They will create a sort of symbolic pre-science of the inner psychic functioning, represented by the struggles of the hero assisted by the deities (superconscious intentions) against the demons and the monsters (subconscious intentions). Animism already had legendary fabulations and complex tales relating the actual struggles of the hero-ancestors during lives held as exemplary . Elaborating on these legends, mythical narrations will progressively reach the plenitude of symbolic language.

Since the era of magical cultures and cosmic allegory precedes the advent of mythical cultures, the symbolic pre-science of inner motivations must be seen as the *product of a long evolution taking place in the depth of superconscious imagination.*

B. MYTHICAL CULTURES

1. POLYTHEISM

The evolution of the "deified father-ancestor" animistic image implies the evolution of the human spirit which is finally personified by the "Father-Spirit" mythical image, a symbol of the spiritualizing force immanent to the pyche.

Now the evolution of the spirit is the biogenetically profound problem of the evolution of the thinking species. In this respect, the development which takes place between animism and symbolism is far more significant than the difference—important through it be—between polytheism and monotheism. The latter both use—as we will show—a common symbolic language. Evolutionary progression unites them in the ability to express more clearly than animism could do, the essential fact of human life, namely: *intrapsychic conflicts between the motivating intentions.*

It is thus imperative to begin by analyzing the processes of symbolization and the meaning of the typical symbols that are shared by the two forms of mythical thought; this is the only way to effectively prepare a methodical deciphering of the symbolic passages included in the biblical texts. At the dawn of symbolization in polytheistic cultures, "God-the-Spirit" is still scattered among a multitude of deities personifying the various positive qualities of the human soul and spirit. Thus, in Greek mythology, Zeus symbolizes lucidity of spirit; Hera, love and warmth of soul; Athena, ethical courage and sublimating combativity; Apollo, the god of health and brother of Athena, personifies the goal of sublimating combativity and the condition for psychic health: harmony of desires. This personifying representation, which goes beyond our few examples and covers all the positive qualities, demands a complementary symbolization which, contrary to the symbolization of sublimating and spiritualizing forces, personifies the negative qualities of the human soul—the "demonic" forces—symbolically represented as enemies of the deities. The wealth of fabulation, especially in Greek mythology, lies in the diversity of mythical themes, each one representing another aspect in the struggle between positive and negative figures and these struggles succeed in symbolizing in a detailed manner the inner conflicts taking place in the soul between vitally meaningful or senseless intentions.

The battlefield—in fact, the psyche itself—is symbolically projected outward, an inescapable consequence of the symbolic process. "In the psyche," needless to say, there are no persons but only motivating functions.

And the reverse holds true: the symbols created by superconscious imagination *can in no way actually exist outside of the inner psychic life.* What does this mean except that deciphering symbolic language is impossible without an *introspective method* and provided that the latter first studies and knowingly elucidates the functioning of inner motivations? This preliminary definition of the method to be used implies a rigorous scientific honesty, precluding easy and fanciful interpretations.

The evolutionary transformation of animism into symbolism is essentially based on different manners of representing motivating intentionality.

With mythical thought, the inner human intentions that animistic mentality had projected onto animals and objects, cease to be invested in such a magical projection and are concentrated again in the human soul. Contrary to animism, mythologies no longer deal with benevolent or malevolent spirits scattered in nature; their underlying meaning concerns *only man and his vitally meaningful or senseless motivating intentions.* But symbolic language remains fictional and veiled. Thus it can only proceed through reprojection of human motives onto fabulous figures—at times superhuman and at times subhuman—which are but inventions of the ethical superconsciousness's symbolizing imagination.

Freed from the primitive animistic projection which was very limited since it had to content itself with attributing a pseudointentionality to actually existing animals, mythical fabulation acquires a new dimension in its expression. It ventures into the creation of a multitude of imaginary beings, be they half-animal and half-man or half-man and half-god.

At the dawn of the symbolizing era—for instance in Egyptian mythology—even positive deities are still represented by half-man half-animal beings. In more evolved mythologies, the man-animal combination is used exclusively to personify monsters and demons (in Judaic Genesis, for instance, the talking serpent). Animals, in their turn, become symbolic characters in mythology. They reappear under the form of attributes stressing the features of such or other deity: (for instance the eagle of Zeus, symbolizing lucidity of spirit and the majestic flight of creative imagination). Due to the double process of mythical personification (reconcentration of the various intentions in man and reprojection onto fabulous beings that are freely invented), symbolic language is able to create an unlimited number of combinations which can symbolize the slightest shades of human motivations.

Besides imaginatively created beings, all living beings, objects, elements, natural phenomena become, for the sublime imagination of myths, means to symbolize the forces that animate man: rightly or wrongly motivating intentions, as well as the essential good or evil resulting from them. Heaven becomes the symbol of the superconscious, the sun becomes the symbol of warmth of soul and lucidity of spirit, illuminating truth. The stars symbolize guiding ideals. The moon, spellbinding star of the night, represents the subconscious temptations which are at times seductive, at times, frightening; dreaminess, absentmindedness and their unhealthy consequences such as changes of mood, whims, irritability. The earth and its vegetation (fruits) become the symbols of the many earthly desires. The underground regions (Hell) symbolize repressed desires laden with guiltiness and remorse, the insidious cause of the "infernal" pathogenic torture. Mountains with their summits and chasms symbolize the possibilities of elevation and downfall of the human soul. Storm and thunder represent the "intrapsychic storms," excesses of tempestuous affectivity and its ruminations, punctuated by "thunderclaps" symbolizing guilty warning. Lightning becomes the symbol of clarifying thought which discerns the motives of vital error while being at the same time the thunderbolt punishing unrepentant culprits.

Thus does symbolic language acquire the amplitude and flexibility apt to describe all the shades of motivations *and above all the essential phenomenon of psychic functioning, namely the transformation of the sublime into perversion and of perversion into the sublime.* All the symbols representing perversions can be turned into symbols endowed with a sublime meaning through the addition of positive attributes:

- the winged dragon (emblem of China): sublimation of monstrous perversion;
- the serpent pouring its venom into the cup of salvation: victory over vanity;
- the fish of the oceanic depths (equivalent of the underground regions) and the fish pulled out of the water: symbol of sublimating achievement, especially symbol of the purifying intention in primitive Christianity, etc.

By the same token, symbols with a sublime significance can be turned into negative symbols: for instance wine, symbol of sublimating impulse and Dionysiac wine, symbol of frenzied desires and drunkenness of soul.

It is impossible to give all the vocabulary of symbolic language and the precision of its grammar due to the flexibility of meaning (as shown above). All these means of expression—which will later be exemplified through the deciphering of biblical symbols—enable symbolic language to formulate precisely what is meaningful and senseless in the inner *motivating calculation*[4] and its search—right or wrong—for satisfaction, a calculation that ceaselessly takes place in the unconscious depths of man. This being the case, ancient mythologies already made up a genuine *pre-science* of the *inner psychic functioning*. They are the extraconscious expression, the superconscious explosion, *of the essential truth immanent to the human psyche*. This is not yet the moment to study the biogenetic explanation of this astonishing finding. It will suffice to stress here that when the species became conscious—or rather half-conscious and half-extraconscious—and thus exposed to a hesitating choice, it could not have survived without being guided by ethical superconsciousness. Taken in this way, the multiplicity of deities characterizing polytheistic mythologies is far from being a gratuitous superstition. Benevolent deities represent the *harmonizing forces* immanent to the human psyche; malevolent deities symbolize the *disharmonizing forces*. (In Greek mythology, for instance, Hades, the king of the subconscious, represents the law ruling over the repression of guilty desires. The consequence of repression—symbolically personified by the daughters of Hades—resides in the Erinyes, symbols of remorse resurging forth from the subconscious to ceaselessly hound the guilty man, i.e., the man who is not in harmony with himself. The only refuge where the culprit can find a remedy—where he can be rescued from the pursuing Erinyes—is, symbolically, the temple of Apollo, god of harmony).

Myths give us to understand that human life is in essence a struggle and an ethical adventure.

---

[4]*Psychologie de la Motivation*, Petite Bibliothèque Payot, 1970. See note 16 in chapter 3: *Le Calcul Psychologique*.

Man himself is represented under a mythical aspect. He is typified by the *hero* who, with the help of the deities (his own positive qualities) should *in himself* and for his own good, fight against *senselessly exalted desires* personified by *tempting demons and devouring monsters* (devouring passions of the subconscious).

In accordance with mythical imagery, the immanent demand for harmonious unification is transcended and appears as the expression of divine will.

Mythical imagery empowers the deities to mete out rewards and punishments. This transference is psychologically valid and sensible since the deities symbolize the determining motives of activity be they healthy or unhealthy, vitally satisfying or dissatisfying.

Due to the imaginative transference of the immanent ethical demand to the deities, the essential destiny of man and the fate of the community seem, in the mythical perspective, to depend on divine will.

Each people's vision creates a crystallizing core able to influence positively the ethical struggle of each member of the group.

All the processes of symbolizing imagination are used to strengthen the suggestive and sublimating power of mythical images. Symbolic personification in the form of heroes and monsters enables man to see and touch, as it were, the insidious dangers of his inner struggles. The fabulous narrative moves the imagination through the peripeties of the story. Poetization adorns the deities and the fighting heroes with all possible aesthetic attractions as well as ethical qualities: the hero whose courage is indomitable does not retreat before the wiles and treachery of tempting demons, nor does he step back in the face of the monsters' brutal strength and frightening ugliness.

Superconsciousness, having been able to create the images, is thereby capable of understanding their hidden meaning. Not that it understands them consciously, but rather it experiences them in their emotional impact. *Worship of the deities becomes a powerful motivating force.*

Thus, in accordance with the myths, man the fighting hero, defeats demons and monsters *with the help of weapons lent be the deities.* His victory is symbolically "thanks to the gods." In fact, he conquers through the strength of his own vital impulse[5], provided however that this impulse, which animates men with varying degrees of intensity, is sustained by the suggestive force of mythical images.

In this perspective one can say that the gods of the polytheistic peoples, even though they had no actual and personal existence, *did really and truly live. They lived in man under the form of vivifying forces, under the form of animating intentions.*

---

[5]In French, *élan* or *élan animant*, a word used by Paul Diel to express that all living beings—and therefore man—are animated by a mysterious force. The translators chose the English "vital impulse" or "impulse" to render the dynamic concept of *élan*. Elan would have led to confusion (with Bergson's *élan vital*).

The deities die when the soul of man dies: when the demons and monsters (the exaltation and multiplication of material desires) overcome the essential desire of harmonization. Zeus does not live anymore: he does not inspire anyone. When the souls of individuals die, cultures die. This does not prevent other deities from appearing, inspiring souls anew and enabling them to create new cultures. The history of the past is, in essence, the history of the gods, their life and their death and the history of the life and death of the cultures they successively inspired.

The study of mythical symbolism leads us to the problem of the life and death of cultures. But the historical succession of cultures includes the essential destiny of the human species: *its past and future evolutionary genesis.* The problem of symbolic language and of its underlying significance goes far beyond the individual and even the social scope. It concerns the evolutionary destiny of mankind. The deepest mystery of human life is the existence of the superconscious symbolization that founded the ancient cultures, including our own culture, presently in a state of complete decadence.

The cause of the life and death of polytheistic cultures is the same as the cause of the life and death of monotheistic cultures.

The narrative facade of the polytheistic myths could not have sustained the cultures: only the underlying truth they express was able to do so. The death of cultures is caused by the decadence of souls and spirits that have forgotten the underlying truth without which mythical tales would be nothing but a dead letter. "The letter kills . . . only the spirit [underlying truth] is alive and life-giving." The agony of vivifying truth is a long process. Cultures die out, societies go on to live in a state of progressive decadence. They can even seem to be thriving due to the increased refinement of their civilization that is overly concerned with the material organization of collective life. But since it has lost all reference to the meaning of life, excessive material needs—deemed to be the only purpose in life—become in fact the cause of its decadence: they pit societies against one another—a constant theme of the Old Testament—and man against man—a constant theme of the New Testament.

2. MONOTHEISM

a) The Symbol of the "One God"

Monotheism is an evolved form of polytheism. What evolved in the first place was the "God" symbol. All other differential traits are only a consequence of this. The difference is not in the underlying meaning of the symbolization, but solely in the facade of the narrative in which the multiple gods are condensed into an only God and the demons and monsters into one adversary of God, the fallen spirit, personified by Satan.

Our central theme in the preceding pages has been the persistence of

a common underlying significance—the immutable ethical truth—
which has not changed since animism. In our day and age, it seems
quite clear that the gods of the polytheistic mythologies were not—
contrary to the beliefs of ancient peoples—real persons. Yet, we still
believe in the personal existence of an only God. Unlike our time, the
ancient world had two forms of theology: one for popular belief, and
the other reserved for a handful of initiates.

Centers of initiation called "Mysteries" existed in Egypt, Greece, and
among all highly cultured peoples. The word "Mysteries" indicates that
the teaching was meant to awaken emotion in the face of the mystery of
universal harmony into which man, for his own essential good, must
incorporate himself through means of self-harmonization, leading to a
living awareness of *immanent ethics,* i.e., true religiosity.

Fully accepting their responsibility and vocation, the priests of the
Eleusis Mysteries, for instance, revealed to those who were capable of
understanding it, the true foundation of the myths' symbolization: i.e.,
the mystery of death and life, the nonexistence of personal gods, and
their meaning with respect to the human soul's positive intentions. To be
sure, the priests did not explain mystery (though this is precisely what
popular theology pretends to do) and even the ethical meaning was not
conceptually explained. Lacking a detailed knowledge of symbolic language, they used a teaching method that had its source in the survival of
the ancient emotion which had been able to create mythical fabulations
and thus they were capable of grasping intuitively the enigma of the
hidden meaning and of conveying it with the help of suggestion.[6]

Nowadays, we have neither initiates nor initiating priests. Nothing
can be found except popular beliefs based on a literal interpretation of
the texts or, conversely, skepticism caused by this interpretative error.
Symbolic exegesis is just as opposed to belief as it is to skeptical doubt, a
fact that is a hindrance in the search for the hidden truth, all the more
so that this truth includes, mythically condensed, not only the meaningful side of life but also the senseless side, both of which are—as is
symbolically expressed—immanent to human nature. This brings
about—or should do—a genuine desire to investigate the problem but
there is also a risk of arousing anxiety at the disturbing prospect of
baring the psychic depths.

Our culture, rooted in the biblical texts, always thought itself superi-
or to the ancient polytheistic cultures, and it still does. And so it is,
since its symbolization is more evolved. And yet, it is not, because it
lacks the deeper vision reserved for the initiates. Popular and profane
theology (profaning the underlying truth) imposes a verbal belief in the

---

[6]See *Symbolism in Greek Mythology* (Shambhala, 1980). It must be pointed out though that
the mysteries of Eleusis are only mentioned in the first edition of the original *Le Symbolisme dans la Mythologie Grecque* (Payot, Paris).

affirmation of the texts according to which God himself, taking a human form, came down from heaven in the person of his only begotten Son in order to bring to mortals the message of salvation. How can one not acknowledge that these are only symbols, all the more so that the ancient gods also used the human form to come down to earth and reveal to mortals what they had to do in order to be saved?

One thing is certain or should be so: theological interpretation is based on a misunderstanding of the ancient "Son of God" symbol. Symbolically speaking, every man is a "son of God." But no man and no god can be at the same time fully god and fully man. Even if he actually existed, an all-powerful God could not produce such a miracle. Because this is an irreversible definition, a man who would be God could not be a man like all the other men. Whether one acknowledges it or not, the texts are only symbolic. Hence they share in the truth and beauty of all symbols.

However, *the most decisive errors of popular theology* do not stem from literal interpretation but from the need to defend it with the help of contrived dogmas that have nothing more to do with the texts. We have to stress it from the outset: the most glaring of all dogmatic errors has to do with *salvation, the tidings of joy brought by the Messiah.* According to the literal interpretation of theology, the tidings of joy— central theme of the Gospels—*would be the promise of survival after death, in the presence of God, which is to be granted to the believers and refused to all the generations that lived before the advent of Christ.* This dogma leads to absurd conclusions, all the more objectionable that they are in total contradiction with the prophetic revelations of the Old Testament. Not only is God unfair towards the polytheistic peoples who lived before the advent of Christ. They are according to dogma, and no matter how they lived—often with great merit— forever excluded from afterlife in God's presence. But what is astonishing here—and beyond any possible discussion—is that the only God, if he exists as a person, *already existed during the pagan era.* Did he deliberately hide himself while being fully aware of pagan mankind's error? And what about the prophets of the Old Testament, and the Chosen People? Are they also to be excluded because they lived before the advent of Christ? According to literal interpretation, God personally spoke from Heaven and into the ears of the prophets. Why did the prophets, to whom God had revealed his will, not say a word about immortality (unknown throughout the Old Testament)? Why did they only talk about the threat of a temporal punishment for the disobedient people? The Old Testament threat is a symbol with underlying significance and so is the message of salvation in the New Testament, though the message is not a promise of immortality.

What matters here is to understand the meaning of the glad tidings in the Gospels, the essential problem concerning the destiny of mankind. *What is the symbolic meaning of the good news?* This is the central problem of this study of symbolism.

Such is the dilemma: either the texts are beyond human reason and its critical power and we must accept literally all the illogical texts from the history of Genesis down to the affirmation that God himself came down to earth in the form of his Son (while remaining in Heaven in the form of the Father) and that the men who killed God are assured of a superabundant grace. If this is the case the symbolic exegesis must be rejected. Or else, all the illogical or supernatural passages from Genesis to the Ascension are symbols which can be explained. If this is the case, the whole dogmatic system collapses. This is undoubtedly what believers fear most, preferring as they do the so-called profundity of miracles to the search for truth. However, research does not really expect to convince believers. The problem has a much greater significance. One must persist, not in order to cast affective accusations, but to reveal the age-old error. One must, no matter how painful it is, put one's finger on the source of the trouble by diagnosing its causes and effects so as to find the remedy that will show to man what he must do to ensure his own salvation while he is alive, without any help from priests or dogmas, but in conformity with mythical truth.

If the dogmatic problem is erroneous—and how could it not be?— piety for the true meaning of the texts should overcome piety for error, no matter how long its rule has lasted and how many its faithfuls are. Emotion in the face of mystery is a far deeper and more manly religious feeling than the sentimental delights sought in the ceremonial and infantile relationship between man-the-child and "the Father in heaven," a relic of magical and animistic beliefs. And how could love of truth not bring more joy than love of absurdity?

Theology failed in its attempt of unification by imposing a belief in absurdity (*credo quia absurdum*) and by making this the supreme virtue. All it achieved was the dissociation of beliefs as is proven by the present situation. No religion was ever split into so many sects, each with its own theology and with no other common factor than the dogma of God's personal reality. The dissociation is even found within the Mother Church itself. There is no other remedy than giving up the dogmas, relics of the medieval night. In fact, many believers concoct their own private theology since they deem themselves too evolved for the dogmas seen only as a necessary control over the masses. But even the latter do not believe anymore in the dogmas. They submit—for want of something better—just as they accept any type of convention.

b) The Biblical Texts

(1) The myth of Adam, common foundation of the Old and New Testaments. From a historical point of view, monotheism is the summit and completion of the mythical era.

Polytheism was an adumbration of monotheism. The only God was foreshadowed in certain pagan mythologies, notably by the Egyptian "Rashunter Amon" and Greek "Triopas Zeus" symbols. The Hebrews' monotheism may have been prepared and influenced by their stay in Egypt. According to the texts, God is surrounded by a multitude of angels, Satan by a multitude of demons, relics of the multiple deities and monsters of the polytheistic myths.

Biblical writings—especially those of the Old Testament—are not purely symbolic, but somewhat epic tales. They do relate historical events, though the latter are mingled through and through with symbolic elements having an irrational and fabulous façade. Now, in polytheistic times, there were similar tales, for instance the Iliad and the Odyssey—however remote their connection with the Bible—showing the history or a stage in the history of a people who was influenced and guided by the intervention of the deities. The Old Testament relates the incidental history and essential destiny of the Hebrews, a people "chosen" by God, a symbolic expression for the constant reference (in the biblical myth) to the essential meaning of life, symbolized by the constant intervention of God, his promises and threats of punishment, which are essentially valid for all peoples down to our times.

The culture of every people falls into decadence through oblivion of its mythical foundation. Decadence is, in symbolic terms, punishment. One could consider the Old Testament as a kind of essential sociology, which explains its abiding capacity to arouse interest. The New Testament relates the decadence of Israel fallen under the Roman yoke, "given by God into the hand of the foe," and the advent of the Messiah, who renews the immutable truth violated by the error of the Pharisees defending dogmatic interpretation: "Moses said . . . ," "It is written. . . ." The Gospels complete the theme of the Old Testament (essential fate of the entire people). They show that in the midst of decadence, each man is personally called to "rebirth" to a meaningful life in truth by following the example of the "Son of Man," who is *Son of Adam* while being symbolically "Son of God," having found anew faith in the Eternal God by freeing himself from the dogmatism of his childhood. The two Testaments are an indivisible entity: the myth of the fall of the human soul and its possible elevation, a symbolic theme including the history of the decadence and rebirth of cultures. (The fall of Adam and the decadence of societies express the same theme: oblivion of the spirit and exaltation of material desires.)

The myth of Genesis, common foundation of the Old and New Testaments, is quite different from all the other texts.

The account of Adam's fall is an uninterrupted succession of symbolizations while the other narratives of the Bible relate historical facts with here and there illogical fabulations bearing a hidden meaning. Since the Old and the New Testaments are a follow-up and a historically documented development of the underlying significance of Genesis, deciphering the latter must supply the key to the understanding of the biblical texts.

Now all the symbols in the story of Adam are, in their deep significance, analogically linked to the hidden meaning of polytheistic symbolization, no matter how different the narrative's facade happens to be.

Moreover, the underlying meaning of the Judaic myth of creation is perfectly identical with the hidden significance of the Greek myth of creation.[7]

Taken literally, the myth of Adam compels us to accept at face value the most incredible thing: *because of the disobedience of one man, God would have condemned all of mankind from generation to generation.*

Yet it is not as if the fault of the first man were so serious as to be unforgivable; according to the façade of the myth, Adam seduced by the serpent would have eaten from the fruit of "the Tree of Knowledge."

What could "Tree of Knowledge" mean? Why would its fruit be forbidden?

How can an apparently venial fault call for a punishment seemingly so disproportionate and unfair?

Apologetics (dogmatic justification of literal understanding) is compelled to admit that this an insoluble enigma. But the understanding of the text depends on the solution to the enigma: the message of Christ announces the pardon of the fault of Adam called "original sin."

This sin is the origin and the key to all the biblical events from man's fault to the crucifixion, when God offers himself as a sacrifice to cancel the original fault. Now the original fault and the punishment are, necessarily and by virtue of their illogicality, symbols.

God is a symbol, the talking serpent is a symbol, Adam is a symbol, Paradise is a symbol, the Tree of Knowledge is a symbol, the forbidden fruit is a symbol. All is symbol. What matters is to understand what is meant by "sin." Only such an understanding will show whether the punishment for the original sin is just or not.

Now the understanding of the original sin, of its punishment and of the reward granted to the men who have purified themselves from the initial sin, will show not the justice of the God-Person, but the justice of the God-Mystery: Creator and Judge of men. It will show that Adam's fate is a symbol of the destiny of every man who is essentially failing, a destiny accomplished during man's lifetime by way of immanent justice.

Here is the essential hidden meaning of all mythologies which monotheism raised to the highest degree of significance since the

---

[7]*Ibid.* (chapter on Prometheus).

"Creator" and "Judge" are united in one sole personifying symbol whose meaning is the mystery of existence in which the mystery of human life is included: man's accountability for his own vitally right or wrong intentions, his responsible choice between good and evil. This mythically and actually true meaning of monotheism—the foundation of our culture—has been misunderstood and this is the essential cause of present decadence.

(2) Symbolic pre-science and science. Thus it seems that the thesis or rather hypothesis to be proven has now been defined.

In order to verify it, it is necessary to tackle the tremendous problem of symbolic thought.

It would be quite wrong to think that this study aims at a return to the ancient foundation of all cultures. There is no hope that a young people bearing a new mythology can still emerge.

In the distant future, when the existence of a symbolic language will be accepted and understood according to its underlying truth, the nations' mythologies, masterpieces of the superconscious, will be exhibited in museums, as testimonies worthy of veneration.

Culture will no longer be founded on the symbolic pre-science of inner motivating intentions but on *the science of life:* the science of inner conflicts and the science of the biogenesis of the human half-conscious, half-extraconscious psychic functioning which includes evolutionary phenomena but also involutionary dangers since both govern human destiny. The more these essential data will become precise and extensive, the more precise and extensive will also become our emotion before the unfathomable mystery of existence.

The deepest and more essential cause of present decadence is, as we all know, the conflict between science and religion.

What other remedy could there be save a reconciliation between true religiosity and true scientific spirit? Believers consider religion as the only barrier against the danger of sciences which are accused of concerning themselves solely with material needs. This reproach is justified because the science of life (psychology, sociology, evolutionary biogenesis) imitate the methodology of physics—the model of all sciences—and thus deprive themselves of a method appropriate to the specific object of their research, i.e., the subject, man as a being animated by motivating intentions.

Physics and the wonders of its technological applications show what the human spirit is capable of producing when it is methodically guided. But they also show the dangers of civilizing progress when it is not sufficiently guided by a controlling spirit. In the past, the control was exerted by the symbolic pre-science of the inner psychic functioning; in the scientific era, it should be taken over by a science of the inner motivating functioning. Based on its own method which can only be introspective, the science of motives should prove its true value by supplying the key to mythical pre-science, thereby reconciling science and religiosity and providing the only effective defense against the abuse of physics' technical inventions; the latter are not a consequence of scientific progress but of the wrong intentions which are immanent to human nature.

The purpose of the present research is to prove that the "original sin of human nature" does in fact exist but is a biogenetic phenomenon, symbolically figured in the biblical myth of Genesis: the "original sin" symbol complements the "God-the-Creator" and "God-the-Judge" symbols.

The "original sin" of the myth points to an essential weakness proper to the human species that has become half-conscious, insufficiently conscious and thereby fallible. *Considered in the totality of his psychic functioning, man is not only weak; he is also strong. His strength will overcome his weakness only to the precise degree in which evolutionary impulse will lead him to full consciousness, able to consciously and knowingly understand the intentions of the ethical superconsciousness as well as the pathogenic intentions of the subconscious* (both being liable to express themselves in the symbolic language of extraconsciousness).

The immanent biogenetic weakness will not be overcome—and thus quite naturally forgiven—except through the merits of man in a struggle deliberately undertaken against wrongly motivating intentions (a struggle symbolized by deities and monsters) which are the inner causes of wrong individual actions and wrong social interactions.

Only once we have deciphered the Genesis myth (and not before) will we be able *to understand the significance of the mythical elements scattered throughout the two Testaments.* It would be imprudent and even impossible to undertake right away the deciphering of the Genesis myth. Not only are there too many prejudices against this, but also too many objections which are quite understandable in the present state of affairs with regard to our concepts of psychic functioning.

These objections can be summed up by a major question: *How can one admit that there is a mythical pre-science, product of an ethical superconsciousness that should be supposed as omniscient, at least with regard to inner conflicts and their meaningful and senseless solutions?* Extensive preparatory work is a must.

In order to introduce an understanding of the Genesis myth, we will first have to analyze the meaning of the central symbol, i.e., "God the Creator of the Universe," so as to unlock at last the significance of "God-the-Judge-of-Man" symbol.

Above all, we will have to show that mythical wisdom and its unifying vision of the problem of our origins uses the expression "God-the-Creator" to describe the unfathomable mystery of existence of both the world and life. Mystery is not what we do not yet know but what the human spirit—whatever scientific progress may take place—will never grasp. The most decisive scientific advance will be to knowingly understand the limits of human reason. Such a limitation, consciously understood and accepted is the only way for the human spirit to open up to the emotional impact of religiosity.

Only a common wonder before the mystery of existence and life can reconcile sciences and religions whose insane conflict is the essential cause of our present decadence stemming from a generalized disorientation.

The following pages cannot be described by any of the usual classifications offered by the materialistic and spiritualistic systems. We have just stressed their incompatibility with both *theism and atheism*. This incompatibility remains the central theme of all analyses directed against the psychopathic consequences—theistic moralism and atheistic amoralism—invading all aspects of practical life. All our analyses will start from this central theme and lead back to it. Such a back and forth is not a gratuitous repetition. It stems from the necessity to unveil the various causes of man's glaring error (be it psychological, sociological or biogenetic) but also, and especially so, the analogical ties uniting and unifying all the enigmatic truths that are hidden in the symbols we propose to decipher.

These developments are not *pantheistic*. They do not identify God with the world. On the contrary, they are based on a clear distinction between the real world and the "God" symbol. Neither are they *agnostic*. For while they insist on the fact that mystery cannot be grasped by reasoning, they prove that reason is perfectly capable of understanding the God-symbol and of explaining its origin and significance. Nor are they *rationalistic* because they are based on the existence of symbolic extraconscious thought (superconscious and subconscious) whose functioning is illogical and irrational.

They are neither moralistic nor amoralistic. Their sole purpose is to prove the biogenetically immanent existence of ethical values.

CHAPTER II

THE SYMBOL OF "GOD-THE-CREATOR"

A. THE SYMBOL OF "TRANSCENDENTAL INTENTIONALITY" AND THE REALITY OF IMMANENT INTENTIONALITY

There are two aspects to the "God" symbol: one is metaphysical (intentional creator of the universe), and the other ethical (God's intention with regard to man). These two aspects are reduced to one if we bring them back to the underlying truth of all symbols: human intentionality.

The ethical aspect of the "God" image concerns the imperative of superconsciousness which is really immanent to the psyche and imposes the harmonization of human intentions under penalty of guilty anxiety.

The metaphysical aspect concerns the manifest harmony of the universe. Man cannot imagine it except in the transcendental—metaphysical—form of a supernatural and all-powerful intentionality.

The metaphysical image of a "creating deity" does not correspond to any reality except to the emotion felt in the face of the unexplainable origin of the existing universe. The "Intentional Creator" is necessarily imagined as existing beyond the limiting conditions of human life, i.e., in the other world. Projection onto the other world is not—at least in its mythical origin—a metaphysical speculation but a symbolization based on spatialization (even outside of space itself) and on personification. The spatial beyond is necessarily completed by a temporal beyond, namely: the image of immortality.

All that is appears and disappears except for the immutable ethical truth (the imperative of harmonization) and the immutable fact of a harmoniously organized universe. Man himself is nothing in the vastness of universal existence except an ephemeral being fated to disappear, which does not preclude a meaning to his life: for his own essential satisfaction, he must incorporate himself into the harmony of the universe.

The image of the "creating deity" is the symbol of appearance and disappearance, a symbol of the mystery of life and death.

Spurred by superconscious emotion, mythical imagination goes beyond the boundaries of space-time existence which is the only given reality. But in so doing, it does not look in any way for a logical explanation; it dreams up an answer which is illogical but symbolically veracious insofar as the meaningful orientation of human intentionality is concerned.

The "Creator" image is in fact a creation of human imagination and is necessarily anthropomorphic. Superconscious imagination can create a metaphysical image but it cannot make a reality out of the imagined "Creator."

Human thought should understand this in order to avoid attempting to explain that which cannot be explained (by the concepts of absolute Spirit or absolute Matter), and in so doing destroy the deepest emotion of the human spirit and soul, an emotion that creates and sustains a motivating influence: the ethical intention of self-harmonization.

The name of "God," if it is not misused, has absolutely no other meaning than emotion in the face of the unexplainable.

B. GOD-MYSTERY AND THE "NAME OF GOD"

For symbolic pre-science, as understood in its deep intention, the name "God" is a word, a term coined to describe mysterious intentionality.

This being understood, it is just as absurd to pretend that "God" (mystery of intentionality) does not exist as it is to believe that he exists personally under the transcendent and quasi-human form given to him by the mythical facade. This is time to introduce a few preparatory remarks. The Latin word "Deus" (meaning "God") is akin to the Greek "Zeus." This means that these various terms define one sole "Divinity" though the personifying images which give shape to the "name of God" are quite different among the various peoples.

If this is the case, it should be clear that we do not have to credit any of these images and any of these names with an existence outside of the common emotion that superconsciously created them.

Now it so happens that the Latin work "Deus" is synonymous with "Jovis." According to etymological rules one could hypothetically suppose that the transformation of the first letter of these two Latin names (D to J) shows a shift that had started with a more ancient Hebrew root, which would authorize one to go back from "Deus" to "Jeus" (Jesus) and "Jovis" to "Jehovis" (Jehovah). Only a thorough etymological study could determine whether these comparisons are valid or not.

However, there is a criterion of validity that has nothing to do with semantic rules. It is based on the *underlying wisdom of languages,* which goes far beyond their conventional use.

Enigmatically locked in the roots of words, linguistic wisdom is a psychological pre-science which—just as mythical wisdom—can only have a superconscious origin.

It is important to clarify this linguistic phenomenon which poses a problem of no lesser magnitude than mythical symbolism. Showing that there is a *superconscious linguistic wisdom* is all the more necessary that it can add an auxiliary means to the methodology of myth deciphering, a means which will be used many times in the following pages. The fact is that linguistic wisdom is frequently used in mythology as a complement to the psychological meaning of the symbols with significant names for the deities, heroes, monsters and demons.

For instance, it is enough to lend an attentive ear to names such as "Medusa"[1] or "Chimerae" to know—even before deciphering the detailed narrative of the myth of Perseus (in which Medusa is involved) and Bellerophon (where Chimerae appears)—that these monsters symbolize "seductive" and "chimerical" temptations (imaginative exaltation) which the hero, in order to free himself, must fight in his own deliberating psyche.

How then could linguistic wisdom have coined—on the basis of the symbols—these meaningful names and adjectives and so many others if it had not pre-scientifically known the existence of the psychic faculties symbolized in such a fashion as well as the danger or asset they represent for psychic health?

C. LINGUISTIC WISDOM

Language has two functions which must be clearly distinguished in order to study symbolization.

It is a means of social and utilitarian communication, based on concepts, but it is originally an imaginative and symbolic means of expression of psychic life and its significance. What is involved in the term "meaning" is twofold: evolutionary *direction* and vital *value*.

Figurative and symbolic expression preceded the formation of psychological concepts. But all psychological concepts (to think, to feel, etc.) were originally created on the basis of introspection because it is quite clear that I must first know that I myself think before acting in order to conclude from the actions of others that they too think before acting, that they—like me—are animated by feelings, intentions, motives. I suppose—in fact I know—that others have intentions (inner tensions) that are benevolent or malevolent as far as I am concerned. I could not know their shades of meaning if I had not first discovered them in my own self. Now if linguistic wisdom and mythical wisdom express the motivating intentions that are shared by all men, they must both be founded on a preconscious introspection and therefore sym-

---

[1]In French, *méduser* derived from *Méduse* means to seduce, fascinate, mesmerize, also to stun, petrify.

bolic language is translatable into conceptual language. This must also be true for the "God" symbol that we are studying now.

The fact is, however, that reducing the "God" symbol to the psychic function it represents, arouses the most decisive resistance against symbolic exegesis, though it is absolutely necessary whether one likes it or not. It is essential in order to fight not only against theism but also against atheism. Resistance here is undoubtedly due to two main reasons: on the one hand the symbol of the "creating deity" representing all the meaning and value of life touches the deepest emotion of the human soul; on the other hand, the symbol is always downgraded into a pseudoexplanatory concept by metaphysical speculation (be it theological or philosophical). Now logical conceptualization—too often only pseudological—is in all fields requiring depth of thought, the most effective way to bypass the difficulty in order to obtain the most unshakable conventional adherence. All concepts have this in common: they run the risk of becoming nothing more than abstract clichés, labels pasted on existing phenomena—be they quantitative and extensive or qualitative and intensive (psychic intention). Psychological terminology is the main victim of this downgrading to the level of concept-cliché extended to the pseudoobject of metaphysical speculation, namely the "divinity" image mistaken for a real person. The difficulty encountered in understanding symbolic language is mostly due to the vagueness of psychological terminology downgraded to the level of clichés.

There will be throughout this study references to the ancestral linguistic wisdom which is a precious instrument for defining psychological terminology. Its conformity with mythical wisdom will at the same time offer yet another proof of the underlying psychological truth of the symbols. But we must, already here, when the question is to determine the actual existence or nonexistence of "God," intentional "Creator of the world," refer to the linguistic wisdom included in the word "existence," in order to fix its boundaries since it is valid only for natural and actual phenomena that are immanent to space-time.

The term "existence" includes two meanings: perceptible existence (the external world) and sensitive existence (the inner intentional world).

In the first of these meanings, the term is the most abstract of concepts. It indicates the factor which is common to all the spatio-temporal phenomena, regardless of their various modalities. In the second one, the term is the most concrete of concepts: I exist, I feel myself existing.

Such distinctions help us perceive that it is not proper to use the term "existence" with a third meaning which would point to a transcendent Being, called "God." At least, one should acknowledge that this could no longer be an actually existing being; "actual" is synonymous with "existing" and is applicable only to immanent phenomena. The "God"

Being does not actually exist though he does so imaginatively since only imagination can go beyond the limits of existence and of thought.

Though it is entirely fictitious, the (necessarily anthropomorphic) image must be emotionally significant; that is to say: the created "God" image has the value of a symbol. The God-Symbol really exists, but it is immanent to the psyche on which it has an emotional impact.

This psychological analysis is confirmed by linguistic wisdom. "To exist" is in Latin "ex-sistere" to be ex, expelled. Out of what? Out of unnamable transcendence, in other words: out of mystery. The latter, being understood not as an entity, substance, or person but as a vacuum, devoid of any tangible significance, devoid of any distinctive attribute, of any tension, of any intention, of any modification. Existence is thus imagined as being "expelled" out of the infinite harmony of silence.

"Expulsion" can be equated with "emanation" which is alluded to in the root of the word "exist"; it is not a reality but a linguistic image, and it brings us back to the personifying image of the myths, the "Creator" symbol.

Neither the linguistic image nor the mythical image are explanatory. Language is compelled to name the unnamable, and in so doing it anthropomorphizes it. "Creating expulsion" is not an adequate term because it presupposes a modification, a tension, a volition, an action, and this degrades the mystery of the Origins and transforms it into a modifiable modality.

The mystery of the Origins does not exist as such; it does so *only for the human mind* and its limited capacity for understanding. It exists only through man and for man.

All the philosophical terms applied to mystery, such as "Spirit," "Being," "Substance," "The One," "Essence," etc. either materialize or personify it.

Even the word "mystery" is an abstract materialization running the risk of becoming a falsely concretizing personification, a belief in a transcendent Entity one is tempted to credit with modal qualities (good, just, etc.), activities (Creator, Judge), a dwelling (Beyond, Heaven). Only mythical images, understood as symbols have the right to personify, verbalize, attribute and localize, and precisely because personification and localization are specific means of symbolic expression. In Existence, nothing is absolute. Compared to Existence, absolute mystery— absolutely transcendental mystery—is *absolute nonexistence.*

The mystery of Mystery is that the phrase "absolute nonexistence" is synonymous with "absolute existence." For it is precisely the Absolute that is nonexistent. According to linguistic wisdom, "absolute" means: devoid of any solution.

What exists is mystery immanent to existence: the harmonious organization of the universe and human emotion in the face of this mysterious aspect which includes everything that actually is: beings and things. (The root "uni-" contained in the word "universe" denotes the mystery of unifying organization, i.e., harmonizing organization.)

Therefore it is essential to clearly distinguish:

- *Emotion in the face of the unexplainable origin of the universe and its organization, which is the only genuine religiosity.*
- *The mythical "God-the-Creator" symbol.* Moved and inspired by religious feeling, human imagination creates the anthropomorphic image of an "intentional Creator" called "God."
- *The error consisting in mistaking the symbolic image for a reality.*

The fact is that this confusion ends up by hypostatizing the "God" image, by attempting to explain that which cannot be explained and by eliminating the feeling of mystery. The symbolically true image is surreptitiously transformed into a "God" concept, object of metaphysical discussions.

Symbolic metaphysics is not explanatory but meaningful. On the contrary, *postmythical explanations dealing with the existence or nonexistence of God are vain metaphysical speculations.*

Wrongly inspired by the metaphysical image, man—being psyche and soma, spirit and matter—is tempted to explain the "Creating Principle" either under personifying form of an all-powerful and actually existing Spirit or under the reified form of an omnipotent Matter. The two attempts at explanation go beyond the given facts of existence in a manner which is no longer only symbolical but realistic. In reality neither absolute spirit nor absolute matter exist. To believe one or the other of the pseudoexplanations to be in conformity with the requirements of the human mind, can only bring about incessant quarrels which are the result of the misunderstanding of the symbolizing imagination at work in myths. Theism and atheism, spiritualism and materialism, though they are antagonistic, are united in a vain attempt to explain the mystery of the Origins of existence.

For theism, God actually exists outside of real space, in a metaphysical Beyond. Atheism believes that the creating principle resided in matter. The latter—uncreated—is supposed to have always existed. Instead of spiritualism's space outside of real space, materialism proposes time outside of real time, which is pure metaphysical speculation. Eternity itself is nothing but a mythical symbol. *God-Mystery is neither transcendent to space nor to time but only to human reason. God-Image, on the other hand, is not transcendent to reasoning. Human reason is perfectly able to explain the mythical image "God" according to its symbolic origin and its significance.*

Human reason should become aware of its limited competence when faced with the mystery of the origins of existence. It should endeavor to decipher the enigma of symbolic language in order to dispel the confusion between God-Mystery and God-Image, so as to strengthen emotion in the face of mystery.

Insoluble problems arise from the error that confuses the "God" image with a concept, and the *Name of God—a pure concept—with the living God, i.e., emotionally experienced mystery.*

The biblical texts show "God" at times as pure Spirit, and at other times as a Spirit endowed with a body. These two images are symbols, a fact which is clearly spelled out in the texts.

Outside of symbolization, the actual existence of a pure Spirit is unthinkable and even unimaginable. Does it float in the air? Where, in which space? Without a body, without perceptive organs, how could it listen to man's prayers? How, if a pure spirit, could it talk, how could it reveal itself to man? All beliefs in the transcendental existence of God refer to a revelation described in the texts, but which is only symbolically supernatural. Did God actually talk in Hebrew to the Prophets? And even if such had been the case, the human mind could only have grasped the inconceivable message in an inadequate manner within man's limited capacity of understanding; in other words, the message would in any event have only a symbolic and anthropomorphic value. (In the dialogue between Jesus and Nicodemus, God is in fact represented as floating in the air: "The wind blows where it wills." But this is a very ancient symbol of the vital impulse animating more or less intensely every individual, though its inspirational force is rarely strong enough to cause man to be "reborn" out of his banal and conventional uninspired state as is the case with Nicodemus.)

Thus if "God-the pure-Spirit," transcendent revealer, is unthinkable outside of the symbolic image, "God-endowed-with-a-body" is a mythical image which is still more unthinkable and unimaginable. Either we are confronted with a real body or a ghost body: a purely symbolic fiction. But how could it be a real body, which in order to be real would have all actual body functions such as nutrition and digestion?

Blasphemy? Of course not! Blasphemy—or as Scripture says, *abomination*—is precisely the literal interpretation of the mythical fiction. The abomination (spoken of by Solomon at the consecration of the Temple in Jerusalem) is denounced throughout all the biblical texts. God is the Invisible and the Unnameable. It is absolutely forbidden— outside of symbolic thought—to give him a concrete representation, be it a statue or a portrait. Yet, one must name God in order to talk about him. But one speaks only about "the name of God." God is too great, says Solomon, to be housed in the Temple (where people talk about him), "The earth is his footstool," an image attempting to express the Incommensurable. Jerusalem (Hebrew culture) will be destroyed—as will all cultures—when the abomination is set in the Temple, when the "name of God" is mistaken for the living God. We cannot quote here the many biblical passages pertaining to this central theme. They are all summed up in the first commandment: "You shall not utter the name of the Lord your God in vain." To utter his name in vain—which is called "abomination" by Solomon—is to utter the name without any reference to mystery.

What could be more vain than the pretension of metaphysical speculation which not only makes vain usage of the name "God" but which, ignorant of its symbolic significance, deems itself competent to discuss the existence or nonexistence of the indisputable mystery called "God"?

D. SYMBOLIC AND ANALOGICAL THOUGHT (THE MYTHICAL "AS IF")

How can we talk about mystery without further investigation? The question is to know whether investigation can avoid getting lost in speculation. It is therefore essential—here more than ever—to analyze the human mind and the limits of its competence.

If the human mind goes all the way in its questioning, it will unavoidably have to pose *the ultimate question: how is it that the universe exists and that its survival is ensured by a harmonious organization?*

Human understanding—if it believes itself competent to tackle the problem of the Origins—is compelled to consider the organized universe as an effect for which it seeks the cause. However, contrary to all actually existing causes (which are themselves effects of preceding causes) the "cause" of the Origins, instead of being only relative should be absolute: *causa sui*. Whether one calls it absolute Spirit or absolute Matter, one refers in both cases to an actually inexistent, unreal, metaphysical cause. *Reflection, without being aware of this, has insidiously lost its way in a flight of the imagination.*

It is not superfluous to recall here the wisdom of language: In French, to speak is "causer" (which also means *to cause*). To speak in an intelligible and intelligent manner means to look for actual causes. But causal reflection and flight of the imagination are not radically separated. The wisdom of language expresses it by describing the reflective function through synonymous terms indicating its varying degrees of clarity: I think, I deem, I believe, I imagine, I fancy. Thus it can happen that what we mistake for conclusive thought is only fanciful aberration.

However, besides causal and logical thought, the human mind also uses an intuitive and analogical form of thought that, while imaginative by nature, is far from being only fanciful aberration.

Just like logically causal thought, analogical thought is a reasoning tool.

It is reasonable to think that each existing phenomenon—by this we mean a phenomenon included in space-time—is subject to the necessity of disappearance and thus becomes the cause of the effective appearance of a new phenomenon, which in turn will disappear and produce of necessity its own effect: the effective appearance of a new ephemeral phenomenon, and so on and so forth. Taking note of the uninterrupted chain of cause and effect is the attribute of logical intelligence. But it is just as reasonable to foresee that all phenomena—since they are included in space-time—must be analogically organized in spite of their modal diversity and must therefore compose together a harmonious whole: a universal organization.

Who created the harmony of the universe?

This question goes beyond intellectual speculation, according to which the existence of the universe would be the effect of a *causa sui*, a pseudological answer which is a late product of philosophical thought. The *causa sui* is impersonal and has nothing to do with the mythical symbol of "God-the-Creator." As far as myth is concerned, God is not an impersonal principle of existence, he is a person who is animated by intentions and this intentionality does not only concern the creating act of the past but the permanent activity of the Creator with regard to his Creation. The mythical answer is an *analogical conclusion* comparing the creation and organization of the universe with the intentional creation of any human work. The human mind[2] confronted with the problem of the Origins, is compelled—as it has always been compelled—to note that *it is "as if" a superhuman mind had created the harmoniously organized universe and "as if" it went on watching over its creation.*

Now this "as if" is the underlying significance of all types of analogical reasonings, mythical symbolism being only one of a special kind. *If it is so,* no investigative effort would be superfluous in order to bring to light the difference between the analogical "as if"—a purely comparative image—and the "it is so" denoting the existence of an actual fact.

There are three forms of harmony that are harmoniously linked to one another:

- harmony of thought: truth;
- harmony of feelings: love;
- harmony of will: harmony of motivating intentions and thus of meaningful activity.

Scientific hypothesis is a form of analogical thought: it is seeking, through superconsciously guided intuition, the universal links—the laws—that bind seemingly heterogeneous phenomena. (Thus, for instance, there does not seem to be any link between the fall of bodies toward the center of the earth and the harmonious motion of the stars, as long as the mind has not brought to light the analogical link, i.e., the law of gravity: the attraction of masses.) The mind, through a kind of

---

[2]See note 1 in chapter I.

superconsciously guided intuitive clairvoyance, based on harmony which is the law of laws, assumes as a hypothesis that *it could be so,* and does not say, until it has been proved, that *it is so.*

The common feature of all forms of harmony is that they are true and beautiful. Beauty is a truth that moves us without any need for proof. Since all is included in the beauty of universal harmony, all that is can be analogically compared, on condition however that comparison uncover a striking analogy between two phenomena apparently devoid of any link. This is the case in *poetic metaphor.* The examples are countless and there is no need to dwell on this point. What deserves to be noted, though, is that the New Testament frequently uses poetic analogy in the form of parables: "To work in the vineyard of the Lord," for instance; the work of the wine grower is analogically compared with intrapsychic work. This would only be a poetic metaphor if the poetry of the analogy were not amplified by the underlying symbolic pre-science. During the polytheistic era, wine was already a symbol for sublimation (and bread a symbol for spiritualization). However, one must first understand pre-science in order to grasp the psychological meaning of the analogy which nevertheless remains a parable since the word "Lord" does not belong to symbolic vocabulary.

The point to emphasize is that through the symbolical expression of myths, analogical thought reaches its highest intensity of significance. Symbolization compares analogically intrapsychic conflicts with external struggles. The positive and negative intentions of the psyche are analogically personified in the forms of deities and monsters. According to the facade of the narrative, the vicissitudes of the battles are poetic analogies; but in the underlying significance, the vicissitudes contain a pre-science of the inner psychic functioning, adding to the beauty of the story the psychological truth based on the laws of harmony and disharmony. *The facade of the story is only an "as if", the underlying truth affirms, "it is so".* It ascertains that harmony of intentions is a source of joy and disharmony a cause for anxiety.

This brings us back to *the question of the origins* to which there is no adequate answer without an analysis of analogical thought.

Analysis shows that just as logical thought, analogical thought is only valid for existing phenomena, among which the most impressive is the immanent harmonious organization manifest through nature. Analogical conclusion being characterized by its ability to compare seemingly heterogeneous phenomena and to group them in a harmonious unity (harmony being unity within multiplicity), it is absolutely necessary for the compared phenomena to be immanent to existence, otherwise the comparison has no intelligible meaning. This also holds true for symbolic analogies in which the common factor of comparison is the immanence of the inner psychic functioning.

Now there is one and only one symbolic analogy—though it is shared by all mythologies—which goes beyond the elements of existence: the image of "God" Creator and intentional organizer of the universe. This is a cosmogonic analogy and not an analogy based on psychology. The anthropomorphic personification which is valid for all the other mythical symbols remains here an "as if" which can never be confirmed. Yet metaphysical analogy, in spite of the lack of a definable meaning, is not senseless. Quite the contrary, since it implies the deepest meaning of manifest existence: the awareness of an infinite and undefinable mystery.

Here is what the biblical God says and it is the revelation of revelations: "I am who I am," a symbolic expression meaning: do not doubt my unnameable existence for I am more than existing. Life and existence are only the forms in which I reveal myself to human understanding. They are my manifest appearance; may I be manifest also in you during your life and through your life. Experience me in the very depths of your being. Fear the unfathomable mystery of your existence. But be also reassured. No harm will befall you except that which you bring on yourself by forgetting me. Make me live in you and I exist for you, though I am an undecipherable mystery.

The ethical symbol of "God-the-Judge" is inseparably linked to the metaphysical symbol of "God-the-Creator." However, while the metaphysical "as if" implies its own negation, i.e., "it is only as if" but *it is not so,* the ethical "as if" pertains to an actual reality: the possibility of psychic harmonization. *The ethical "as if" has the bearing of a scientific hypothesis calling for a proof of its reality.* "God-the-Judge" is the symbol of the superconsciously immanent ethical law, immutable truth, law of harmonization: when man is in a state of inner disharmony he experiences the ethical law through the self-judgment of guilty anxiety intimating that he should—for his own essential good—actively prove the possibility of harmonization through self-control of his motivating intentions in order to change guilty discord into agreement with himself. Since *it is so,* the ethical "as if" represented by "God-the-Judge," but in fact a psychic phenomenon, is equally probable through the deciphering of myths insofar as they represent, in symbolically exteriorized struggles, the inner conflict and its harmoniously happy or disharmoniously anguishing result, an essential reality for every man and for all men.

Emotion in the presence of the mystery of creation becomes a superconscious voice symbolized by the "God-Judge" image. The abomination described in the Old Testament does not only pertain to idolatry (metaphysical speculation) but also to its consequence: loss of the ethical sense of superconsciousness (split into excessively good or moralizing intentions and excessively evil or banalizing intentions). Just like the Old Testament, the New Testament opposes metaphysical idolatry and its consequence which destroys the ethical sense. The meaning of the Christian myth is summed up by a sole formula: "Heaven is in you." If Heaven is in us, its resident, "God," is in us just as are "Hell" and "Satan."

What we really have "in us" are the disharmonizing intentions shamefully hidden in the subconscious, and also the harmonizing intentions of superconsciousness. (Though it must be noted that the terms "superconscious" and "subconscious" like the phrase "in us" are only "as if" expressions that are linguistically spatializing and whose underlying significance are the functional dynamics of the psyche. The understanding of the biogenetic origin of the extraconscious processes will be developed in a subsequent chapter.) Is it possible to raise to the level of consciousness the secret conflict of extraconscious motivations? In our day and age, this is indeed the way one has to ask the ultimate question implied in the symbols of "God-the-Creator" and "God-the-Judge."

Theological spiritualism and atheistic materialism are not the result of an emotional contemplation of nature. They are the products of abstract speculation. The spiritualist pores over the texts and misunderstands their symbolic intention. The materialism of *the sciences of life* observes nature without any emotional contemplation. Thinking that this is a criterion of objectivity, the materialist interprets nature and man on the basis of the subjectivity of his underlying antispiritualistic metaphysical prejudice that makes him believe in a creating matter. Metaphysical speculation begins as soon as the symbolically profound "as if" is turned into a flat explanation: "it is so" or "it is not so." Such is the twofold error ambivalently bonding theism and atheism.

The theist affirms: it is not only as if a God had intentionally created the world, it is so. The atheist affirms: it is not so; the intentional aspect of nature, though manifest, is in fact nothing more than an illusion and the product of chance. Theism and atheism are confronted with the finalistic intentionality of nature. But instead of acknowledging its mysterious aspect, they endeavor either to explain it through God and his creating intentionality or by rejecting God and denying any intentionality—even human intentionality—thus turning all nature into an automatism and life—including human life—into the epiphenomenon of a "Matter" endowed with omnipotence. How could this be anything but a *credo quia absurdum?* "Matter," an abstract concept, is pseudologically proposed as a creating reality and confusedly identified with concrete matter: the atom. Where does the very mysterious organization of the atom come from? Should it not be clear that by granting only an epiphenomenal dimension to the whole of the intentional functioning of the psyche—and thus to the psychic function which is the human spirit and its explanatory intention—the materialism of the sciences of life, in order to remain logical would have to declare that the doctrinal product of its own explanatory reflection is nothing but a negligible epiphenomenon?

Spiritualism and materialism, theism and atheism, all have an arsenal of arguments—or quibbles—to justify themselves. It would be futile to enter into the details of their dogmatic discussions. What matters is to stress their common error: the imaginative leap surreptitiously taking the mind beyond the competence of human reason, limited by the unexplainable, to the unlimited realm of delusions and beliefs. Only mythical imagination, with its symbolic "as if" proposition may transcend the mystery of the Origins which is indissolubly linked to the *immanent mysterious aspect of all that is, man included.*

Chapter III

The Problem of Methodology

A. Philosophical Epistemology

Epistemology is the fundamental research for a sure and indisputable foundation of human thought and for the methodological principle of its research. As such, epistemology is opposed to all forms of metaphysical speculations, be they spiritualistic or materialistic.

Materialists of all types, being ignorant of the meaning of the term "metaphysics" which belongs to the philosophical vocabulary, usurp it and misuse it in order to condemn any investigative effort going beyond the immediate data obtained by the observation of materially perceptible objects. The fact is that they themselves go beyond the immediate data by introducing the metaphysical concept of an absolute matter endowed with creative powers, so as to deduce from it the solution to the basic problem pertaining to the origin of the world and life and its meaning.

As a matter of fact, epistemological research—its progress and errors—constitutes the essential history of human life: the research for an indisputable foundation of ethical values. In this understanding, which is not only theoretical, it is fair to note that the most ancient form of epistemological investigation—already rooted in animism—was the image of the creating deity and its symbolic "as if."

Throughout time and in all great cultures, philosophical meditation was born in opposition to theological epistemology proposing belief as an indisputable certainty, a foundation that was too doubtful not to end up by unsettling the guiding values. Up to our time, the history of thought remains full of controversy. In order to safeguard the ethical values, philosophy abandoned theological terminology borrowed from mythology which had become suspicious. Instead of talking about deities and referring to beliefs, philosophy while still in its pre-epistemological form, presupposed the existence of an "absolute Substance" or a "supreme Being" and tried to shore up its new beliefs with rational proofs. It is therefore not surprising that "Substance" was finally replaced by the idea of a pre-existent material substance.

Having as a sole method of analysis intuitive inspiration, the various attempts at philosophical synthesis remain divergent systems, at times spiritualistic (concerned with grasping the "Being" of the world), and at times materialistic (concerned with understanding the changing nature of the world). Each system offers another foundation for values. However—and this is *the most remarkable fact in philosophy*—in all cycles of culture, the insoluble contradiction always led to *a self-criticism of the mind: an epistemological philosophy or critique of knowledge* showing a profound sincerity on the part of the great guiding minds that were the true philosophers (as the name implies: lovers of wisdom). Epistemology periodically questioned not only theological dogmas, but the competence of the human mind: is it capable or not of finding a valid answer to the metaphysical question?

In our culture, epistemological self-criticism of the mind started with Descartes's *cogito*. To set the present study in its historical context would not mean taking a speculative detour, since—in order to clear the way—both spiritualistic metaphysics and materialistic metaphysics must be opposed. This clarification is all the more necessary that nowadays materialism refers itself to Cartesian philosophy and its *cogito* which—with the *Discourse on Method*—was the beginning of a long era of epistemological (i.e., methodological) reflection that remained unfortunately incomplete and was finally overwhelmed (as must be proven) by the advent of a new scholasticism replacing belief in an "Absolute Spirit" by belief in an "Absolute Matter."

The question is to find out why and how the formula "I think, therefore I am" (I am mind, therefore I exist first of all as a thinking being) was finally turned into a counterproposition that can be summed up in the following formula: "I am matter, therefore I exist as an automaton" (without being subject to guiding values). The purpose of this clarification is thus not only theoretical but highly practical.

The criticism is only directed at the materialism of the sciences of life and does not pertain in any way to the methodological foundation of physics. In physics, materialism is only a working hypothesis. As such, it is perfectly adapted to the object of the study which is limited to the finding of the laws ruling the spatial motion of inanimate objects.

Physics does not pose the metaphysical problem of the origin of the bodies (matter) or of the laws (spirit). However, as a man (and not only as a specialized scientist), a physicist can be tempted to go beyond the limits of his science. He will answer the metaphysical question by introducing—as Newton did—the "Demiurge." It should be evident that in Newton's mind, the "Demiurge" or "Clockmaker" is only an anthropomorphized image devoid of any real explanatory value, since in fact, as a physicist, he explains the workings of the World-Clock on the basis of immanent laws and not on that of a transcendent Clockmaker. The physical world exists and works "as if" the Clockmaker had manufactured it once and forever and did not have to intervene anymore, which is precisely the mystery. Awareness of an immanent mystery (or better yet, of a mysterious aspect in existence) is far from being occultism. The latter, a type of vague and confused thought, is in fact the absence of a clear distinction between mystery and phenomenon, and it is in such a way that the materialism of the sciences of life becomes a dogma just as scholastic as theological spiritualism.

The old theological scholasticism and its spiritualistic metaphysics were founded, as we know, on the affirmation that the only certainty is the belief in a personal existence of God.

Descartes opposes this belief with doubt. Belief—whatever its object—is only a function of the human psyche, a kind of imaginative thought, necessarily vague to some degree. The only certainty, as the *cogito* posits, cannot therefore be reached through any belief (and surely not through the unprovable metaphysical belief in an absolute spirit), but only through the effort of the human mind to free itself from any metaphysical prejudice. To do so, the mind (which undoubtedly exists) should try to understand *the limits of its competence* and the suitable means of its discursive process (Discourse on Method).

Now the mind will not become aware of its limitations and its means until and unless it has subjected itself to a *self-critical research* which, through the very nature of the problem in question, can only be introspective. Thus, starting with Descartes, epistemology, methodical self-criticism, the need to define *a theory of knowledge* became, instead of metaphysical speculation, the central theme of philosophical meditation.

It is not possible here to go into the details of the tremendous effort of self-analysis—more or less introspective—that was developed on the basis of Descartes's *cogito* by the British empiricists (Locke, Berkeley, Hume) and by German criticism from Kant's *Critique of Pure Reason* to the contributions of Fichte and Schelling and finally to Hegel's *Phenomenology of the Spirit*.

What we want to stress here are the common features of those researches. In the first place, they all endeavored to prove that the "In-Itself"—which is precisely "Metaphysics"—that underlies all things (the perceived world) is a *mystery beyond* both our perception which is limited by space and time and our thought, restricted to searching the causal modifications ruling all existing spatio-temporal "things."

Epistemological philosophy thus admitted quite rightly on the one hand, mystery (called the "In-Itself") and on the other hand, existing phenomena (thought and perception, psyche and word, spirit and matter).

The other common feature is that epistemological philosophy—though unaware of it—takes the problem of knowledge away from the metaphysical plane and brings it within the realm of *psychological study*.

Such an approach calls for an analysis of the human spirit[1] which is a psychic function. In this respect, it must be said that all these attempts of self-analysis of the spirit—though very valuable—were based on an inadequate introspective method, since at that time the extraconscious (superconscious and subconscious) was unknown and therefore also the importance of symbolic language.

It would be unfair not to list in this all too brief outline one of Descartes's great successors, though he remains a somewhat unique and isolated case. Spinoza, in his *Ethics*—which gives a magnificent overall view—included all aspects of the epistemological problem: mystery which he calls "Substance", its two manifest "Attributes" understanding and extent (spirit and matter), and the "Modalities" or causal modifications (due to the constant interactions between spirit and matter). The *Ethics* ends up with an attempt at establishing morality on the psychological analysis of the motivating intentions underlying the life of the feelings.

Epistemological philosophy and its theory of knowledge did not succeed in definitely superseding scholastic metaphysics and its theology. The persistent influence of the antimetaphysical meditation started off by the *"cogito"*—though it remains subjacent—can be felt in all the fields of our present life and not only on the theoretical plane.

All present philosophical trends stem from Hegel's philosophy and his *Phenomenology of the Spirit.* For Hegel, spirit is preconscious; it is an immanent phenomenon: his phenomenology attempts to prove that the human spirit is a product of evolution and that its special function is the valuation of desires (material and sexual), which implies the ethical phenomenon.

It remains true that the Hegelian system does not take sufficiently into account the constant interaction between the two existing phenomena—spirit and matter. That finally led to a reversal of the relationship between spirit and matter. The latter was given a primary importance. The introduction of the belief in an absolute matter was meant to do away with the necessity for epistemological investigation. Absolute matter was thus erroneously thought—in lieu of an absolute spirit—to be the unique certainty on which any attempt at explanation should be based. Abandoning epistemological self-analysis, the various doctrines of modern philosophy are characterized by a common trend: they are only concerned with existing phenomena from which however they exclude the valuating spirit, deemed to be an unimportant epiphenomenon. Ethical values—guides to practical life—are thus declared nonexistent, unless they are seen as social conventions (Existentialism, Phenomenology, Marxism, Structuralism).

Such a progressive neglect of epistemological investigation led to for-

---

[1] See 1 in chapter I.

getting the essential acquisition of the notion of mystery present in the "In-Itself" concept. The "In-Itself" of philosophical epistemology was, however, only a theoretical notion, devoid of any emotional warmth in the face of the *mysterious aspect* of all that is, emotion that extends or should extend to the mysterious aspect of immanent values—their immutable truth—, constant theme of mythical pre-science, and its "as if" pertaining to the existence of a God, who creates and enforces values.

Man's explanatory spirit, guide of human activity, should discover the biogenetic immanence of harmonizing values so as to knowingly reconcile human valuations and the harmonizing intentionality immanent to all of nature, the most basic of phenomena, though its origins remain mysteriously unexplainable.

The purely phenomenological and existentialistic explanation necessarily confuses ethical values and the material conditions of social life, a reversal leading to a wrong overvaluation of material desires and to the cynical excesses of our time.

Being radically opposed to mythical pre-science, all the *sciences of life* are now deeply influenced by materialistic philosophy: psychology limits itself to the study of behavior and neglects the inner motivational causes; physiology attempts to replace the failings of psychology with the study of brain matter; psychiatry sees the "illnesses of the mind" as nothing but a somatic disturbance; sociology states that the individual is completely shaped by his material situation and the influence of the social environment. All the materialistic disciplines of the sciences of life declare themselves to be followers of the *cogito* and the *Discourse on Method,* forgetting that the "I" of the *cogito* is the *individual,* the valuating spirit of every man and of all men: the inner motivating life of each one of us, sole essential criterion of the vital value of each person, and thus of the vital value of all people and their social interactions.

There is no doubt that the advent of *depth psychology* must be understood as the indispensable reaction against the degradation of the individual and his inner life. Studying the extraconscious depths, it is in the process of discovering symbolizing thought and its superconscious pre-science regarding the immanent origin of ethical values and the deep significance of the "God" symbol. As a reaction against all types of metaphysical speculations, depth psychology's investigation has as its main object the study of guilty feelings. What are these feelings if not *an inner self-criticism,* too often repressed and falsely justified? *Guilt is the mind's self-criticism (pre-scientific, pre-philosophical, pre-epistemological) with respect to its own errors, be they theoretical or practical.*

Seen thus, psychology of the extraconscious depths is also a remote heir to philosophical epistemology. Yet, only too often, the various schools of psychology remain subject to the influence of materialism and its phobia of introspective self-control. This necessarily leads to looking for a remedy for "the illnesses of the mind" only through social adjustment while neglecting essential adjustment to the immanent superconscious ethical sense. In order to find a solid basis, psychology of the extraconscious depths should free itself from materialism and its phobia of introspection. *Does not the undeniable fact of a self-control in the form of guilty warning prove the existence of a more-than-conscious psychic process* which has always been known by linguistic wisdom and called "ethical conscience"? Can anyone deny that we deliberate before we act? *And what is this inner deliberation if not a ceaseless introspective self-observation?* Psychiatry acknowledges this but sees it as an excess of self-love, vain egocentricity, illness of the mind, morbid lack of objectivity, the cause of psychopathies. The truth is that there is such a thing as morbid introspection and it does pose a problem of epistemological depth. Epistemology would be unthinkable if the human mind was, by its nature, incurably falsifying the truth about itself. *For epistemology is an objective self-criticism of the mind or it is meaningless.* Philosophy and its "Critique of Knowledge" (search for the criterion of objective knowledge) could not tackle this essential aspect since it had no awareness of the extraconscious depths; this is the task of depth psychology which must reopen the study of this problem in all its magnitude. In this respect, we must point out again that here lies the central problem of all mythologies; for they are—as we have stressed many times—a prescientific depth psychology.

As a matter of fact, the existence of a morbid introspection is the clearest proof of the complementary existence of a lucid and healthy introspection. The human mind is, by nature, prone to error; but due to its spiritual and sublimating side, it is a tireless seeker for truth. This evident fact enables us to replace the somewhat arid term of "epistemology" by its actual significance: *love of truth and joy of knowledge.*

What could be the inverse and adverse principle, immanent to psychic functioning, that deprives us of the love of truth about ourselves and the joy of knowledge, above all knowledge of ourselves (never perfect but always perfectible)? The subconscious is not what we do not know or we cannot know, but what we do not want to know because it is too painful. The whole problem of epistemology is thus led back to self-criticism of thought which should be able to discover the deep and hidden motive of the anxiety regarding the truth about ourselves, i.e., what causes phobia of introspection.

This obsessive subconscious motive is vanity (*vanitas:* vain, vacuum). "Vanity, vanity!" exclaims Ecclesiastes. Not all is vanity. But all our thoughts and all our actions are threatened by vanity if we do not defend ourselves against morbid introspection with the help of lucid and healthy introspection.

Vanity is the mother of all vices. Being excess of self-love, its egocentric subjectivity downgrades the life of the feelings to a swarming of spiteful resentments that are falsely inculpating, exacting and provocative, offended or triumphant, plaintive or aggressive, overladen with rancor and jealousy, indignation and vindictive ruminations. Without any exception, all the perverse feelings—pitting man against man—are the byproduct of vain self-exculpation and excessive inculpation of others (individually and collectively), leading to mutual accusations which—based on false justification on all sides—become the motivating cause for all hostile interactions. Would this insidiously hidden vanity be *the secret and central motive* of all false motivations and all false interactions? Would not greed of material desires, the main culprit in social disorders, be itself one of the nefarious consequences of egocentric vanity? Would this be the meaning of Ecclesiastes's cry of despair to the "chosen people," symbol of all peoples, all communities of mankind? Ecclesiastes sums up the prophecies of the Old Testament pertaining to hidden motivations and their destructive consequences, by denouncing their unsuspected common cause.

The life of the feelings would not become perverted if man did not become deaf to the call of the spirit: in other words, to the call of the immanent ethical superconscience and its imperative of harmonization. Vain self-justification—call it deafness of the understanding or blindness of spiritual lucidity—by repressing the message of the superconscience—the feeling of guiltiness—thus becomes the guilty cause, the fundamental *illness of the mind,* while the degradation of the feelings into spiteful resentment is only an effect. Vanity—imaginative exaltation, morbid self-interpretation—becomes the cause of a morbid interpretation of all the elements of existence: it imaginatively exalts all the desires (material, sexual, pseudospiritual) beyond any possibility or realization and mistakes this initial error for unquestionable proof of a limitless vital impulse. Its insatiability can only be fulfilled by the *ideal absolute* (be it absolute spirit or matter), and *perfection.* Since the absolute is unthinkable and perfection impossible, the imaginative oversatisfaction due to vain hopes, creates its own disillusions which are themselves unlimited, and which can end in despair about oneself and life.

The means available to a vain mind for arguing and fallacious justification are unlimited since the beliefs it takes for certainties are the product of an unbridled imagination delighting in aping the veracious conclusions of genuine thought. Its favorite guises are pseudospirituality and pseudosublimity, but also and conversely, the cynical effrontery of banalism mistaking itself for a supreme judge of life and its meaning.

All forms of triumphant vanity have the potential to become ruling ideologies and to meet unanimous approval due to the lack of a genuine criterion of objectivity. Their compromises and quarrels breed pseudomorality, demoralization under two contradictory forms: exalted moralism and banal amoralism.

Such are the grave defeats—though they are never final—that the love of vain lying inflicts on the love of truth and the joy of knowledge.

B. The Error of Philosophical Epistemology

The awareness of an immanent possibility of vain error adds to the Theory of Knowledge a dimension that philosophical epistemology had totally omitted.

The problem is no longer only to find out whether thought is capable of truthfully grasping the world of objects. The central problem of the Theory of Knowledge is to find out whether it is possible or not for thought, insofar as it remains lucid, to detect and correct its own tendency to fall into vain error. The corollary of this epistemological evidence is the fact that such a correction can only be achieved through introspective self-observation and self-control. The motive for introspective self-control can only be the superconsciously immanent self-objectifying impulse, intensified to the point of love of truth about oneself to such a degree that it can defeat the subconsciously obsessive excess of self-love which is vain subjectivity. Love of truth, far from being a doctrinal verbalism, finds and proves its effectiveness through epistemological research. "I am because I think." To be sure. But what is the purpose of thinking if I refuse to think myself through? What is essential is not to know that I am but *who I am.* If I dare not take upon myself this essential function of my thought—self-knowledge—the refusal clearly stems from a kind of counterspirit which surely one has to diagnose as obsessive vanity compelling one to love, rather than the real self (criterion of real existence), a flattering image, a ghost of the real self.

Seen thus, the existence of vanity is quite evident. But it is the very characteristic of vain blindness to obsessively push man to believe in the pseudoevidence of its nonexistence: the vainer one is, the less one believes oneself to be so. Thus vanity was never diagnosed outside of mythical and linguistic pre-science. Myth has given us the "serpent" symbol to show how venomous vanity can be. Linguistic pre-science also points to it as the very principle of senselessness: "vain, devoid of sense." The attempt to minimize the existence of vanity is manifested even in daily language which tries to hide its importance under weaker terms: "fatuity," "futility," "ostentation," etc., the intention being to see it as a shortcoming with no more importance than any other. False and vain overvaluation is even confused with pride, though the latter is precisely the opposite of vanity: just and moderate self-valuation, in accordance with real qualities.

However, the need to bring into epistemology and its search for fundamental truth, the introspective study of vanity and its multiple forms of false motivation, has even deeper roots.

Vain self-oversatisfaction and its power to disturb the objective process of thought are anchored in the biogenesis of the thinking being. "I am (man) because I think." Considered from the biogenetic viewpoint, man is the only thinking animal. Since he is not guided anymore by preconscious instinct, he is compelled to think consciously—and if possible, knowingly—in order to find his bearings in the world which provides his living environment. Man is not pure spirit. He is, first of all, an intentionality directed towards the world which is indispensable for his subsistance. His thought is a means of orientation: his intentional goal is to obtain the satisfaction of his vital needs. The objects of the outer world become the objectives of man's thought because they are initially objects of his desires and of their demand for satisfaction.

Adapting desires to objective reality is nothing more than correctly judging promises of satisfaction and threats of dissatisfaction. Through right or wrong valuation, desires—often potential desires only—become inner motives for the interest invested in external objects and situations. All these motives of future actions (preparing the acquisition of the object or flight in the face of difficulty) are part of a ceaseless deliberation kept in a state of alert either by the *presence* of the perceived object or by its imaginative *representation*. All the vital problems linking man to the outer world are—at least originally so—psychic problems of satisfaction or dissatisfaction. All the *attention* given to the outer world—be it perceptive, imaginative or cognitive—is due to the *intention* to extract satisfaction from it.

The search for satisfaction is the root of all motivating intentions. The search of the spirit is directed toward its specific satisfaction: truth. Love of truth and joy of knowledge—foundations of epistemology because they are the supreme satisfactions—are the most evolved manifestations of the biological need for satisfaction. To understand the biogenetic importance of the search for satisfaction (material, sexual, and spiritual) is *an integral part of epistemological research.*

The intentionality of the whole of nature—mysterious as it is—becomes a phenomenon that can be defined on the basis of the quest for satisfaction which dictates to life a hierarchy of immanent values. Materiality and sexuality are basic values, indispensable for survival. However, life would be nothing but a swarming of obscure intentions if, starting from the biological basis, the pyramid of values rising from one evolutionary step to the next up to the level of man, it did not attain the superior values of the human spirit (superior in their intensity of satisfaction): the superconscious intentionality to understand what is true in order to achieve what is right, i.e., the ethical principle of satisfaction.

The biogenetic evolution of the inexorable search for satisfaction clearly points to the subconscious involutionary danger of vain blindness. Vanity, imaginative exaltation with regard to oneself, attempts to penetrate all the motivating intentions and thereby all activities. It infiltrates all thoughts, all ideas, all ideologies, and all idealisms. It downgrades feelings to the level of sentimental or spiteful resentments, will to the level of pseudosublime volitions that are either plaintive or aggressive. It threatens to invade the entire inner deliberation which is the human function of search for satisfaction. Vanity, the primary false promise of satisfaction, exerts a magical, I-magical, imaginative seduction because it is imaginatively all-powerful and promises the satisfaction of all desires no matter how absurd and impossible. The sight of vanity evokes horror in our inner eye and this is caused by anxiety in the presence of rising guiltiness. The pseudo-omnipotence of vain imagination is in fact a biologically deep weakness arousing the warning of ethical superconsciousness; but guilty self-dissatisfaction is then repressed and hidden from superconscious control. Thus, from repression to repression of its guilty aspect, it insidiously creates a terrifying mirage, a ghost of the self which is obsessively preferred to the genuine self, the latter being progressively destroyed and hated because it is a living reproach. Is there a man, who in the secret of his inner life, has not experienced the horror of these swings from vanity to guiltiness and guiltiness to vanity?

As painful as it is to acknowledge this, consciously and knowingly, I know—in spite of myself—that this concerns me. I know this superconsciously. After all, could not *vain discord between imagination and reality* be a constant though hidden state of mind? It would of course vary depending on the degree of intensity of inner discord. This is the essential illness! A split hidden in our very depths! A ceaseless temptation to self-overvaluation, self-justification accompanied by an excess of inculpation of others, of situations, of life itself, exaggerated complaints, false motivations, erroneous and morbid deliberation! Monstrous truth! Unavowable truth! To be sure. But it is unavowable only for our vanity and for that very reason it is an essential truth, a healthy truth, an epistemologically profound truth. Here is what has become of me because I believed that it was enough to think in order to be genuine. When will I understand at last the truth of truths, the certitude of certitudes: to grasp the truth, *one must become true oneself, and how can this happen without controlling one's motives?* Tremendous hope: if the fault is in me, I can amend it myself. Having become what I am—a liar to myself—why could I not become more objective? On the sole condition however not to transform this tremendous hope into an absolute hope, a vain hope for perfect liberation. A modest project, too modest perhaps? Absolutely not! Never modest enough not to demand permanent self-control, which is the only way to prevent a meaningful project from deteriorating into an excessively good and therefore senseless intention, liable to lapse again into vain superiority. The struggle against vanity experiences defeats but it also knows victories. This is the truth expressed by the wisdom of myths as well as by the wisdom of language: "The greatest victory is victory over oneself."

Since this is in me, is it not in all of us? Ultimate question of objectivity. What acme of vanity, what madness even would we not all perceive if anyone attempted to make us believe that his most hidden intentions were free of vanity, unhampered by any influence of the subconscious, that he knew them perfectly well, and that he deemed himself therefore to be the most just and most truthful of all men! Thus if by common consent of judgment, the man who considers himself free of vanity is the vainest of all, does it not follow that a vain lie exists in all of us? Do we not all have rare moments of objectivity during which, in the presence of an all too visible failure, vanity collapses, when—even for a fleeting moment, in a glimpse of lucidity—we see the smugly justified horrible truth (that we are vain) as the motive of our wrong actions and interactions? Does it not happen during these rare moments of involuntary lucidity, that faced with a too painful reality, our eyes close convulsively in a significant twitch? It is the inner eye shying away from what it sees?

The most dangerous transgression of the ever present vain seductions is that they twist love of truth into hatred of truth and joy of knowledge into anxiety in the face of self-knowledge. The Theory of Knowledge cannot be content—as philosophical epistemology proposes—with exclusively searching for criteria of objectivity with regard to the external world. By far the most important epistemological research concerns the conditions of an objective self-knowledge: the struggle against the magical seduction of vanity, which is impossible without becoming aware of the inner motivating deliberation.

C. PSYCHOLOGICAL EPISTEMOLOGY BASED ON THE STUDY OF INNER MOTIVES

All the themes that will be developed later have as a foundation and a goal the development of the previously demonstrated considerations, which is why we have to sum them up here. The essential purpose of the preceding developments was to suggest emotion or awe in the presence of the mysterious aspect of existence—religiosity—which is *the only foundation for certainty* because it is opposed to metaphysical speculations, bearers of beliefs that provoke doubt. All the same, one must be careful—we will never stress this enough—not to nominate what is mysterious into a mystery *the* mystery, and be tempted to credit it with explanatory attributes.

Bearing this reservation in mind, we can say this: existence is the manifestation of mystery. Mystery is not partially but wholly manifested through the totality of existing phenomena. What follows is the axiom pertaining to the economy of thought: by imposing on itself the discipline of explaining only what can be explained—the totality of existing phenomena—the mind is on the methodical way leading to its total satisfaction—joy of knowledge—though that will never be perfectly achieved since perfection and the absolute are not part of existence.

The economy of thought is disturbed if one does not exclude from the effort of explanation what is unexplainable in itself. It is also disturbed if one excludes from the explanation any existing phenomenon, and it is deeply disturbed if one omits the explanation of the motivating functioning of the psyche.

The principle of existence is duality: space-time, extension-intension, world-psyche, object-subject, appearance-disappearance, life-death, satisfaction-dissatisfaction, joy-suffering.

All existing dualities are the various manifestations of the fundamental duality: spirit-matter. This is the initial discord. The whole meaning of existence is to transform this discord into agreement, into harmony. Such a salutary transformation is possible since neither spirit nor matter exist absolutely as such, nor are they absolutely separate. There is no spirit without matter, nor is there matter without spirit. Being complementary phenomena, spirit and matter exist only in relation to each other. Their relativity lies in the fact that from atom to man, spirit is the preconscious organizer of matter, and thus the dynamic principle of evolution. Since this is so, we tend to believe in an omnipotent Spirit who is supernatural and superhuman. The initial discord, instead of being peacefully turned into harmony, becomes insuperable when one believes either in an absolute spirit or in an absolute matter. From this stems the basic epistemological error: instead of explaining all the existing phenomena with the exclusion of the unexplainable organizing intentionality, each one of the beliefs claims to explain the absolutely unexplainable mystery and excludes from its explanation either the evolutionary modalities of matter or the evolutionary modalities of spirit.

The human spirit[2] is at the same time the explaining function and a modality to be explained. The self-explanation of the spirit, the condition for self-knowledge, is the indispensable complement to knowledge of the outer world. Since the spirit is one of the multiple functions of the psyche, its capacity for self-explanation is inefficient and its essential goal—self-knowledge—cannot be achieved without studying all psychic functions. This is impossible without objective self-observation.

Self-observation brings to light the existence of a permanent deliberating introspection, which is the most essential phenomenon of human existence because of the motivating force it exerts on all activities. The latter are meaningful or senseless depending on whether the motivating intentions be vitally right or wrong, harmonizing or disharmonizing. The organizing unification of the preconscious spirit becomes "incarnation" with the emergence of life. Already, in the animal (animated

---

[2]See note 1 in chapter I.

being), the spirit penetrates the soma-matter (flesh) under the preconscious form of instinct. In man, the incarnate spirit is dispersed in
motivating intentions and commands the activities of the soma. Since
intentions are not always conducive to harmony, the initial discord
between spirit and matter reappears as a tension between spiritual and
material desires which can be brought, through means of imaginative
exaltation, to the pathological excess of a promise of absolute satisfaction either of the spiritual or material desires. This morbid dualism,
futile and devoid of meaning, vain and guilty at the same time, is
necessarily due to the perverse mix-up of excessively good and bad
intentions escaping the control of the spirit and thus subconsciously
obsessive. But since the preconsciously organizing spirit with its mysteriously harmonizing intentionality is manifested throughout nature,
how could it not also be manifested in human nature? It is the superconsciously immanent mystery: *the call of ethical superconsciousness.*

Man's task is to organize himself psychically and he cannot do so
without an introspection capable of elucidating the conflict of motivating intentions.

This is the truth which is at the same time epistemologically, mythically, biogenetically, and psychologically profound. Man is a thinking
animal. His only salvation is to think himself and his life in truth, and
since truth is the opposite of vain lie, *salvation is victory over vanity.* The
biblical myth states this: it relates the defeat of Adam seduced by the
serpent-vanity. It formulates the condition for victory: "Let the light
(superconscious) shine in the darkness (subconscious)."

It seems that psychology should limit itself to talking about health
and remedies, about illness of the mind and conditions for psychic
health. But the psychology of the extraconscious depths must—or
should—take upon itself the task of establishing the most undisputable
proof of its scientific value: the methodical deciphering of the superconscious explosion of truth represented by the mythologies of all the
peoples. In so doing, it realizes to its own wonderment that the central
theme of symbolic pre-science is the link between salvation and psychic
health.

Such a proposition is certainly too unusual to be easily accepted,
which is why we have had to pursue it down to its epistemological
foundation, the latter being impossible to establish without taking into
consideration all the forms of human thought: not only conscious
thought, but also extraconscious thought (subconscious and superconscious); not only logical thought but also and above all, symbolic
thought.

Just like actions, thoughts can be rightly or wrongly *motivated.* This
is precisely why epistemology must be based on the study of inner
motivations.

Epistemological study leads back to the study of symbolization. Deciphering only one myth, even the biblical myth—core of the erroneous beliefs of our time—would not suffice to convince people, i.e., to overcome the countless motives of resistance.

Only the proof of *the universality of symbolization and of the universality of the method of deciphering* will, we hope, be strong enough to prevail or at least to bring about a salutary reflection of the human mind about its own weaknesses. In order to establish the proof of universality, it is important to amplify the confrontation of the biblical myth and the pagan mythologies, which has hardly been touched on so far. The purpose of such a confrontation is to stress the analogies—and even the identical features—linking the underlying significations in spite of the diversity of the narratives. This is especially so in the case of typical symbols such as "Heaven and Hell," "Life and Death of the soul," "Resurrection of the soul" (during life and not after death), "heroic struggle" (against vain subconscious temptations).

In order to prove this universality, no repetition could be superfluous as long as it brought a significant clarification.

CHAPTER IV

THE UNIVERSALITY OF SYMBOLIC LANGUAGE

A. VICTORY OVER VANITY IN GREEK MYTHOLOGY: THE HIDDEN MEANING OF THE MYTH OF PERSEUS

Perseus, the victorious hero of Greek mythology, attacks a monster called "Medusa." Seen face to face, the seductive monster—*médusant,* which in French means fascinating or mesmerizing—is terrifying. No mortal can look at her, can confront her without being paralyzed with terror at her sight unless he is protected by a succoring deity.

Athena, the Olympian deity, lends her mirror-shield to the hero. Perseus captures the image of Medusa in the protective mirror. Thus his hand is guided without him having to submit to the petrifying look. The hero is able to decapitate the monster.

This is only a brief summary of the story of Perseus[1]. In fact there is a wealth of episodes, each symbolically completing the underlying significance of the myth. For the sake of a preliminary understanding and in order to avoid getting lost in details, it will be prudent to first clarify the meaning of this brief summary and even to confront it with episodes taken from other mythical tales so as to introduce the analogical parallelism. The purpose being to prove that there is an underlying psychological pre-science which is universally shared by all symbolizations, the method used for deciphering will be to replace each of the images by the psychic function it symbolizes. It would obviously be impossible to base the science of the psyche on the deciphering of myths. Quite to the contrary, such a science must first be established[2]. Our deciphering, however, can enlarge the science of motivations, especially when it comes to its healing techniques. In this respect, Greek mythology is especially enlightening because of its multitude of heroes

---

[1]*Symbolism in Greek Mythology* (Shambhala, 1980).
[2]*Psychologie de la motivation,* Presses Universitaires de France, Collection Philosophie Contemporaine 1969, Petite Bibliothèque Payot, 1970.

and the struggles in which they are involved. Each struggle brings up a new aspect of perversions and the effective or ineffective means of confronting them.

One should bear in mind the indispensable condition for accuracy: the narrative's facade must be deciphered image by image, and once the significance of a symbol has been discovered, it must be tested so as to show that the meaning remains always the same through the most diverse mythologies, so that the translation of the myth of Perseus will be a preparation for deciphering the symbolization in biblical texts. In the face of such rigorous standards, any refusal to acknowledge the cogency of the method would be nothing but a sign of bad faith.

Since all the mythical characters represent positive or negative qualities of the human soul, Medusa is the symbol of vanity. Vanity alone can be at the same time seductive and petrifying. No man would be vain if he did not find in this the most seductive self-satisfaction, and all men are horrified at the sight of such a monstrous truth. The significance of "Medusa-vanity" is stressed by symbolizaton: her hair is made of serpents. She represents the subconscious vanity of Perseus. If he were exempt from vanity, he would have no need to fight her. The goddess Athena represents, as we know, wisdom and the combative force of the spirit. For the spirit to be combative, it must want, and dare, to confront vanity. Athena—since she arms the hero for the struggle—represents the superconscious impulse of Perseus.

Thus the myth expresses the inner conflict in Perseus' psyche between the superconscious (love of truth) and the subconscious (anxiety in the face of truth). Anxiety would petrify him with horror when seeing himself such as he is, liable to seduction by vanity (inner petrification, stagnation of the vital impulse), if the love of truth were not strong enough to bear the avowal of his vain weakness. Thus it is his own superconscious combativity that lends to Perseus the protective weapon, the shining shield of Athena: the mirror of truth.

Instead of vainly looking at himself, thereby falling prey to the seductive and horrific mirage, Perseus captures the image of Medusa—his own vain image—in the mirror of truth. Since everything takes place within the psyche, the mirror-shield itself must represent an intrapsychic force. What else could it symbolize but the objectivating force of introspection (demanding that one sees oneself such as one truly is)?

Vanity must be diagnosed introspectively: we have to accept once and for all that we have to look at our own true image so as to be able to undertake the most difficult and decisive of struggles.

The mirror of truth symbolizes consciously accepted superconscious truth. Only the avowal of vanity's existence and of its terrible danger will be able to strengthen the vital impulse, which is the indispensable condition for a voluntary and fearless introspection. The myth of Perseus sums up in one single struggle the constancy of the introspective effort needed to achieve a salutary self-control; far from reaching absolute perfection, it remains relative to the intensity of the vital impulse.

Providing however that vanity is not grafted onto transient victories: *victory over vanity must not be turned into vanity over victory*. This danger stemming from victory over vanity is undoubtedly the most astonishing testimony to its seductive force. The myth expresses it symbolically: the severed head of Medusa retains its power of fascination. The second part of Perseus's myth shows how the exemplary hero manages to overcome the insidious danger of his transient victory.

Because this theme is fundamentally important for the understanding of the functioning of inner motivations, it will be useful to introduce here the story of a hero who, precisely because of his temporary victory, becomes definitely prey to vanity.

Bellerophon, victor over the Chimaera (imaginative exaltation and its chimerical promises) *yields to the most absurd temptation of triumph: he dares to attempt the conquest of Olympus and the unseating of Zeus in order to take his throne*. The Chimaera is a monster with the body of a he-goat, the head of a lion and the tail of a serpent: the chimerical promises of imaginative exaltation are made up of the perversion of the spirit (serpent), sexual perversion (he-goat), and material perversion (whose domineering and voracious threat is often represented by the lion).

The threefold danger of perversion is also depicted in the myth of Medusa. She has two sisters. The three monsters are called the Gorgons. Medusa or vanity, who is the monstrous distortion of the spirit, rules over her sisters who symbolize material and sexual perversions. Medusa is the one who, through vain overvaluation (or undervaluation) rules by monstrously exalting (or inhibiting) the otherwise natural desires of sexuality and materiality. She is queen of the Gorgons.

Victory over the Chimaera denotes that Bellerophon has freed himself from the chimerical promises of the exaltation of material and sexual desires. In this long intrapsychic struggle, the hero is guided by his own sublimating impulse. This is expressed by the symbolic facade of the myth: Apollo (god of harmony and health) lends him his weapons: the bow and arrows. (The arrows represent the rays of the sun, and symbolize therefore the force of elucidating spirit: sound valuations.) Moreover, the hero is given Pegasus, the winged horse of Apollo.

The horse symbolizes impetuous desires. According to the previously described symbolic process, the winged horse signifies therefore their sublimation, the elevation of the soul. (It is only quite later, and through a misunderstanding of the deep meaning, that Pegasus became—in Plutarch—"the horse of the Muses".) Carried into the air by Pegasus (sublime flight, soaring enthusiasm, the opposite of perverse exaltation), Bellerophon is unaffected by the chimerical promises. He kills the Chimaera "with the help of the arrows" (with the help of his own lucid valuations). But his lucidity becomes cloudy. The victory over chimerical vanity turns into vanity over victory, into the senseless pretense to conquer Olympus with the help of Pegasus and to take Zeus's place: to be a pure spirit. There is only one psychic motivation corresponding exactly to such a mythical image: the excessively good and moralizing intentions leading to unbounded asceticism: the exaltation of the spirit towards the absolute and the excessive contempt for material and sexual desires even in their natural and healthy form. The absurd intention to reach absolute perfection (Olympus) converts the positive significance of Pegasus (sublime and harmonizing elevation) into its negative form (false elevation of exalting imagination). In the myth, Bellerophon is condemned by Zeus—i.e. the immanent superconscious law—to be thrown into Hades (the Hell of Greek mythology). This means, in psychological terms, that the senseless desire to conquer the absolute becomes the cause of decisive downfall. Bellerophon (the man whose vital impulse is strong but who exalts it excessively, i.e., beyond his limited strength) will remain *all his life* prey to the "infernal" tortures of his excesses (under the vain sway of his subconscious: imprisoned in the subconscious).

The myth shows Bellerophon, victim of his madness, tied by serpents to an endlessly spinning incandescent wheel. The symbolic image represents as one and the same, both vain attachment to the task of the spirit exalted towards the absolute and immanent punishment for such unachievable exaltation: the incandescence of the "infernal fire," symbolizes the burns of guiltiness, of suffering that is as exalted as the task is excessive. What cannot be achieved, since excessively good intentions always fail, provokes guilty obsession. The spinning of the wheel on which the head rotates now upwards, now downwards, symbolizes the state of mind of the tormented man, self-torture: the excessively good intentions of elevation persist only to be followed by repeated relapses. Vertigo of the soul. The seductive exaltation of vain hopes periodically collapses in self-despair (mythically represented by "the infernal torture").

Here, as usual, the deep psychological meaning would be totally misunderstood if one believed that the "sin against the spirit" (unseating Zeus) and the quest for the absolute which are incompatible with human strength (vain attempt to climb mount Olympus, i.e., Heaven) are to be punished after death (life in Hell). In psychological translation, the "infernal torture" of alternating between pseudoelevation and downfall is the punishment for rebellion against the superconscious law, a punishment meted out during life through subconscious channels. Since defeat (Bellerophon) and victorious achievement (Perseus), punishment and reward, are attained through extraconscious channels (subconscious and superconscious), the conscious is unaware of the law of immanent justice which is illustrated by the confrontation of the two myths.

The myths of Bellerophon and Perseus are complementary: one shows the decisive defeat caused by vanity; the other represents decisive victory over vanity. This analogy of contrast is underlined by the symbol of "Pegasus" which appears in both mythical tales. *From the body of Medusa decapitated by Perseus rise and fly—free at last—Pegasus, the winged horse (sublime imagination) and Chrysaor, the gold sword (incisive force of the spirit).* Now through the final defeat of Bellerophon, the symbol of Pegasus took on a negative significance (vain flight); Pegasus was captured and devoured by Medusa.

The meaning of these images does not become fully comprehensible unless we take into account the fact that—just like the deities and the monsters—the mythical heroes represent the strengths and weaknesses not only of each man but of *all men, of mankind.* In this enlarged meaning, Perseus becomes the symbol of an essentially combative mankind. Medusa also acquires a significant meaning going beyond the hold individually exerted over Perseus. She is not only his deep-seated vanity; she becomes vanity ruling the world. (Etymologically, Medusa means "she who reigns".) She symbolizes universal evil, the evil tormenting the whole world and consisting in a magically seductive confusion inciting mankind to yield to the lures of terrifying evil, so much so that it becomes the norm of life and even—acme of falsely justifying resignation—the most attractive good. Vain stagnation, petrification, "death of the vital impulse"[3] is felt as the most attractive liberation *from essential responsibility* and its imperative: the combative impulse. In the enlarged signification of the myth, Perseus turns general resignation into liberating combativity. He turns evil into good. The introspective subjectivity of individual victory acquires thereby the importance of an objective achievement concerning *the salvation of the world.* The victorious weapon, the mirror of truth, reflects the objective image of the seduced world, the image of Medusa as principle of evil. But being captured in the mirror of truth, Medusa, vanity, the principle of evil (in the biblical myth: the prince of the world, Satan) can be vanquished: these are the glad tidings. The myth of Perseus stresses this transposition of the subjective value of liberating introspection into an objectifying force which concerns mankind in general, by the image of the liberation of Pegasus and Chrysaor, symbols of the forces of sublimation and spiritualization that had been captured by vanity, by Medusa. Perseus, representative of combative mankind, frees the spirit which had become powerless and gives back to the vital impulse the strength of sublime flight, enthusiastic impulse, which is the opposite of imaginative exaltation.

---

[3]Translators' Note: See note 5 in Chapter I.

However, the forces symbolized by Chrysaor and Pegasus are, since they yielded to vanity and were devoured by Medusa, characterized as inferior when compared to the much more effective weapon of Perseus. He frees them but they are of no help to him. They take flight. Having always been in existence, they were devoured, since only too often they are nothing else but good intentions, ready to collapse. To be sure, there are men whose spirit is a trenchant weapon but it is rarely made of gold (symbol of spiritualization). And it is on Pegasus's back that Bellerophon flies up to conquer Heaven.

The only truly effective weapon is the shield of Athena: the mirror of truth, introspective insight, lucid introspection. (Though there is a morbid introspection which is nothing but vain self-contemplation.) The Greek ideal of *the happy medium* is radically opposed to the excesses of asceticism and its exaltation directed toward the absolute (pseudo-sanctification). The happy medium is determined for each individual by the degree of intensity of his impulse. In the biblical myth, the hero endowed with an exceptionally intense impulse accomplishes the "Ascension into Heaven" (sanctification).

The Greek ideal of the happy medium, understood as dynamics in conformity with the vital impulse, is in no way inferior to the biblical ideal. The underlying meaning of Perseus's myth is a proof of this. When it is understood in all its extent and depth, it shows that the only way not to go beyond one's impulse (nor to stay behind it) is to keep it in a state of constant struggle against vanity, a salutary struggle which is the very meaning of life. The means to achieve this are the theme of the second part of the myth of Perseus.

Having vanquished and decapitated Medusa, *Perseus carries away the head which has kept its monstrous power of fascination,* (symbol of the persistent and even increased danger of yielding to seduction and magic petrification). Neither Medusa nor the severed head exist. Thus the image means that the hero carries with him and in him a warning of the persistent and permanent danger and he is—because of this—now able to confront his own vanities without being terrified and without being subjected to magic seduction since he is always ready to admit their existence; he will not let himself be imaginatively led by the false promises of vain self-valuation.

The head captured in the introspective mirror means the awareness—having the value of a diagnosis—of the existence and nature of vanity (victorious awareness since vanity can only survive in the darkness of the subconscious); the head, in the hand of Perseus, constantly exposed to objective self-observation (purifying introspection) means the indispensable daily experience: detailed confrontation of the awareness—first admitted in a general way—with the many small temptations of daily life. Only the daily experience—imposed upon Perseus by the head he carries away—will keep awake his authentic combative impulse. The head thus replaces—and in a more effective way—the image of Medusa captured in the mirror of Athena. In the hand of Perseus, the head of the defeated Medusa becomes itself "mirror of truth." Perseus does not vainly give up Athena's help. Quite to the contrary, he subjects himself even more effectively to the superconscious inspiration symbolized by the goddess.

But the severed head has a much deeper significance yet, since the struggle of Perseus symbolizes the combative impulse of mankind. Perseus carries the head, not as a vain trophy, but in the full pride of his victory. The myth represents victory in one sole decisive battle, but in fact the symbolically exteriorized fight is a long introspective struggle against his own vain temptation, and victory is never final. The severed head, or vanity, will not overpower Perseus but only on one condition: that he remain too proud to become vain of his passing victories in the introspective struggle he undertakes when carrying away the magic head. The courage to carry the head away, humble pride, the avowal that the struggle has to be continued, thus becomes the most characteristic feature and the most remarkable difference when one compares the ethical courage of Perseus and the guilty vanity of Bellerophon who is also a symbol of mankind. What could make mankind proud of itself in spite of centuries of defeats, if not the persistent combativity symbolized by Perseus? He shows the defeated head to the enemy, not to paralyze him but in the hope of arousing his pride, the only way of overcoming vanity. "Look, here I am, but here you are also, all of you. This is an aspect of myself, but it is an aspect of you too. Dare to look, it is not invincible"!

But the vanity of the world refuses to hear and to see. It is petrified with horror. This is described by the myth *in the encounter between Perseus and the giant Atlas,* who also represents mankind and is the symbol of its banalization. (Giants are throughout Greek mythology the symbols of brute force, opposed to the forces of the spirit.) Atlas the Titan bears more easily the crushing weight of the earth (earthly desires and their banal exaltation) than the sight of the truth. The banalization on which the world rests, is a gigantic distortion which is as poorly diagnosed as vanity because it is in itself a form of vanity. Vanity cannot stand the sight of vanity. In the myth, Atlas refuses hospitality to Perseus. Perseus shows him the head of Medusa so that he can recognize himself in it (so that he can understand the motive for his refusal of hospitality). But Atlas, bearer of the world, is too weak to stand this sight. He is paralyzed with horror. Perseus is the mythical victor over the vain temptations personified by Medusa and Atlas.

The struggle against vanity goes on until the death of Perseus. It will never end. It goes on after the death of the hero on a larger and higher plane, thus stressing that this is the essential struggle of mankind. *At his death, Perseus bequeathes the head of Medusa to Athena who attaches it to her mirror-shield.* The final image carries the significance of the myth to its highest intensity.

It is not anymore Perseus inspired by Athena, but the inspiratrix herself, the immortal goddess of truth, who shows to mortals that victory is possible over subconscious lies, principle of evil itself. The head of Medusa—even attached to the aegis of Athena—remains magically alive. Showing that victory is possible for man and mankind, the goddess of Truth, symbol of wisdom and combativity of the spirit, invites the man who is willing to meet her, to recognize himself in the magical head in order not to become petrified. Recognition turns the eternal monstrous truth into eternal salutary truth. "Recognition" is another word for "gratitude." Awareness must arouse recognition or gratitude so that—thanks to the moving inspiration which is both active and activating—paralyzing fright can be transformed into the joy of self-knowledge.

Perseus, the victorious hero, is—in the myth—taken up to heaven and becomes a star symbolizing the guiding ideal. Neither Perseus, nor Medusa nor Athena nor the mirror-shield exist as such. They represent the strengths and weaknesses of the human soul: the hope of every man and of mankind (Perseus) to overcome vanity (Medusa) by the strength of the vital impulse (Athena) with the help of elucidating introspection (mirror-shield).

The only way to strip the severed head of the monster of its persistent magic power depends on our vital impulse. We are the ones called to resolve the essential dilemma. In our psyche there is an ongoing struggle between Perseus and Medusa, between impulse and stagnation (unless our vital impulse is dead, death of the soul "petrified by Medusa"). Impulse cuts off the head of Medusa, stagnation revives it. Since this is the case, we are lacking the exemplary strength of Perseus who was able to carry away the head and could look at it face to face. The bequest made to Athena of the vanquished head represents comfort given to our wavering strength through understanding of the example left by the victorious hero who, in the end, is symbolically deified. In continuing to show us the head of Medusa, mark of the victory of the man Perseus, the goddess of Truth does not cease to remind anyone who cares to see and understand that victory (albeit a limited one) is possible over vanity, the principle of evil: glad tidings, tidings of salvation.

B. SALVATION

Who is Perseus? A symbol. A character of immortal significance. An eternal truth (eternal in that it is immutable in time and not in the metaphysical understanding of the word, "extratemporal"). The eternal truth of salvation, a possibility immanent to human existence.

The representations of this eternal truth vary with the different mythologies; the underlying psychological meaning remains the same: victory over vanity. Only the signifiers—the characters, their names, and their adventures—vary from one culture to the other. However, even the fabulous façades remain, in spite of their multiformity, united by such a typical feature that its presence alone compels us to admit that we are faced with a myth, faced with a story representing symbolically the essential truth: *with the help of a deity, the hero (who is often the son of a deity whose essence is either positive or negative) confronts or is confronted by a monster or a demon.* Most of the heroes die in the struggle.

If one solitary myth—in this case the myth of Perseus—represents salvation, or in the case of Bellerophon means essential perdition, we have no choice but to acknowledge that all the tales of the past which include the characteristic constellation (hero, deity, monster) are myths we can decipher. The key to this deciphering is the understanding of the principle of symbolization: the struggle of the hero symbolizes victory or defeat in the intrapsychic struggles experienced by all men. The hero represents mankind.

Biblical texts contain the three typical characters. In Genesis, the "original sin" committed by the hero symbolically represents mankind's weakness. In the Old Testament, the hero is "the Chosen People." In the Gospels, the victorious hero is Jesus Christ. Symbolically deified, Son of God, he is in fact a fighting hero and thus comparable to Perseus, the victorious hero.

Comparable but not identical. An analogical comparison includes common features and differential traits. If there is an analogy between the myths of Perseus and of Jesus, one has to admit the superconscious vision has evolved. And the evolution lies in that the underlying meaning is clarified and verbally formulated: "I have sanctified myself." Purification from the hereditary sin is suggested by the tempting seduction of the demon Satan personified by the serpent-vanity. Would victory over vanity be the meaning common to the myth of Perseus and the life of Jesus? Would the glad tidings of salvation contained in the Gospels be identical with the hidden meaning of Perseus' victory?

Should the answers be affirmative, the biblical texts would be raised to a level where there is no more room for the quarrels of the historians about the actual existence of Jesus. Even if he did not live, what matters is that the mythical vision was able to create and recreate the guiding image of the victory of the superconscious impulse. If one believes in the literal interpretation, there can be no legitimate comparison between the message of Jesus and the victory of Perseus or the victorious struggles of other mythical heroes.

To believe is to know nothing; more than this: to believe is to refuse to know, and especially to know anything about symbolization.

The message of joy would not be an exemplary victory, acquired during life against vanity ruling the world—"I have overcome the Prince of the world"—but would be the promise of life eternal with Jesus in a transcendent Heaven, a reward granted to faithful believers. On the other hand, the unbeliever is threatened with eternal survival with Satan, and delivered to the fires of Hell, which is a rather horrifying message. Other mythologies have developed different eschatological images. Surely it would be absurd, for instance, to accept the "transmigration of souls" as a reality. It does not prevent the image from being at least as eloquent as that of the symbol of an eternal punishment, image of despair which cannot be separated from the hope of eternal reward. Hope and despair are brought back to their right proportions, if one is willing to understand that "Eternity" is not an endless time, but a metaphysical symbol, an unimaginable image, the meaning of which is intemporal mystery: the mystery of death. On the other hand, the mystery is manifested through temporal life and its highest manifestation is sanctification: decisive victory over the "demon" vanity.

The life of the soul—its combativity—is the meaning of life. This meaning is not transcendental. It is immanent. God himself, if he existed personally, could impose nothing else but the ethical principle: essential combativity. Since this is the case, the "God" symbol is symbolically distributing reward and punishment. In fact, reward and punishment are meted out during life through the superconscious and subconscious channels. From the ideal of elevation and its joy in harmony (mythical Heaven) just as from anxiety provoking subconscious disharmony (mythical Hell) stem the hierarchy of values: the gamut of positive and negative values.

In symbolic spatialization, elevation in the air (up to Heaven) or fall to the ground (descent into Hell) are represented as a tremendous distance. On the other hand, in psychic reality, the imperishable joy of superconsciousness is not spatially separated from the subconscious and its "infernal" torture. *The elevations and falls of the soul are not extensive but intensive:* they signify the degree of intensity of the struggle between the vitally meaningful and senseless intentions. The meaning of the "ascent into Heaven" symbol can be formulated as follows: the hero, thanks to the exceptional strength of his spiritual combativity, attains during his lifetime the eternal truth: the imperative of harmonization of intentions, which can only be achieved through victory over the principle of evil, the "Prince of the world" of banal vain exaltation. (In the myth of Perseus, the "Prince of the world" is personified by the "support of the world," the Titan Atlas.) Harmonization of desires is an indispensable condition for joy since it alone can put an end to the inner conflict and its torturing anxiety. Bearer of the joyful news, the victorious hero is symbolically immortalized (taken up to Heaven) because his example—as a guiding ideal—remains eternally true, forever inscribed in the superconscious memory of mankind. Whether the hero is called Perseus or Jesus, whether he actually lived or was mythically created by mankind's superconsciousness, his example—real or imagined—will not cease to exert throughout all the errings of human generations its vivifying and activating influence.

This psychological significance remains invariably true, whether it be consciously understood or not, whether the victorious hero be, in the course of the centuries, replaced by other characters with a similar meaning, whether the message be wrongly interpreted or even whether the masses, deaf to superconscious understanding, go on living under the yoke of subconscious deviations, in the grasp of "the Prince of the world."

Whether the subconscious danger be called Medusa or Satan, whether the victor be Perseus or Jesus, the enemy to fight remains invariably, "eternally," vain temptation whose most monstrous form is not exaltation directed toward the spirit (nervosity[4] leading to mortification of the matter-flesh) but exaltation of the "carnal" desires, banalization[5] leading to the "death" of the animating impulse, mythically called "death of the soul."

The major obstacle to understanding the universality of symbolic language and to its translation into psychological terminology stems from the fact that banalization (just as vanity in general) is not diagnosed as an illness. Because of its frequency, it is considered as the very norm of human existence. Only symbolic pre-science diagnosed it as essential perdition, seductive and petrifying, as the Greek myth put it, or in the framework of the Christian myth: imaginative exaltation, subconscious blinding personified by the demon Satan, the Prince ruling over the multitudes, the intrapsychic principle which determines, which motivates banal, egocentric and aggressive activities.

What Satan achieves symbolically is actually done by the imaginative exaltation of desires: it whispers to the inner ear its vain promises of satisfaction, its temptations which destroy harmony and drag seduced men into terrible struggles for material goods, making man the enemy of man. Jesus is a fighting hero because he opposes to the hatred of the world, the only remedy: victory over egocentrism, the message of love. Though not the absolutism of exalted love of the spirit (through which Bellerophon thought that he could conquer heaven), nor the sentimentality of exalted love for others. "Love your neighbor as yourself," i.e., love yourself first of all, do yourself the good of fighting restrictive egocentrism, conquer the demon vanity, and you will love your neighbor in proportion to your victory. Love your essential self above all else, know yourself and you will live in the joy of essential knowledge (sym-

---

[4]Diel distinguishes three levels of mental disorder: *nervosité, névrose,* and *psychose,* which have been translated as "nervosity," "neurosis," and "psychosis."

[5]See note 3 in chapter I.

bolized by "the kingdom of God is within us"). The victory of the fighting hero is above all a victory over himself ("I have sanctified myself"; would a god need to sanctify himself?). Like Perseus, he dared to see himself in the mirror of truth. Like Perseus, he showed the truth to the world that refused him hospitality. These victories unceasingly repeated over the hatred of the world (hatred that he accepted without letting himself be dragged into it though he foresaw and predicted his tragic end) make of him the symbol of love. The symbol is misunderstood if, through sentimental love, one falls into calling him "sweet Jesus" even though—in his own words—he did not "bring peace but a sword," the trenchant weapon of the spirit, (Chrysaor in the myth of Perseus). His victory over vanity—exalted self-love and guilty hatred of others—can only be solitary, intrapsychic, since the world that lives under the rule of the "Prince of evil" has neither been conquered nor convinced (on the exterior plane). Men who were "dead in the soul" inflicted on him a decisive defeat: death of the body. This makes his heroic example all the more moving. A real man, he chose death of the body rather than death of the soul. Never was there greater injustice because never was there such a just man. But the greatest injustice is to make of him, through misunderstanding of the mythical "as if," a real god. For the profound truth conveyed by the myth and at the same time self-evident, is that he was not one. Counter to the symbol "death of the soul" we find the symbol "life of the soul": it is inscribed in the possibilities of human nature that the animating impulse lives or dies during the existence of the ephemeral self. In order to grasp the meaning and the scope of the message of joy, one must understand the meaning and the scope of the myth of the soul.

C. The Symbol of the "Immortal Soul"

The myth of the soul—of its life and death—is the central theme of Scripture. The misunderstanding of this central myth's significance is the major cause of dogmatic error. It is true that this error becomes forgivable due to the extreme condensation of symbolic language which includes in the myth of the soul the two aspects of mystery: the mystery of manifest life and the unfathomable mystery of death. The mystery of life is—in psychological terms—*the animating impulse*. The most important psychological fact—mentioned many times—is that the impulse can "die" (lose its harmonizing force), which is essential perdition mythically symbolized by "death of the soul" during life (banalization). Yet, in spite of the possibility of "death" during ephemeral life, the soul is imagined as being immortal.

The indisputable fact is that *life and its impulse cannot have come out of total nothingness. It is thus unthinkable that the principle of life (animation) return after temporal life into nothingness.* Though terms such as "to come out" and "return" are anthropomorphisms for the "fate of the soul" before and after death, even superconscious symbolic thought can only offer an inadequate and unreal image. Symbolization in fact, foresees only the conflicts (life or death of the impulse) of *psychic life that, being as ephemeral as the body to which it is inseparably bound, cannot survive it.* Animation—in that it is not only a psychically manifest impulse— belongs to the mystery of life and death. Only the metaphysical "as if" can deal with it; just as the metaphysical symbol gave of the mystery of creation the personified image of "God-the-Creator," it gives of the mystery of animation a personifying image: "the immortal soul."

Since symbolization is characterized by personification and spatialization, mythology creates a metaphysical image according to which the immortal soul dwells in the body during life and returns after the death of the body to a transcendent Heaven, a symbolic place, to live— as a symbolic character—in the presense of "God-the-Creator" who is himself a symbolic character, while it will live—in case of demerit—in "Hell," the symbolic place of eternal punishment.

The metaphysical image of the transcendent survival of the soul after death becomes superstition, just like the metaphysical image of "God-the-Creator" if one mistakes the symbolical "as if" for a reality. The superstition is compounded if one confuses soul and psyche. The soul is a personifying symbol, the psyche is a reality: the personal self of each one of us. Such a confusion leads to belief in the eternal survival of the ephemeral self. From this confusion stems the decisive error, which is no longer a theoretical but a practical one. For in truth, reward and punishment are not meted out after death but during life. This is the essential truth represented by the psychologically significant symbol: life and death of the vital impulse during the existence of the ephemeral self.

All the confusions vanish if we make a clear distinction between the metaphysical symbol "eternal life of the soul after death" and the psychological symbol "death of the soul during life." Such an essential distinction is difficult to establish and to understand because the symbol of "eternity" includes almost constantly in the biblical texts, especially in the New Testament, two meanings: eternal life after death (metaphysical symbol) and eternal truth of the immutable ethical law immanent to psychic life, i.e., self-knowledge, the struggle against vanity.

In the psychological meaning of the symbol "life eternal," *man can during his temporal existence live eternally* (in an eternal way: in accordance with the immutable ethical law) or he can die in his soul and spirit to the eternal ethical truth. But, also during his life, man can be reborn from the loss of his essential desire, from the "death" of his animating impulse. The soul can revive, rise again. This rebirth is an elevation of the soul and spirit: *resurrection achieved during life and not after death.*

Linguistic wisdom—here as elsewhere—agrees with the psychological pre-science of the myths. It expresses the universal truth through the common root of the words.[6] To be born again means to be born to a new knowledge of the spirit, to be born in the spirit and by the spirit (through the spirit of truth and out of love for truth). The "Old Adam" must die—in us—for the soul to be reborn. The ancients already expressed the "eternal truth," the possibility of victory and rebirth, by the symbol of the "Phoenix being reborn out of its ashes," symbol equivalent to "rebirth through lustral waters." But it is quite clear that the rebirth is not effected "thanks to" the symbolic rite. It is achieved thanks to the purification of intentions. The message of joy is joy in and by knowledge before it can exert on the intentions and thereby on the actions, its moving ethical power of renewal.

Insofar as the biblical texts are concerned, here is one quotation chosen as an example among countless others expressing this common truth: Ezekiel 18:27-28 (JB): "When the sinner renounces sin to become law-abiding and honest, he deserves to live. He has chosen to renounce all his previous sins; he shall certainly live; he shall not die." The condition for rebirth is clearly expressed: "he has chosen",[7] he has looked into his own subconsciously hidden intentions—essential causes of "the death of the soul"—with his introspective sight, the only means of knowledge enabling him to make his choice. "Light must shine in the darkness" of the subconscious. What lives or dies during the life of man is "Light": the immanent truth of the ethical superconscience and of its harmonizing impulse; its spatializing symbol being "the Kingdom of Heaven within us," and its personifying symbol being "God in us," the divine element in us.

As long as the inner motivational intentions remain subconsciously hidden, vainly repressed and falsely justified as meaningful, valid and just, the universality of mythical pre-science will not be understood. Heaven (except in its metaphysical sense) is the symbol of *life on earth* insofar as it is superconsciously motivated. Hell is not underground, it is *life on earth* such as subconsciously motivated men make it for themselves. *The dead souls do not live in the underground Hell. Men endowed with dead souls live in this world. Their subconsciously motivated interactions make life on earth—symbolically speaking—infernal.*

D. THE ANIMATING IMPULSE, A PHENOMENON IMMANENT TO THE PSYCHE

The preceding analyses are summed up in a threefold meaning contained in the "Heaven vs Hell" symbol:

---

[6]In French, to be reborn is *renaître* (from *naître*, to be born) and to know is *connaître*.
[7]Even clearer in French: *il a ouvert les yeux:* he has opened his eyes.

1. *Metaphysical Significance:* representation—with the help of the mythical "as if"—of man's fate after death, symbolic spatialization of the "places" of reward and punishment, symbolic personification of the animating impulse ("immortal soul"), symbolic temporalization (Eternity).
2. *Psychological Significance:* an ethical bearing; the psychic processes: Heaven, symbolic place of superconscious harmony and joy; Hell, symbolic place of subconscious disharmony and its anguished torture: essential destiny of the individual during his life (life or death of the animating impulse).
3. *Social Significance:* the "Kingdom of Heaven" announced to all men of the world, message of joy opposed to the "Kingdom of Prince of the world, Satan." Hell is life on earth under the rule of collective banalization.

Literal exegesis precludes the understanding that the "dead souls" do not live in an underground hell but on earth. It is thus compelled to interpret the symbols of "Heaven and Hell" exclusively in the the metaphysical sense, ignoring the psychological meanings, be they individual or collective. There is therefore a misunderstanding of the message of joy of the Gospels: *In the midst of generalized decadence, the individual man can, insofar as his vital impulse enables him, be reborn from his symbolic death, be reborn to the immanent meaning of life and its value.*

The three meanings are complementary and inseparable. Symbolization deals only with the concrete life of the individual, of every individual, of all individuals. But concrete life includes metaphysical anxiety, fear of death. The mythical dream would be incomplete if it did not answer this question. Symbolization uses the image of the superposition of psychic processes in order to constitute an image of superposition of the fabulous places in a life after death. Drawn from the conflict between psychic processes, the metaphysical image of a resurrection in the beyond thus projects onto the afterlife each and every feature of the essential givens which are immanent to the actual life of the individual: symbolic death (banalization) and the *immanent* possiblity of resurrection during life. We are faced therefore with one single image of psychological significance and it deals with the essential merits or demerits of the individual, every individual, all individuals. Hence the social significance: Hell on earth, collective banalization; Heaven on earth, solitary sanctification, guiding ideal valid for every individual, though it only shows a direction, and is only approachable through the dynamics of sane motivation (without moralizing overtension) according to the individually limited impulse of each person. No one can know the limits of his own vital impulse. The happy medium consists in exercizing it actively so that it can, little by little, grow to its genuine strength. What matters is not to reach the goal but to be on the way.

Excessively good intentions run the risk of overtension toward the absolute (we shall see further on how to avoid this without falling back into banal laxism).

These conclusions, based on the deciphering of the most typical symbols with the purpose of establishing the proof of symbolization's universality, have such an importance—and are at the same time so diametrically opposed to accepted beliefs—that it will certainly not be superfluous to stress them even more vigorously.

One of the oldest symbolisms proves with extreme clarity that indeed "Heaven and Hell" symbolize above all the inner psychic functioning. *The symbolism of fire* is found in all mythologies. The image has the advantage of representing the psychic functioning not through a spatial superposition of the psychic processes, but through the functional dynamics of "combustion" which is able to express better the energetic processes of the constant struggle between the superconscious and subconscious motivations.

The animating impulse is represented by the ascending flame. The elevations and falls are symbolized by the sparks that rise and fall. The energy of combustion is significant of the inner deliberation. The fuel is, in this instance, supplied by the surrounding demands, i.e., by the desires (material and sexual) connecting the psyche to the environment. If the deliberating combustion is under control, the ascending flame (vital impulse) is able to sublimate and spiritualize the desires; their energy is turned—in this image—into warmth of soul (love) and lucidity of spirit. But, if on the contrary, the intrapsychic "combustion" is under poor control, the fire turns into a destructive conflagration (a psychic inflammation: imaginative exaltation). The banal exaltation of material desires overfuels the fire and instead of being an ascending flame, it becomes a devouring blaze, so that in the end nothing is left but ashes (death of the soul). The psyche is symbolically thrown into "the eternal fire" which smokes, devours, and chokes (imaginative vapors, devouring passions, choking anxiety).

The biblical texts do indisputably make ample use of the fire symbol. Jesus is "the light coming down from Heaven to enlighten the world." Light—the message of joy—"shines in the darkness" where men with dead souls live in the realm of the Prince of the world. Satan rules over the living and not over the world.

Here is a biblical image, a decisive argument in itself through its translation into psychological language: "Heaven," symbol of superconscious joy; "Hell," symbol of subconscious vanity. "Jesus descended into Hell to save the dead souls." Can one believe that the savior of souls, a man of flesh and blood—even if he were a god—was able to go through the layers of the earth? And even if one wants to believe this, why would he go down to the underground Hell, supposing that it exists? The text talks about "dead souls" and not about the "immortal souls" who, according to dogma, are living there. Why save them, since they—another supposition of dogma—are sentenced by God's verdict to stay there eternally? Is it conceivable and believable that he crosses the earth's layers on the way back, followed by a procession of dead people brought back to life?

The truth is that, like the "ascension into Heaven," the "descent into Hell" is a very ancient symbol. Its psychological meaning is twofold: banal downfall, or conversely, (in accordance with the symbolic language process) victory over subconscious temptations (exploration of the subconscious: elucidating introspection). According to the façade of the various myths, many pagan heroes "descended into Hell," for instance in Greek mythology, Orpheus, Theseus, and Heracles. Theseus, lost in the underground region (subconscious erring), sits down exhausted on a stone and remains stuck to it (typical symbol of banalization). On the other hand, Heracles, also exposed to subconscious temptations emerges victoriously out of Hell.

Just as Jesus is the savior of the "dead souls" of banalized people, Heracles saves the dead soul of Theseus: he helps him get off the stone and rises with him out of Hell. When we reject the outside wrappings (the narrative façade), what is left is the core: the psychological truth. The theme of essential victory is taken up in the twelve works of Heracles, symbols of his constant struggle against intrapsychic temptations. His final victory is stressed by a most eloquent symbol: the hero throws himself into the fire (purifying flame). Like the Phoenix, his soul (his vital impulse) is reborn from the ashes during his life. After his death, the victorious Heracles is raised to the rank of guiding ideal: he goes up to Heaven (Olympus) where he dwells among the gods. The descent into Hell and the ascent into Heaven of Heracles express, more clearly than the "rising up to the firmament" of Perseus, the significant analogy with Jesus' ascension after his death.[8] As to the "descent into Hell," the meaning becomes clear through the introduction of the significance—individual and social—which has already been analyzed: living on earth, the hero of the biblical myth has sanctified himself, i.e., he has, like Perseus, overcome his own subconscious temptations by recognizing them as vain and empty (we shall see later what these temptations are). He has, just like Heracles, purified himself by self-knowledge (introspective descent into the subconscious Hell). His achievement, in retreat and solitude, would remain incomplete—and even suspicious—if he did not dare, in spite of the foreseeable mortal danger, leave his solitude, his beatitude (superconscious Heaven) to bring—by word and example—to the "dead souls" living on earth in the Hell of banalization the message of joy, the message of possible

---

[8]*Symbolism in Greek Mythology*, Shambhala, 1980.

rebirth; at that time, such a message could only be expressed in pre-scientific and symbolic language.

The underlying analogies connecting the myth of Perseus to the story of Jesus extend—in spite of the differences in the narratives—to all the important features of the mythical accounts of the life of the two heroes.

Jesus symbolically is, just like Perseus the victor of Greek mythology, son of the spirit impregnating—under the guise of a cloud—the earthly woman. Here is one of the most ancient symbolisms: fecundation of the Matter-Earth by the Spirit-Heaven. Uranus (Spirit-Heaven) impregnates Gaea (Terra Mater) through rain which is symbolically the "fecundating sperm." Jesus tells the Pharisees: "You are children of the devil," which shows clearly that the filiation is symbolic.

Jesus is in fact—and he says so—a man like all the others, son of man, son of Adam who is the symbol of the fallibility of human nature falling too easily for the false promises of the temptor, the serpent Satan.

If one could show that being son of Adam, Jesus, just like Perseus, had to purify himself from the principle of evil through an introspective struggle, before fighting the world that lives under the rule of evil, the proof of an analogy between the two myths should be considered as conclusive. This introspective struggle will have an identical significance to that of the "mirror of truth".

E. THE TEMPTATION OF JESUS

According to Mt. 4:1, and Lk. 4:1, Jesus is tempted by the devil. Can one believe that the devil approaches him in person and under the form given to him by imagination: lolling tongue, horns and hooves, hairy and dark? This image of the devil belongs rather to folklore. But all folklores contain references to genuine symbolization. Even if we have no knowledge of symbolization, we know that the features given to the devil have a psychological significance: the hanging tongue characterizes the liar and his false promises; the horns and the hooves symbolize sexual perversion, the animal hide is a genuine mythical image symbolizing the monstrous bestiality of banalization.

The detailed account of Jesus' temptation has all the features of a myth's façade (hero, deity, demon) with one difference however: the hero is at the same time "Son of God," and "God in person," specific symbol of Christian mythology. Another difference deserves to be mentioned: in the myth of the temptation of Jesus, the conflictual situation of inner deliberation is not symbolized by a physical fight with symbolically significant weapons (arrows, shields, etc.). The nature of the deliberation is represented by a dialogue between Jesus and Satan, in which false promises of satisfaction are confronted with victorious valuations of the superconscience.

The typical symbols contained in the dialogue and its setting (desert, mountain) enable us to decipher the meaning of Jesus' temptation.

This underlying meaning is the foresight of the dangers that he will inevitably provoke by announcing that his "kingdom is not of this world" (though it is neither of the other world, the "beyond"). It is the kingdom of his solitary joy from which he came down to bear witness to its reality for the men who live in the "kingdom of Satan, Prince of the world." Messiah of the Spirit, he must convince, under penalty of death, the people who, having misunderstood the prophecies announcing a liberator, live in the hope of "a Messiah according to the flesh" who would free them from the Roman yoke. By disappointing the people and confronting "the powers that be" (superstitions, institutions), i.e., conformism, he cannot but be aware of the fate he will meet in the event of failure which he foresees. He knows the horrible form of execution then in use. Alone against the whole world, how could he not be in anguish, were it only for a moment? The myth shows that, in his heart of hearts, Jesus falters. He has a fleeting temptation to betray his mission. The myth—here as everywhere—sums up in one sole confrontation the intrapsychic struggle against anxiety and its false temptations of escape which must have periodically haunted Jesus' intrapsychic dialogue, i.e., his inner deliberation. The images show clearly the nature of these promises and that of the "weapons of the spirit" (elucidating introspection and liberating value judgements) with which Jesus, the fighting hero, succeeds in defeating the temptation of the demon in his own heart ("I have overcome the Prince of the world").

According to Mt. 4:1 (JB), "Then Jesus was led by the Spirit out into the wilderness to be tempted by the devil." The symbolic "wilderness" is not the real desert (John the Baptist, for instance, did not preach in the desert where nobody could have heard him nor were there Jordan waters to baptize with). The symbolic wilderness is the desert of the world where the banalized people live. Ths significance is identical to the symbol "Hell on earth."

The spirit ("the Father-Spirit") is his own superconscience which leads him out into the wilderness of banalization to test his resistance to temptations instead of remaining alone in his beatitude. (This meaning is even clearer in Lk 4:1 (JB): "Filled with the Holy Spirit, Jesus left the Jordan and was led *by the Spirit* through the wilderness.") Mt. 4:2 (JB) "He fasted for forty days and forty nights, after which he was very hungry." The figure "four" symbolizes earthly life exposed to temptations. After having fasted for a long time (forty days and forty nights) and resisted temptations (symbolically, he fasted), he was hungry. The day symbolizes lucidity and valor, the night symbolizes cloudiness, risk of losing one's combative lucidity, which means that during his long fast he had hesitations (nights). They become stronger, the tempter approaches.

Mt. 4:3 (JB): "And the tempter came and said to him, 'If you are the Son of God, tell these stones to turn into loaves.' " The stones are the symbol of the desires of banalization; the bread symbolizes the food of the spirit; hence the messianic symbol: "I am the bread of life. He who eats me—he who feeds on my word and example—will enter the Kingdom." Now the word and example of the "Son of God," of "the One who was sent" have a precise meaning: the promise that any man resisting the vanity of the world, the false promises of the tempter, will live in the kingdom of joy.

The false promise tempting Jesus in his heart of hearts (symbolically expressed by the temptation of the devil) has—in its psychological meaning—the implication of a compromise: Jesus is brushed by the idea that he will remain Son of God and messenger of the Spirit even if he tries to gather the people by resigning himself to play the role of a "Messiah according to the flesh" (offering stones instead of bread) in order to finally insure his real mission. He is able to reject the temptation. But it repeats itself insidiously and more and more clearly a second and third time.

Verse 4:
"But he replied, 'Scripture says:
Man does not live on bread alone
but on every word that comes from the mouth of God.' "

In his own deliberation, he fights the tempting compromise by reminding himself that the immutable truth does not tolerate half-measures. For man to live (instead of dying in his soul) he needs a truth "coming from the mouth of God": truth dictated by the superconscience, freed from any false and lying justification.

Verses 5-6:
"The devil took him to the holy city and made him stand on the parapet of the Temple, 'If you are the Son of God' he said 'throw yourself down; for Scripture says:

        'He will put you in his angels' charge
        and they will support you on their hands
        in case you hurt your foot against a stone.' "

With the help of the spirit's weapon (just valuation opposed to false promises) he rejects the temptation and feels in a state of elevation (on the parapet of the Temple). But instead of being a full acceptance, the elevation is still nothing more than a good intention with an underlying anxiety in the face of the consequences of its achievement.

This second temptation is, in spite of the difference in images, identical to the previous one, with only one slight change. The Temple of Jerusalem is the symbol of the Covenant with the "eternal God" (Covenant synonymous with harmony; the eternal God is the personification of the immanent eternal superconscious truth: the law of harmony, supreme promise of joy). He must first be party to the Covenant, i.e., his character formed by all his sublimated motivations must bind him to the eternal truth before he can be "Son of God"; as long as he remains in a state of anxiety, he cannot be the messenger of joy. It is not the devil who really puts him on the parapet of the Temple; it is he himself who tries to rise to this task. But since the devil does place him there symbolically, it is nothing but a diabolical temptation: an exalted task. Exalted elevation is the cause of downfall (symbol of banalization). But to "throw oneself down" is to totally abandon the highest plans of elevation. This is more serious than the first temptation. Yet, the content remains the same. He still hopes that the downfall will only be temporary. The angels (symbols of just valuations) will come to help him during his fall. God (his persistent impulse) "will put him in their charge, and they will support him on the hands" (symbol of activity) "in case he hurts his foot" (symbol of the soul and its bearing in life) "against a stone" (symbol of defeat of the soul in banalization).

Verse 7:
"Jesus said to him, 'Scripture also says:
You must not put the Lord your God to the test.' "

The temptation of the devil is an attempt to deceive the superconscience (God). In his introspective deliberation, Jesus can clearly see the absurdity of believing that he is "Son of God" once and for all, and so can let himself fall without suffering the consequences. It is then that emerges from the depths of his subconscious—clearly expressed by the images of the ultimate temptation—the most deeply hidden motive of his hesitations, a motive which is not exclusively anxiety in the face of his destiny as Messenger of God; the devil is the symbol of *imaginative exaltation* "whispering" to the intrapsychic its limitless promises, the main cause of his quasi unlimited seductive power, making of him a Prince before whom the whole world prostrates itself. Therefore, son of man, son of Adam, Jesus will not be victorious without having been subjected to the ultimate assault already announced by the proposal to "throw himself down." It is renewed, but this time there is no vain hope that angels would come to his help is he deliberately threw himself down, if he definitively renounced his mission as Son and Messenger of God. He overcomes the tempting idea that by accepting to be the Messiah according to the flesh, why would it be impossible to defeat the Romans, and—who knows?—the Roman Empire, an easier feat after all than defeating Satan?

Verses 8-9:
"Next, taking him to a very high mountain, the devil showed him all the kingdoms of the world and their splendor. 'I will give you all these', he said, 'If you fall at my feet and worship me.' "

The very high mountain from which can be seen all the kingdoms of the world and the hope of possessing them, of conquering them with the help of the devil, is the acme of imaginative exaltation brought to the point of absurdity. The underlying significance is diametrically opposed to the preceding imaginative exaltation where "the devil made him stand on the parapet of the Temple." The image of the very high mountain (higher than the Temple) expresses—and quite clearly so—the intention to renounce "the glory of God" for the glory of the world. To prostrate oneself, to worship the devil (subconscious temptations) means to kill the spirit, to die in the soul, to free oneself perversely of all hesitations. (The image does recall in a way the pseudosublime attempt of elevation which caused the downfall of Bellerophon.)

Undoubtedly, no other man has ever found himself confronted with such a tremendous problem whose attempts at a solution reveal clearly the summits and abysses of the human soul, vainly tempted to confuse summits with abysses and abysses with summits. In his deliberating introspection, Jesus dares to go to the end of his liberating endeavor. From one victorious step to the next, though ever again in danger of relapse, his combative impulse is armed to repulse the final assault when, coming from the very depths of the subconscious, emerges—finally unmasked—the obscure seduction in all its horror and absurdity. Deliberately faced, it can be defeated (Perseus's "mirror of truth").

Verse 10:
"Then Jesus replied, 'Be off, Satan!'
For Scripture says:
'You must worship the Lord your God
and serve him alone.' "

In psychological terms: be gone, yourself, give up all the absurd promises and the exalted anxiety of the subconscious and listen only to the promises of the superconscience. This is the full acceptance of his mission and his foreseen destiny. Having defeated in himself the egocentrism of vanity, he has the right to bring the message of joy to the world: vanity can be defeated.

Verse 11:
"Then the devil left him, and angels appeared and looked after him."

Then, anxiety leaves him. All his energies are positive again (angels) and thanks to elucidating introspection, they are at his service and reinforce the combativity of his impulse: better to die in body than to die in soul.

The underlying significance of the myth of the temptation sums up the essential truth, the universal common meaning of all mythologies. It would be hard to understand the myth of temptation—or any symbolization in general—if one did not take into account the fact that there is here as always, besides the personification of motives and the spatialization of images, a *temporalization* summing up in a single encounter the conflicts of deliberation, which are in fact stretched over a long period of hesitation. Very often the fabulous account sums up the entire life of the hero (who symbolizes mankind), representing thus through victory or defeat, one or the other typical constellations of the conflict between superconscious and subconscious motivations, characterizing the human soul. From this we deduce the fundamental principle of decoding the myths: once the core has been brought to light, the hidden meaning understood, the fabulous façade is only a shell we must discard so as to prevent the images (which tend to persist because they are concrete and visual) from being mixed in a confusing way with their psychological understanding.

In the Christian myth where the fighting hero is Jesus, this tendency of the image to persist is especially linked with the symbolic image "Son of God and God come down personally from Heaven." According to its psychological meaning, the temptation of Jesus is a special case in the universality of the intrapsychic conflict between the superconscious law of joyful harmony and the subconscious law of anxiety provoking disharmonies: the essential truth which is the common core of all myths and mythologies. The myth of the temptation brings the universal law to a level of intensity and exemplarity which is humanly the most moving. Is shows how seductive vain temptations can be, but also how powerful is the victorious impulse immanent to human nature. The vital impulse of Jesus has an unequalled strength; it is quasi-superhuman and ideally guiding, but it remains misunderstood without psychological decoding. Emotion is downgraded to the level of sentimentality (sweet Jesus) if one sees the combative man as a supernatural being (misunderstanding the mythical "as if").

The emotion acquires, on the contrary, a far stronger impact by the implication in the Gospel according to Luke that the struggle against temptations is not definitively over: "Having exhausted all these ways of tempting him, the devil left him, to return at the appointed time" (Lk 4:13, JB). The seeming contradiction between the narratives of Matthew and Luke disappears when we take into account the fact that mythical temporalization is entitled to sum up the final victory in one single encounter, though it is in truth the apex of an entire life devoted to the essential struggle. Anxiety always renews its attacks against the man Jesus (Mount of Olives; his cry on the cross: "why have you forsaken me?"). He feels himself abandoned by his own strength of resistance. But at the moment of the agony, the final victory is triumphantly expressed in his cry of acceptance, a cry which is not addressed to a transcendent God but to himself: "Forgive them, for they do not know what they are doing!" *Ecce Homo.*

From our comparison of the story of Jesus with the myth of Perseus, we can easily deduce two stages in the essential victory: self-purification (struggle against Medusa and Satan), and the message that victory is possible: the message of joy (struggle against banalization in the world: the head of Medusa in Perseus's hand; the victory of Jesus over "the Prince of the world"). Neither victory over the self, nor victory over the world is final; they both imply the permanent combativity of the impulse.

In the mythical image of the struggle against the vanity innate in each one of us, and thereby in the world, all the psychological truths of human existence are summed up. The universal psychological truth concerns the inner deliberation be it just or morbid. The immanent significance and value of life is right deliberation which consists in fighting and defeating the vain seduction and its morbid consequences, in order to reach harmony—thanks to the superconscious impulse—and its joy which can only be achieved through the spiritualization—sublimation of the desires binding man to his environment. Spiritualization is the formulation of just value judgements (free of vanity) bringing about a sublimative formation of the character, the elimination of resentments and, consequently, a sensible bond with the environment and especially with the social milieu.

Perverse seduction turns the solicitations of the environment into exalted and anguished temptations—into unhealthy intentions—motives of perverted actions. The insufficiently combative spirit reaches the point where it is enslaved to perversion. It is degraded in false valuations and false justifications of the false valuations. The degraded man, deaf to the call of the superconscience, vainly believes himself to be just while he acts unjustly. The fallen spirit is, in mythical terms, the demon living in man, troubling him and in the end, "killing" his essential combativity. It is the principle of evil, the seductive Satan. Speaking in psychological terms, the inner function which is falsely seductive is *imaginative exaltation*. It aggravates the innate tendency to be seduced to the point of becoming pathogenic and ambivalent. Perverse imagination exalted toward the spirit, overloads material and sexual desires with guilty anxiety and ends up morbidly inhibiting them. When banally exalted toward matter, imagination overvaluates the sexual and material solicitations to the extent of seeing in their exclusive fulfillment the only meaning and value in life. In its two ambivalent forms (moralism-amoralism), imaginative seductibility—an illness of the valuating spirit—is the principle of demoralization. It saps the vital impulse, it undermines its combativity, it chokes it, "kills" it.

The mythical victor is the "Son of the Spirit," unique in the sense that he incarnates in the soma-flesh and even in his activities, the eternal truth, the immutable guiding ideal. Being reborn to eternal truth, he makes his psyche into a "dwelling for the Father." The Father "lives in him" and superconsciously dictates to him his intentions and his works.

Sanctified by the immanent strength of the Father with whom he is united, he is as free from the seductions of the world as from its threats. His unwavering soul is free from anxiety in the face of life and death. Having defeated vain and guilty egocentricity, he bears the adversity of the world without sentimental complaints or accusing resentments. He loves his essential self and he loves the essential self of others (not the vain self). His love is combatively manifested in the message of joy inciting others to fight in themselves the essential enemy: banal and vain temptation, perverse seductibility. (This universal truth is also offered, outside of symbolization, through the words of Buddha and Lao-Tze.)

F. The Various Aspects of the Universality of Symbolization: Historical, Psychological, and Cosmological Aspects

1. Historical Universality:

the mythical pre-science of all the deliberating psychic functions is the foundation of all cultures.

2. Psychological Universality:

the pre-science of all the deliberating psychic functions is expressed in the detailed representation of the ceaseless transformation from the sublime into the perverse and the perverse into the sublime (elevations and falls) and of the superconscious foresight of the causes (motives) and consequences (actions). The preconscious representation of the diversity of motivating constellations based on the laws of harmony and disharmony appears clearly in Greek mythology where it is illustrated by a multitude of heroes and their adventure. No other mythology is as rich in its teachings.[9]

Monotheism, which sums up all the positive and negative values in the struggle between one sole hero and his adversary Satan, stresses in the clearest possible way the essential theme: *fall and elevation*. The specification seems to be less detailed, yet it is expressed thoughout the texts by the words of Jesus, especially in the many parables.

3. Cosmic Universality:

the spatializing superdimension (Heaven-Earth-Hell) of the elevations and falls of the soul creates images that are common to polytheism and monotheism. Mythical dream invents *fabulous places* which are just as nonexistent as the fabulous characters of the half-animals, half-men or half-men, half-gods. The superdimension (Heaven-Earth-Hell) is in conformity with the linguistic spatialization of the psychic processes:

---

[9]Ibid.

superconscious, conscious and subconscious. Moreover, it enables symbolization to include in its universal vision the cosmic conditions of earthly existence. The linguistic concepts of "elevation and fall" are in themselves spatializations. All psychological terminology, be it conceptual or symbolic is spatialization with an underlying significance. It is common knowledge that the concept of "elevation" in psychological terminology means the sublimating intensification of the vital impulse, just as the word "fall" means diminished intensity of the impulse. What is even more important in this context is the fact that not only is the concept understood but also the symbol (fall of Adam) is understood in its psychological meaning with no explanation required. However, the understanding remains vague as long as one is unaware of the existence of the extraconscious processes. It is quite clear that the psyche has no spatial dimension. It constitutes functional dynamics. The processes are not spatially superposed. The linguistic image of their superposition represents the various modes of psychic functioning (logical and illogical: conscious and extraconscious).

The subconscious is nothing but the superconscience blinded by vanity. Since the meaningful or senseless motivating intentions are the product of a ceaseless valuation—be it right or wrong—of the desires (spiritual, material and sexual), the vacillation between lucidity of mind (elevation) and vain blindness (fall) takes place on the level of the inner deliberation (as long as it is not lucidly controlled) constantly and instantaneously, without any crossing of a spatial distance. Heaven and Hell being the mythical symbols of the superconscience's harmonizing valuations and of the subconscious disharmonizing valuations, it is evident that the cosmic distance used by the mythologies to represent the joy of harmonization (ascent into Heaven) and the horrors of disharmonization (descent or fall into Hell) is only an image stressing the vital importance of the judgments that—sensibly or senselessly—determine the value and the meaning of life for every man.

This essential understanding restores the cosmic superdimension (Heaven-Earth-Hell) of the elevation and falls of the soul to their real psychological significance. The psychological fact is that the law of harmony governing human life is only a special instance of the universal harmony, an irrefutable truth which gives to the *universality of symbolic language* a new meaning which is undoubtedly the most profound of all.

Can anyone fail to be moved by cosmic harmony at the sight of a starry sky, moved by the feeling of the unfathomable mystery of existence and awe inspired by the ephemeral nature of human life? The imperative of harmonious incorporation of man in the universal harmony is the central theme of all mythologies because nothing else moves the human soul as much to a feeling of elevation and nothing—except the thought of death—makes one more acutely aware that the vain exaltation of temptations and mundane cares is the downfall of the vital impulse. However, besides the deep but fleeting emotion inspired by the contemplation of the night sky, cosmic harmony and rhythm infallibly rule all conditions of existence. Life is regulated by the day-night alternation. This rhythm, due to the cosmic environment, is in fact more essential to the organization of human existence than the accidental stimuli of the earthly and social environments. The soul, overwhelmed by daily contingencies loses its sense of wonder before the gratuitously insured regularity of cosmic influence. Another reason for this must be mentioned: overintellectualization and its counterpart, pseudometaphysical explanations, detrimental to the awe inspired by the mystery of existence.

From the outset of the mythical era, the motions of the stars inspired symbolization. Sun and moon were personified. Their appearance and disappearance were interpreted as an endless struggle. Day and night became symbols of light and darkness in the human soul. By the personification of the stars, symbolization created a multiplicity of solar and lunar deities representing the positive and negative qualities of the psyche. The deities of the night, because of the magical and fascinating light of the moon, ultimately symbolized psychic seductibility, i.e., imaginative exaltation and its vain egocentricity (linguistic wisdom too, uses words like "lunatic" to describe deviations of the imagination). In order to express more clearly the central theme of "elevation" and "fall," lunar deities were finally transferred to the underground and became infernal deities.

Cosmic images ultimately evolved in a more and more spiritual direction. Lightning, an attribute of Zeus-the-Spirit symbolizes, in its positive meaning, elucidating thoughts, harmonizing valuations; in its negative meaning the thunderbolt blasts, strikes dead: the punishment immanent to banalizing false valuations. All the elements (fire, water, air, earth) are involved in this transformation into a psychological meaning—positive or negative—symbolizing the elevation or fall of the soul. We have already dealt with the positive and negative symbolism of *fire*. *Water* falling down from heaven—rain—becomes the symbol of purification or conversely, symbol of punishment (flood). Clouds become symbols of spiritual impregnation (incarnation of the Holy Spirit in the soma-matter) or negatively, of the darkening of the sun (elucidating thought) by the nebulous ideas of imaginative exaltation. *Air*, elevation in the air, the wings of angels and of Pegasus are symbols of the spiritualizing and sublimating forces, while in their negative meaning, they are the wings of the bat, an attribute of Satan (imaginative pseudoelevation, multiple exaltations). The *wind,* symbol of the divine breath (vital impulse) negatively expresses "the storms of the soul": the fall into ruminations of impotent rage, spiteful or plaintive resentment, vain brooding over schemes of revenge. Does not the wisdom of language stigmatize the vacuity of vain projects by saying "It is all wind, a windbag"? *Earth* where human beings live, becomes "Terra Mater," symbol of earthly desires and their sensible satisfaction; in its negative sense, it symbolizes the exaltation of earthly desires causing either their guilty repression (underground Hell: the subconscious) or their unscrupulous excesses (banal fall: Hell of life on earth).

The symbolism of the four elements is inexhaustibly rich. The few examples we have listed can only give an inkling, albeit one which is sufficient to glimpse their universal significance which underlies the symbolization of all mythologies including that of the biblical texts (myths of the fall of Adam and of the resurrection, synonymous with elevation; myths of the descent into Hell and the ascension into Heaven, myth of the descent of God in the shape of his Son and many other symbols). The spatial superdimension of the ascents and descents, elevations and falls, introduced into symbolization by the cosmic images has a precise purpose; namely, to remind of the moving truth, too easily forgotten, that the conditions of life on earth depend above all on the cosmic environment.

Such a reminder points to a surprising problem which concerns the universality of symbolic language. The relationship between cosmic environment and life on earth is only an infinitesimal part of the conditions of existence and life on the countless planets in each of the countless galaxies. Nothing could be more unlikely and vain than to suppose that our planet is the only inhabited one. From the atom to the cosmic universe, everything is ruled by the laws of temporal existence: harmony and disharmony. The first is the law of appearance, organization, composition; the second, the law of disappearance, disorganization, decomposition.

Supposing that there are other living beings—whatever their morphological aspect which we cannot imagine—on other planets, must we not also suppose that they are all subject to the wear and tear of time? That they are—from the most primitive to the most highly organized—dependent on the psychic phenomenon of satisfaction and dissatisfaction? That appeasement due to the harmony of feelings is periodically disrupted by the awakening of the appetencies that animate them? That the biological requirements of life—similar to ours—are to eat for the individual to survive, to reproduce for the species to perdure, and to evolve when the environment becomes unfavorable to the survival of the species such as it is? That evolution must lead them toward more farsighted lucidity since this is the best means of adjustment? That lucidity—the preconscious spirit that enables them to live—organizes first of all the possibility of orientation in space, i.e., the organs of sense (probably quite different from ours)? That evolution leads them toward orientation in time through a memory linking past, present and future: the condition for conscious foresight which is the indispensable means of more and more lucid adjustment without which life, devoid of evolutionary impulse and threatened by environmental handicaps could not perdure?

To be sure, all that the mind can think or imagine with regard to extra-terrestrial life remains an anthropomorphic analogy. But here the analogy is not in the least metaphysical speculation because it does not transgress the limits of existence. Matter being the same throughout the universe, how could spirit be of a different nature on other planets? The common factor of all errors is the misinterpretation of the relationship between spirit and matter by both spiritualism and materialism. The error here is to make the spirit into an entity, a noun, a substance, instead of understanding that the term only denotes the organizing function undoubtedly manifest in the harmony of the universe, and nothing else. It is certainly more consistent to admit that matter and spirit—the one an extensive quantity and the other an intensive quality—are universally complementary. Quantity and quality, extension and intention do not exclude one another, quite the contrary: their interpenetration is a condition of existence. Preconscious spirit organizes and harmonizes the material universe. On the level of life, this interpenetration constitutes the psychosomatic organism, an evolutionary product of spirit-intensity—tension of the spirit—interiorized in the soma-matter. (The *tension* of the spirit, by its embodiment in the flesh, becomes through evolution *intention* animating the soma: linguistic and mythical wisdom complete one another.)

Since the preconscious spirit which organizes, harmonizes matter clearly becomes more and more conscious on our planet, how could it not also evolve on other planets toward conscious lucidity? (Whatever the morphologies and even the capacities of reflection could be in their diversities, they all remain analogically linked to our somatic organization and our intellect since the universal law of harmony rules somatic organization as well as organization of thought.) Nothing can exist in a state of vitally unsatisfying disharmony except the conscious psyche, and even then it has to hide its guilty dissatisfaction under the pseudo-satisfaction of vanity. What characterizes conscious life is the diversification of the biological drives (nutrition, reproduction) into a multitude of often contradictory and disharmonious desires (myth of the fall of Adam), which, when projected into the future—because of the imaginative capacity of foresight—become the projects and motives of future actions.

This is why the imperative of self-harmonization is the ethical law, governing life which has become conscious (myth of the resurrection). Could the universal truth—fall and elevation—common theme of all mythologies, go beyond the conditions of life on earth? Could the symbolic explosion of the human superconscience be universal in the widest and deepest meaning of the word: truth about the universe?

Given the harmony of the universe—which includes perhaps forms of life that are more evolved than ours—does not the "hell on earth" of our beliefs and of our pseudosciences of life, our ideologies, our quarrels of opinion and the vanity of our discussions represent a collective delusion, caused by the lack of understanding of the ethical truth which has remained symbolically hidden in our mythologies?

SECOND PART

CHAPTER V

GENESIS: THE MYTH OF THE FALL

A. INTRODUCTION TO THE DECIPHERING OF THE TEXT

Symbolization, intuitive knowledge of the psychic functioning, answers man's question: "What must I do with my life?" This is the ethical problem. Vital satisfaction or dissatisfaction depends on its solution.

But before he can solve this problem, man must answer the ultimate question concerning the origin of the world and of life, because only faith in the lawful organization of the world and existence, only the certainty that the world and life are neither incoherent nor due to chance, can arouse man's vital impulse to associate himself with this lawful organization, i.e., to discover and develop the meaning of life— its evolutionary direction—on which its value depends. The epistemological problem and the ethical problem, studied at length in the first part of the book, are inextricably bound. The solution of the first leads to the solution of the second.

This is why the myths of all peoples start with the creation of the world and life, or cosmogony. In its search for an explanation to the mystery of the origins, the human spirit is obliged to project onto the very beginnings of life the duality existing within man, imagining duality to have been "expelled from unity." the latter being seen as the mysterious cause of appearance[1] (or existence) and its duality. The return to unity is, for appearance, its harmony. Appearance is unthinkable without the duality of inner and outer world, psyche and world. But it is equally unthinkable without the harmonious reunification which must always be renewed between the inner and outer world, without which life would be impossible.

These statements are self-evident. They are the basis of the certainty of our thought, they enable us to answer the ethical problem: the search for harmony, unity in multiplicity, is the evolutionary meaning to be given to life. Cosmogonies, just like theogonies, are allegories; they cannot have the precision that symbolic language attains when

---

[1] What Paul Diel calls *l'apparition* has been translated as "the appearance" (of the manifest world).

dealing with the laws ruling the harmonizing or disharmonizing intra-psychic dynamics, the latter being a phenomenon that can be introspectively observed.

They describe that which has never been observed, and which can never be related, not even in science since physics—when it comes to the origins of the world—can only voice hypotheses, and even though these evolve with time, they still remain mere hypotheses. Whatever the progress of physics, it will always remain, even when we take into account the evolution of its discoveries, an anthropomorphic vision which leaves untouched the mystery of the origins.

A cosmogony itself can only be an anthropomorphic description of the successive stages of the appearance of the world and existence, its underlying meaning being:

1. Acknowledgement of the mystery of the origins which is called God (the word God does not imply an explanation but an emotion).
2. Expression of the duality of the world, principle of the appearance.
3. Development of the progressive incarnation of the organizing spirit up to the advent of the thinking being.

These three essential themes are included in all cosmogonies as in all theogonies. As we know now, the first chapter of Genesis was written several hundred years after the second and third chapters. But it is also generally accepted that its oral sources go back to very ancient times. Whatever the case may be, the first chapter fulfills the need to establish a cosmogony which, in psychological translation, means an epistemology, the latter being the only way of giving its true dimension to the ethical problem outlined in the second and third chapters.

The first chapter of Genesis is an account of the creation of the world and life, considered as an explanation of the origins. The first five verses are the epistemological foundation: acknowledgement of mystery and the dual modalities of appearance. Verses 6 to 10 outline the spatio-temporal environment in which life is going to unfold; its development is related in verses 11 to 31. It deals first with vegetation, then animals, then man. A more detailed explanation will be given at a later stage.

The second and third chapters deal with the biogenesis of the thinking being, the biogenesis of the psychic functions which include the ethical problem; man gains access to consciousness but that function not being fully developed, he remains under the direction of the superconscious which is the survival of instinct in human beings; through the more or less constant rejection of this inner guidance of the superconscious, the subconscious—all that a human being does not want to know about himself—comes into being. These psychic functions—conscious, superconscious, subconscious—have all three emerged out of the animal unconscious which still rules the vegetative functions of man.

Man is thus confronted with the necessity of choosing between the imperative of the superconscious, calling for harmony of desires, and the disharmonizing seduction of the subconscious which is nothing else but blinding vanity.

This is not only the theme of the second and third chapters of Genesis, studied further on, but also that of the Old and New Testaments and it is the theme of all mythologies, for indeed the only problem that has always confronted and will always confront man, remains the problem of the death and of the life of his soul. Man can "die in his soul" but he can be born again during his earthly existence.

In the myths of all peoples, man symbolizes the spirit while woman symbolizes earthly desires, each of these symbols being—depending on its attributes—either positive or negative; it is the fundamental spirit-matter pair. The myth of Adam (second and third chapter of Genesis) as indeed the myth of Prometheus, stands on its own even though there are analogical links with all the other myths. They represent the genesis of man, the biogenesis of man's psychic functioning during a decisive stage of his evolution, when the intellect, owing to the importance of its development starts to oppose the spirit. The characters in the myth of Adam represent the detailed relationships between the various psychic functions: God symbolizes the evolutionary impulse, the immanent justice ruling over psychic functioning, the lawfulness of psychic functioning, the latter expressions being equivalent and fundamentally linked to each other. One must recall here that in the Genesis of the world (first chapter), God symbolizes the creative and organizing act. Now the organizer of the world, a symbolic expression, becomes on a human level, the organizer of the psychic functioning, of its lawfulness, of its psychological reality. It is symbolized by "God-the-Judge."

Adam symbolizes the intellect that is more and more subjected to seductive imagination and has forgotten during its development the imperative of the spirit to which, however, it had originally been linked ("God breathed in his nostrils a breath of life, and thus man became a living being"). Eve symbolizes exaltative imagination regarding earthly desires, and the serpent, original vanity. The detailed psychological significance of these symbols will be described later.

Let us also stress that Adam represents, as in all myths, man confronted with the problem of choice: he is a hero similar to all mythical heroes, called by the gods and faced with monsters and demons he has to fight. This significance is included in the previously indicated meaning of Adam as symbol of the intellect because it is the characteristic of conscious man—in fact, half-conscious—to hesitate between the work of the spirit and the excessive attraction of the matter, the appeal of material and sexual pleasures, and such a hesitation is due to the new possibilities offered to him by his intellect.[2] Only when taking on his responsibility as a valuator of material and sexual desires does man symbolize positive spirit which fecundates matter.

The fact remains that the fundamental spirit-matter relationship (man-woman) and all its implication is, in the myth of Adam and the myth of Prometheus, explained by images of such precision that on the one hand several characters are needed to describe all the aspects of psychic functioning and that, on the other hand, one single character can, depending on the dynamics of the myth, embody two antithetic meanings though inherent, both of them, in psychic functioning; for instance, woman, symbol of exalted earthly desires or symbol of purified earthly desires.

It must be said that although this psychological translation of Genesis, is on the whole, based on The Jerusalem Bible in the English text and in the French text on E. Osty's translation, the work could equally have been done with other versions. The uncertainties of the text itself, the variations from one translation to the other, cannot present a real difficulty for the psychological understanding of these documents. Errors of translation from the original Hebrew have unavoidably crept in throughout the centuries, but they cannot destroy the mythical content of the texts.

The preliminary understanding of the psychic functioning, used as a methodical basis for the psychological translation, enables us to find our bearings without hesitation throughout the difficulties of the façade of the narrative. In brief, behind the more or less well reconstituted façade of the Hebrew text, the psychological significance remains because it is what initially dictated the symbolic story. Linguistic studies, comparisons of texts, the historical aspect of the writings, the various eras during which they were set down, their rewriting across the centuries, no matter how interesting all these may be, are not the object of this study which deals only with the psychological content of these texts.

Before undertaking the verse by verse translation, it is necessary to stress the distinction between the façade of the story which can be called the plane of reality and the deep psychological meaning underlying the facade, called the symbolic plane.[3] Certain verses (for instance Gen. 2:17 and 21; 3:1, JB), due to their illogicality, only become understandable once their symbolical façade has been translated into terms describing the psychic functioning. But certain other verses (for instance Gen. 2:24; 3:16–17, 19, JB) appear to be logical, conform with reality and thus seem to have no symbolic significance. They therefore

---

[2]See note 2 in chapter I.
[3]Linguistic foreknowledge is rooted in the intuition of psychic functioning. But the deep meaning of the linguistic plane cannot unfortunately be exploited here since our analysis is not based on the Hebrew texts.

seem to remain outside the scope of psychological translation. This is not the case. In myth as in dream, both being oneiric expressions of man's essential life, creative imagination uses the elements of reality, such as they actually exist when they are apt to represent the calculus of satisfaction and its variations.

Even when creative imagination fabulates, it does so on the basis of elements taken from reality; thus the centaur is an image made of man and horse. It is not necessary for the image to be a fabulation for it to be considered a symbolic image. But every symbolic image has to be translatable in a coherent way into psychological language and to fit harmoniously in the analogical corpus of the translated symbols.

However, when the plane of reality is obvious (for instance: "you shall give birth to your children in pain"), it is still more difficult to free oneself from the images in order to understand their psychological meaning. Man has always considered Adam and Eve as the man-woman pair. In fact, they only symbolize psychic functions which are characteristic of every human being, man or woman. In this vein, being fundmental elements of psychic functioning, they are indeed the ancestors of present humanity and the source of conflict in the human soul. This will be explained later on.

The error of dogmatism is nothing but a literal reading of all the symbolic data ("creation of heaven and earth," "creation of man," "inferiority of woman," etc.). This misunderstanding is reinforced by the logical appearance, in conformity with the reality of these data which have, however, an underlying symbolic meaning. "The letter kills, only the spirit is life-giving," as the Apostle Paul said.

B. Deciphering of Symbolism in Genesis

Chapter 1

Verse 1:
"In the beginning God created the heavens and the earth."

As was explained at length in the first part of this work, when the human mind tries to think of "the beginning," it is confronted with the impossibility of understanding the origins of the world and life. The cause of this created world remains mysterious, undefinable, for only that which is finite, existing in space and time, can be defined. However, thinking about the "beginning" is a necessity for the human mind which looks for a cause for every effect and links every duration to a beginning. The human mind, compelled to name the unexplainable, calls it God; by naming it, it anthropomorphizes it. Not being able to explain anything, but attempting to calm anxiety in the face of the question, "Where do the world and life come from?" the myth answers, "It is as if a real God were the cause"; the world is the lawful effect of this cause. Thus the mind can refer to "the beginning" and appease the vertigo of fear in the face of a duration whose beginning is unknown to us; for the original creating act and the word God, *purely symbolic expressions*, express only one thing: the mystery of the origins; this mystery is nevertheless manifested under the lawful form of the appearance of the world and life. Therefore the "God" symbol also includes the harmonious lawfulness of appearance. The lawful organization implies the dual manifestation of the two fundamental poles which are inherent in all that exists: spirit and matter (the world "spirit" means nothing more than the organizing principle of matter, at all levels). These two principles, spirituality and materiality, are symbolized by heaven and earth, for "in the beginning" nothing can exist except as a potential which will enable the world and life to emerge: organizing spirit, and matter to be organized; these two modalities are distinguished by analysis, but one does not exist without the other, and their complementarity makes life possible.

The first verse is a synthetic vision of what will be developed in the following verses: mystery (symbolically God) from which emerges duality (symbolized by heaven and earth), the principle of all appearance. This appearance will be the entire cosmos, the apparent geocentrism of the myth being itself only a symbol. It is striking to note that in the Hebrew language the word for "universe" is a combination of the two words "heaven" and "earth".[4] This implies that the superconscious intuition at work in the formation of language has always known that the emergence of the world is dual in nature and cannot exist without the manifestation of the two opposite and complementary principles, the spiritual and the material.

This calls for an analogy with the Greek Theogony:[5] "At the beginning, there was chaos, the Abyss," is an image expressing fear, while the Judaic myth stresses faith in the lawfulness of things: the mystery symbolically called God. However, these symbols remain analogically linked since both pertain to the mystery of the origins and both can arouse emotion.

As to the emergence of the world, the Greek myth stresses the conflictual duality of all that is in existence, even on the most elementary level. This is indicated by the revolt of Gaea against Uranus, of matter against spirit, long before the appearance of the human being. The human mind, in search of an explanation of the origins of life, thus extends to the beginning of the world the inner discord that splits man in two, discord between material and spiritual desires.[6] However, one

---

[4]The same applies to the Chinese language.
[5]*Symbolism in Greek Mythology*, Shambhala, 1980.
[6]Ibid.

must note that Eros,[7] the first of all deities, symbolizes in the Greek myth the still undifferentiated vital force including spirit and matter.

As to the Judaic myth, it stresses in this first chapter the harmony established between creator and creation: "And God saw that it was good," a sentence punctuating, as we shall see, each creative stage. The conflict between spirit and matter appears only with Adam, symbol of mankind rebelling against the law of harmony. These visions describing the various fundamental aspects of existence, although they may seem contradictory, are in fact complementary. Duality is the principle of differentiation; harmony, the principle of reunification. Duality would only lead to disorganization if it were not, always anew, overcome by harmony. The latter, being always threatened by duality, can be reconstituted at higher and higher levels, which characterizes the evolutionary phenomenon. Both are conditions of the existence of the universe and life.

Verse 2:
"Now the earth was a formless void, there was darkness over the Deep, . . . "

The preceding theme is developed. The deep, alluded to in Greek mythology as we saw ("the abyss"), symbolizes the unfathomable mystery of appearance. Darkness and the deep are words which express the disorientation of the mind when it strives to reflect upon the origins of the world and life. In search of an explanation, the human mind finds "darkness." No light, no matter where it comes from, is able to help him when it comes to this problem.

The earth, a symbol of matter, the quintessentially tangible element, is devoid of any content, chaos, when one attempts to reflect upon it "in the beginning," apart from what it represents for us now. The spirit cannot have the slightest idea of what it was initially, unless it is an anthropomorphic idea (hypotheses of physics) implying that it is "as if" a human eye had been present when it was formed. Being symbol of matter, or rather of the disorientation of the spirit attempting to imagine nonorganized matter (an impossibility), it does not represent in this verse what it will be in Gen.1:9, when the "dry land" will appear, when it will be "our" earth.

Verse 2:
". . . God's spirit hovered over the water."

Yet, next to the deep, next to this impenetrable mystery, appearance emerges under its two modalities of spirit and matter; it is the spiritual principle and the material principle in their potentiality: the spirit of

---

[7]Not to be confused with Eros, son of Aphrodite, the deity ruling sexuality both in its banalized and sublimated forms.

God, symbol of the organizing spirit manifest throughout all nature, preparing the differentiation of matter, the organization of the cosmos.

The "waters" out of which the first seeds of life probably came are very apt to symbolize, by analogy, potential existence. From this point of view, all is water, all is still formless, but all is potentially fecund. We know how important fecundating water is for agriculture, especially in the countries of the Middle East where the Judaic myth arose.

Thus mythical imagination strives to express through the words "chaos," "darkness," and "deep" the vertigo of anxiety taking hold of it when it evokes the creation of the world and, at the same time, it strives to express its faith in a world in the process of emergence, which is seen, thanks to the evocative power of the human mind, as emerging in an organized form. Mystery and appearance are thus evoked in the same verse because they are in fact inseparable, they are the two aspects of the same phenomenon: mystery is not an entity, it exists only for the human mind; mystery is only the mysterious aspect of appearance. Formulated in a different way, the first verse of the Prologue of John, translated in this work, expresses the very same truth: "In the beginning was the Word, and the Word was with God, and the Word was God."

Verse 3:
"God said, 'Let there be light,' and there was light."

The word of God, symbolically understood, is creative, it creates the universe. No time elapses between creative will and its accomplishment. This is a metaphysical image formed by analogy of contrast with the life of man taking place in space-time and whose every desire implies, to achieve satisfaction, a wait of some duration. The word of God (symbol) is thus at the same time his creative will and the accomplishment of that will: the manifest world, the appearance, "the Word." Thus "light," manifested by "the Word of God," symbolizes the appearance, the visible universe. It is opposed to the "darkness," explained in the preceding verse. The manifest world is for the human mind, light. There, he can perceive in the slightest details the manifestations of the mysterious organizing law. It is revealed to him, as it were, as soon as he gives up the pretense of wanting to know "the cause" of the existence of the world. The manifest world becomes the light because the only way man can emotionally experience the mysterious aspect of existence is to contemplate the lawful organization ruling all that exists, to wonder and marvel at it. On the level of inner deliberation, light is the symbol of the superconscious, and darkness the symbol of the subconscious. By analogy with the preceding explanations, it becomes clear that man is engulfed in the darkness of the subconscious if he tries to explain the mystery or if he wants to eliminate it; in short, if he refuses to accept the limits of the competence of his spirit. On the other hand, he gains access to the superconscious light if he discovers the lawful manifestation of the universe and accepts to live in accordance with this law, accepts the responsibility of living according to his essential desire of harmonization, according to the evolutionary impulse that was already at work in the beginning.

Verse 4:
"God saw that light was good, and God divided the light from darkness."

Symbolically, God approves of his creation, but it is in fact man who creating the myths imagines the approval of God. It therefore symbolizes his own approval when, moved by creation, he grasps that it is organized lawfully. In this way, the human mind, under the revelation of the mysterious aspect of appearance, clearly distinguishes (divides) light from darkness, what is explainable (the modalities of appearance) from what is unexplainable (the mystery of appearance).

Verse 5:
"God called light 'day,' and darkness he called 'night.' "

The words light and day, darkness and night are more or less synonymous. But light and darkness are here, as we have just explained, metaphysical symbols; they do not imply the temporal duration of day and night. Day and night symbolize the rhythm which is necessary for appearance to evolve: the dual conflict on the level of existence, the conflict between organization and disorganization, appearance and disappearance, which is imposed by time and its passage since appearance is a temporal phenomenon. On the specifically human level, "day and night" symbolize the conflict between good and evil, the moral conflict which emerges at the same time as man when the myth, leaving the theme of the creation of the universe, enters the ethical theme: the task of man during his life. For day brings light, symbol of lucidity, and night brings darkness, symbol of disorientation, of affective beclouding.

Verse 5 (end):
"Evening came and morning came: the first day."

Each day of the creation is the symbol of an evolutionary stage; the seeming illogicality of an evening followed by a morning (one could understand very well if it were "morning came and evening came") expresses therefore that each era ends to open on a new promise, a new evolutionary step, a new day, symbol of a renewed hope. This sentence will keep its meaning all along and its translation will not be repeated.

Verse 6:
"And God said, 'Let there be a vault in the waters to divide the waters in two.' "

The waters are, as we have seen in verse 2, the potentiality of all the cosmos and life. In the Oriental vision of that time, the heavens are a solid vault rising over the earth. This vault, this dome, enables the celestial ocean to be kept under control and thus space can appear.

Thus with temporality (verse 5), space is created: the perception of distance, of space, is the product of an evolutionary stage imposed by the need to better elucidate the obstacles to satisfaction. Such a perception enables one to differentiate and order the various elements of the manifest world, the objects to seize and the objects to avoid.[8] Temporality and space are imagined as having been set into place before life appeared, as being necessary for its appearance.

This is again an anthropomorphic vision: that of a preexisting space-time framework in which life would have been set. But to make of this space-time framework a reality is to totally misunderstand the actual vital phenomenon which is that psyche, soma and environment all follow the same evolutionary ascent.[9] In fact, every psychomatic organization creates its own space-time. The perception of a space cannot occur without organs of sense or the psychic capacity to interpret perception. The space-time framework which is proper to man, exists only for him; how it existed without man—what it was—remains a mystery.

But the symbolic process through which the myth imagines a preexistent framework for life is an explanatory necessity, whose purpose is to calm anxiety, because this preexistent framework would be an effect having God for its cause. Referring to a God-symbol as "creative cause" is an act of faith in the lawful organization of the inner and outer world. It soothes anxiety in the face of mystery.

Verse 7:
"God made the vault, and it divided the waters above the vault from the waters under the vault."

After evoking the cosmos, establishing the space-time framework enables the myth to concentrate on the planet Earth; for the ethical question confronting man: "What must I do with my life?" can only be solved within the conditions of his terrestrial life. The waters below will become the oceans, and the waters above, the clouds. This is already a promise of fertilization, of future fecundation: the cycle between oceans and clouds, the dynamics uniting heaven and earth which enable the development of agriculture. This real link is the symbol of the fundamental link between spirit and matter, symbol of the fecundation of matter by spirit which is the constant preoccupation of the myth, a fecundation which will become on the human level, the spiritualization-sublimation of material desires.

Verse 8:
"God called the vault 'heaven.' Evening came and morning came: the second day."

[8]*La Peur et l'Angoisse,* Petite Bibliothèque Payot, Paris.
[9]Ibid.

Thus appear in their reality and not only in their potentiality (verse 1) the two fundamental elements: the heaven (preceding verse) and the earth (following verse).

Verses 9 and 10:
"God said, 'Let the waters under heaven come together into a single mass, and let dry land appear.' And so it was." God called the dry land 'earth' and the mass of waters 'seas,' and God saw that it was good."

In Greek mythology, the great geological cataclysms—symbolized by the Cyclops, the Hecatonchires, and the Titans—fashioned the earth and enabled the earthly crust to form (preparing it to become the nurturing mother of life). So here too, the Word of God organizes earth and sea: real possibilities of life and of its evolutionary development.

"God saw that it was good" (verse 10) has already been translated in verse 4.

Verse 11:
"God said, 'Let the earth produce vegetation: seed-bearing plants, and fruit trees bearing fruit with their seed inside, in their several kinds, on the earth.' And so it was."

Verse 12:
"The earth produced vegetation: plants bearing seed in their several kinds, and trees bearing fruit with their seeds inside in their several kinds. God saw that it was good."

Verse 11 expresses the creative intention, verse 12 the accomplishment of the divine intention, symbolizing mysterious intentionality. With the formation of the earth emerges the initial possibility of life, vegetation and its biological means of reproduction, seeds. The second chapter will deal extensively with the fruit trees and their symbolic significance. These verses, describing the fertility of the earth, already contain man's gratitude toward the nurturing earth.

Verses 14 to 19:
"God said, 'Let there be lights in the vault of heaven to divide day from night, and let them indicate festivals, days and years. Let them be lights in the vault of heaven to shine on the earth.' And so it was. God made the two great lights: the greater light to govern the day, the smaller to govern the night, and the stars. God set them in the vault of heaven to shine on the earth, to govern the day and the night and to divide light from darkness. God saw that it was good. Evening came and morning came; the fourth day."

One could expect a cosmogony to refer to the stars before dealing with vegetation. But this is not the case and it is psychologically explainable. The myth appears during the agricultural era. The farmer's first concern is for the cultivated earth, and as a result he raises his eyes to heaven, striving to understand the determining influence of the stars, especially the sun and the moon, on his work and the organization of his life. The light referred to after the creation of the lights in the preceding verses is thus real light and this confirms that the light of verse 3 is not the light of the stars but, as we translated it, the symbol of the appearance of the world and life. The stars are no longer deities as in the polytheistic mythologies, but have been created by the deity in order to serve man. This represents an evolution in mythical thought. In the manifest world all is dual, life and death, day and night, good and evil; light and darkness will continue to be used analogically by the Judeo-Christian myth to symbolize superconscious harmony and sub-conscious disharmony in the human soul. Still more precisely, the analogy between sun, light, and divinity is implicit in the symbolic expression of Jesus: "I am the light of the world." The stars, symbols of the guiding ideals, lead man in his search for satisfaction; they symbolize the highest values of satisfaction: truth, beauty, and goodness. Only the elements of the outer world and above all the fundamental elements surrounding him and sustaining his life—water, air, earth, fire, light, sun, moon—gave man the materials on which the explanatory and analogical vision of his mind could be exerted. He thus projected implicitly onto these fundamental elements that were quite clearly a necessity for the allegorical description of the creation of the world, the moral content they will acquire later on when the myth will tackle the ethical problem.

Verses 20 to 23:
"God said, 'Let the waters teem with living creatures, and let birds fly above the earth within the vault of heaven.' And so it was. God created great sea-serpents and every kind of living creature with which the waters teem, and every kind of winged creature. God saw that it was good. God blessed them, saying, 'Be fruitful, multiply and fill the waters of the seas; and let the birds multiply upon the earth.' Evening came and morning came; the fifth day."

In these verses, life itself appears. First, life in the waters and in the air. Then the development of this life. This is what the myth calls the deployment of the word through evolution. Psychologically speaking, this is the *progressive incarnation of spirit in matter:* the organizing spirit, by creating species that are more and more highly evolved, manifests and reveals its mysterious intentionality, the finality of life itself in its quest for harmonious satisfaction.

Verses 24 and 25:
"God said, 'Let the earth produce every kind of living creature: cattle, reptiles, and every kind of wild beast.' And so it was. God made every kind of wild beast, every kind of cattle, and every kind of land reptile. God saw that it was good."

These verses will be studied in several stages. In verse 24, earth itself is being inhabited, and it is on earth that the real adventure of life, the human adventure, will unfold.

The fish, the birds, the wild beasts, the reptiles (verses 20 to 25) are not here symbols endowed with an ethical meaning since the first chapter does not deal with ethics, the task of man in life. They do not require therefore a detailed translation but a global translation of their biogenetic significance, the progressive incarnation of spirit in matter. The sentence, "Evening came and morning came," which has punctuated so far every evolutionary stage, is not used between the appearance of the animals and that of man. What could be the reason for such an omission? Although it is quite clear that a new evolutionary stage was manifested by the appearance of man, the myth does stress the biological link uniting man to the animals. Man is the thinking animal. Animals, just like men, are the apparent manifestation of the mysterious intentionality at work in all of nature; thus the evolutionary step separating them does not abolish the evolutionary bridge uniting them. If man has lost the instinctive certainty of the animals, he still remains subject to the organizing law of life: the law of harmony. He will not live satisfactorily unless he finds again, on a higher level, access to harmony; by virtue of this biological need to seek satisfaction, he is more deeply linked to his evolutionary predecessors than he is separated from them.

Verse 26:
"God said, 'Let us make man in our own image, in the likeness of ourselves, and let them be masters of the fish of the sea, the birds of heaven, the cattle, all the wild beasts, and all the reptiles that crawl upon the earth.' "

Man is created in the image of God; this symbol has to be explained at length. The mysterious intentionality which prevails throughout nature is manifested on the human level in a *conscious* way, it is no longer instinctively incarnate in the soma, as it is in the animal; it is diversified in the multiple intentions animating man. Man therefore has an inner experience of intentionality. Among the living beings, he is the only one who can express it in his thoughts, his feelings, his words. To the extent that he is able to experience emotion in the face of this intentionality surrounding him on all sides and which he calls "God," and emotion in the face of his own intentionality, he feels himself directly animated by God, by the mysterious creative intentionality. His own conscious intentions become the most evolved expression he knows of the intentionality of nature, which he calls "God." In this, he feels himself close to God, created in his likeness. Besides this, inversion is a frequent symbolic process. In fact, man created God in his image: he made of him a thinking and willing being like himself. Which means, analogically to what has just been explained: the most evolved appearance among living beings, man, endowed with conscious intentions, is the most adequate organization for representing the mysterious organizational capacity of nature, symbolized by God.

"... and let them be masters of the fish of the sea, the birds of heaven, all the wild beasts and all the reptiles that crawl upon the earth." Man is effectively the master of nature. He is no longer passively dependent on the environment as are animals. Having access to conscious memory, he bears the whole world within himself, in the form of images. The imaginative foresight regarding future possibilities of satisfaction will be accompanied by an intellectual foresight regarding the obstacles to satisfaction and the way to overcome them. Living in a three dimensional time in which past and future are linked by conscious memory, he can draw from his past failures or successes, an experience he will use in the future, thus becoming more and more capable of organizing the mastery of the external world. It is thus that he is "... the master of the fish of the sea...," etc.

Verse 27:
"God created man in the image of himself,
in the image of God he created him,
male and female he created them."

This then is the creation of man as a biological species, male and female, incorporated in the evolutionary stream of life. Being still as it were an innocent animal, integrated in the tribe of hunters and shepherds to which he intimately belongs, he remains more or less subject to the conditions offered by nature.

However, as the myth points out, the creation of the animals is made "in their kind," the creation of the thinking species is made in the form of man and woman. On the human level, the spirit is not incarnate anymore in matter as it is on the animal level in the form of instinct. The spirit and matter modalities symbolized by the man-woman couple are differentiated from one another. The creation of Adam and Eve in the second chapter will develop this differentiation with all its consequences.

Verse 28:
"God blessed them. . . ."

Man is thus approved, "blessed" by God. In psychological terms, man who is still innocent, lives "under the law of God," in accordance with the law of harmony, the law of life. Transgression of this law leads man to know unhappiness and pathological suffering, as will be demonstrated in the following chapter.

Verses 29 and 30:
"God said, 'See, I give you all seed-bearing plants that are upon the whole earth, and all the trees with seed-bearing fruit, this shall be your food. To all the wild beasts, all the birds of heaven and all living reptiles on the earth, I give all the foliage of the plants for food.' And so it was."

In fact, there are no non-seed-bearing plants in nature, as this is a condition for their reproduction. But it is stipulated that to man alone are given the seed-bearing plants, for man alone is capable of cultivating the earth and sowing seed. The animals receive the foliage, the gratuitously given product of the earth, a symbolic image of the animal's dependence on his environment, a very different situation from that of man who will become a farmer. The stress on the exclusive right to seed already denotes man's potential evolutionary future and his mastery to come, over all that lives on earth.

Verse 31:
"God saw all he made, and indeed it was very good. Evening came and morning came: the sixth day."

It is not only "good," but "very good." On the last day of creation God completely approves his work. Man, moved by the mystery of the emergence of the world and life, completely approves the organization of the universe; for he superconsciously knows that the disharmony of the world in which he lives, social disharmony, is bred by the psychic disharmony of each and every one of us, for which each and everyone is responsible. If man is capable of putting himself in harmony with the laws of the universe, interiorly as well as exteriorly, he can only marvel in the presence of universal harmony.

The world thus appears in its inherent duality, the species inhabit the waters, the heavens, and the earth; they multiply, and they lead through successive evolutionary stages to man, the thinking animal.

CHAPTER 2

Verses 1 and 2:
"Thus heaven and earth were completed with all their array. On the seventh day God completed the work he had been doing. He rested on the seventh day after all the work he had been doing."

The creation was accomplished in seven days, a sacred figure including 3, the figure representing the spirit, and 4, the figure of matter; it is the union of the spiritual principle and the material principle, the progressive incarnation of the spirit in the manifest world, the Word. It is then that God rests. With the appearance of man, destiny is passed on from the "creator" to the creature. Psychologically speaking, the creature is now responsible for creation: man will have to take it upon himself, no longer as an unconscious and instinctive animal, but as a conscious being responsible for the evolutionary road to be walked

Verse 3:
"God blessed the seventh day and made it holy, because on that day he had rested after all his work of creating."

As we have already said, this is the emotional approval of man in the presence of creation. Guided by his superconscious (God in him), he blesses the creation of which he is part because he knows, faced with the mysterious preadaptation which links every species to the specific environment it perceives, that this world is such that he can find satisfaction in it. Only the multiplication of his demands can make him incapable of attaining satisfaction, and of wonder and worship of this inner world and outer world lawfully ordained.

No one can violate the law. It has ruled, symbolically speaking, over the creation of the world: in its manifest aspect it governs life and its evolution in the form of immanent justice. *God-the-Creator gives way to God-the-Judge:* this will be the theme of the second and third chapters.

Verse 4a:
"Such were the origins of heaven and earth when they were created."

Verse 4 sums up all the first chapter, the creation of heaven and earth, the manifestation of "the Word of God."

Verses 4b and 5:
"At the time when Yahweh God made earth and heaven, there was as yet no wild bush on the earth nor had any wild plant yet sprung up, for Yahweh God had not sent rain on earth, nor was there any man to till the soil."

It is quite clear that the earth was inhabited before myths were created (eras of animistic cultures); however, for the myth which is no longer epistemological and cosmogonic (Chapter 1) but the myth of the biogenesis of the conscious spirit, the earth had not germinated yet, rain had not fallen yet, i.e., the earth was not considered truly fecund before the start of the new adventure of human life, developed in the following chapters of Genesis and throughout the Old and New Testaments: intellectualization[10] and its danger which have to be overcome by progressive spiritualization.

Verse 6:
"However a flood was rising from the earth and watering all the surface of the soil."

The earth is being prepared to become not only fecundable but tillable because, in the next verse, the thinking being, and here more specifically, the farmer and creator of myths is going to appear.

One could object that in Chapter 1, man and woman had already been created and with them, the environment necessary to life. But in the first chapter, they are symbolic of the human species, without any distinction of the various stages which take place within human evolution itself.

---

[10]See note 2 in chapter I.

This second birth or humanization (verse 7) is, as we shall see, the specific story of intellectualized man; it is an evolutionary stage; in a way, it is a new birth to life (future man will be subject to other births and rebirths). At that point began the mythical era, when man abandoning the wanderings of the hunter or shepherd, became sedentary.

As long as man is a hunter or a shepherd (animistic cultures), he is to a large extent protected, because of the very precarious conditions of his life, against an excessive multiplication of desires.

The sedentary farmer finds himself in a very different situation: through the cultivation of the soil, he multiplies the natural riches of the earth, he becomes wealthy; powerful cities are built, causing the envy of his neighbors; the dispute for material goods starts and it has not yet ended.

Verse 7:
"Yahweh God fashioned man of dust from the soil. Then he breathed into his nostrils a breath of life, and thus man became a living being."

Here, man is a generic term; it includes man and woman at the time when they enter a new evolutionary stage. Man is made of the dust of the earth. The earth is the symbol of earthly desires, material and sexual desires. Man is naturally inclined to seek the satisfaction of his material and sexual desires, elementary grounds of survival for the individual and the species.

But at the same time, he is a creature animated by "the breath of God," by the creative spirit which, on the human level, manifests itself in the essential desire to keep the harmonious organization entrusted to it. Thus man is the child of the spirit, while having been fashioned out of the earth. The analogy with the myth of Prometheus is quite clear.[11] In the Greek myth, the human being, the being who has become conscious, appears under the reign of Zeus, symbol of the ideal of the spirit: the spirit which valuates desires and explains the world. Mythically expressed, Zeus, the spirit of lucidity, of spiritualization-sublimation, creates man: in other words, through evolutionary necessity, man follows the ascent which nature as a whole pursues toward more and more lucidity, thus reaching the capacity to spiritualize and sublimate his desires.

But at the same time, man is made of muddy earth by the Titan Prometheus, symbol of the intellect in revolt against the law of the spirit. These two births express clearly, as does the Judaic myth, the two possibilities offered to man: to listen to his divine nature, the imperative of the spirit or to listen to his earthly nature, the call to the multiplication of desires, of which the intellect is the agent.[12] The fun-

---

[11]*Symbolism in Greek Mythology,* Shambhala, 1980.
[12]*La Peur et l'Angoisse,* Petite Bibliothèque Payot, Paris, 1973 (3rd Edition).

damental duality between spirit and matter is thus clearly expressed on the human level. Spirit is not incarnate anymore in the form of instinct, therefore essential desire—the desire of the harmonizing spirit—and earthly desires can thwart each other. The meaning of man's life is to undertake the new evolutionary stage, to consciously assume the incarnation of spirit and matter and reconcile spirit and matter. In the Greek myth, Zeus and Prometheus, the spirit and the rebellious intellect of man, are reconciled; the intellect then becomes the servant of the spirit and Prometheus is deified.

In the biblical cycle, it is not before the advent of the Christian myth, the fulfillment of the Judaic myth, that Jesus, son of man *having symbolically become Son of God,* brings the message of salvation that reconciliation is possible for each man at his own level between his earthly nature and his essential desire (symbolically the divine in man). Once more, then, the two myths express the very same thing, under different façades.

Verse 8:
"Yahweh God planted a garden in Eden which is in the east, and there he put the man he had fashioned."

Geographically the garden of Eden is the area located between the Tigris and Euphrates, the fertile cradle of the Hebrew people. Symbolically Eden is the earthly Paradise, the place where man, still innocent, is living in the animal paradise, free from the tortures of guilty feelings (the golden age of polytheistic myths). Long evolutionary stages will be necessary between the time when innocent man, animal among animals, lives in the "garden of Eden" and the time when he will little by little become intellectualized, and master of the outer world. The mythical narrative does not give an account of the thousands of years which, in reality, were necessary for this evolution. The mythical narrative uses temporal condensation and concentration of the problem. This is a fundamental difficulty in the understanding of the myth.

The rest of the chapter will enable us to explain more precisely the symbol of "animal paradise."

Verse 9:
"Yahweh God caused to spring up from the soil every kind of tree, enticing to look at and good to eat, with the tree of life and the tree of the knowledge of good and evil in the middle of the garden."

The promises of the earth, berries and fruit, symbols of justified earthly desires, were offered to man; but in analogy with the two births previously studied, two sources of food also appear, differentiated by the new evolutionary stage in preparation. The tree of life symbolizes the essential productive force, the evolutionary capacity that man draws from the biological depths of the need for satisfaction. What has enabled, not only mankind, but every form of organization, to survive, is the inherent desire in all that exists to overcome the unfavorable aspects of the environment in order to subsist, which implies the means and the need to evolve.[13] The tree of life digs its roots into the earth, symbol of the elementary biological desires (feeding and reproduction), and stretches toward the sky, thus representing the push of evolutionary ascent that the various species pursued step by step until they reached humanization.

Next to this tree in the garden of Eden grows the tree of the knowledge of good and evil. It symbolizes the stage in which life has become conscious. Access to consciousness enables man to multiply his desires because, through conscious memory, the entire world is brought into the human psyche in the form of images. The latter, with their accompanying promises of satisfaction, are the desires. The desires in the human psyche are linked up in the form of images and this constitutes man's imaginative capacity to explore the various possibilities offered by the outer world. When imagination includes in its search for satisfaction the obstacles of outer reality that can thwart the desires and when it plans practical means to overcome them, it becomes intellect.

Man no longer lives like an animal, in the here and now, he knows that he is the same one who lived yesterday and will live tomorrow. Thus he projects his past experience onto the future, he uses it to his benefit, managing in this way to control the unfavorable conditions of the environment through intellectual foresight. The intellect is therefore the capacity to act upon the outer world, to alter it, master it, thus enabling an organization of the world unknown to the animal which is subject to the environment. Every step in the mastery of the outer world is a source of new possibilities of satisfaction, thus of new desires. The multiplication of desires on the human level is a tremendous evolutionary step, provided the desires remain under the control of the harmonizing spirit, and provided they do not lead us into dispersing our vital energy and finally into the inability to satisfy them; for the more desires there are, the more they thwart each other, and the more it is difficult or even impossible to satisfy them all. This intensifies the dissatisfaction which is the punishment for this dispersion of vital energy.

As for the animal, it cannot fall outside the sphere of satisfaction, except in the case of the natural dissatisfaction inherent to all that exists and which is quite different from the pathological dissatisfaction that man creates for himself through the excessive multiplication of his desires. It is in this way that the evolutionary stage of intellectualization which distinguishes man from animal leads man to know good and evil: access to consciousness linked to intellectualization is good because it considerably increases the possibilities of satisfaction; but because of its

---

[13]Ibid.

excesses, intellectualization can become the very essence of evil, the source of pathological suffering, involution instead of evolution.

A deeper analysis is necessary: the excessive multiplication of desires, a danger of vital dissatisfaction, is counterbalanced by the essential desire of harmonization (harmony is experienced in the form of desire on the human level, but it manifests its organizing power at the prevital and prehuman level, as previously explained). The essential desire, i.e., the demand for harmony, seeks to reestablish the integrity of the individuals threatened by the excessive multiplication of desires. It is manifested by a feeling of guiltiness, which is the superconscious warning of a vital transgression. The individual in the grip of his excessive desires, can repress the feeling of guiltiness so as to reestablish a pseudoharmony which is nothing more than an illness of the spirit, going from nervosity to neurosis and even to psychosis.[14] The individual can go further, to the extent of killing the inculpating process, the essential desire itself, always in the same vain delusion of reestablishing harmony; he thus reaches banalization, the death of his valuating spirit and of all feeling of humanity.

Deprived of the inculpating process, he allows himself unscrupulously to satisfy his most exalted material and sexual desires, thus becoming the enemy of all, especially of those who, having themselves become banalized, seek satisfaction through the same procedure. The punishment is not only the destruction of their souls, but the death of cultures and the decadence of societies.

On the basis of this understanding of the evil that man brings upon himself by excessively multiplying his desires, it is easier to perceive the good he can bring upon himself. This good is the spiritualization-sublimation of exalted desires; in other words, the dissolution of exalted desires with the help of a reflective work of elucidating valuation leading to a reconciliation with the limiting circumstances of life (exaltation of desires being a rejection of the limitations imposed by the laws of nature). Through spiritualization-sublimation, man finds anew his harmonious integrity, he can satisfy his nonexalted material and sexual desires, he achieves satisfaction. Thus the good that man can create for himself is not only an access to positive intellectualization but the possibility to recover harmony at a superior evolutionary stage, the only genuine hope of mankind. However, the myth of Adam stresses above all access to the knowledge of evil, the fall of man into banalization, while the Christian myth brings the message of joy: the good that man can do to himself through the rebirth of his soul to harmony, through the resurrection from death of the soul.

---

[14]Translators' Note: See note 4 in chapter IV.

Verses 10 to 14:
"A river flowed from Eden to water the garden, and from there it divided to make four streams. The first is named the Pishon, and this encircles the whole land of Havilah where there is gold. The gold of this land is pure; bdellium and onyx stone are found there. The second river is named the Gihon, and this encircles the whole land of Cush. The third river is named the Tigris, and this flows to the east of Ashur. The fourth river is the Euphrates."

It is difficult to follow the description of the river and its four streams as well as their location with respect to the "Garden"; is it at the entrance to the "Garden" or at the exit that the river, promise of fertility, is divided into four streams? Now, from the viewpoint of symbolism, four is the figure characterizing the earth, the Terra Mater, and this garden, fertilized by the river which is itself divided into four streams, is very apt to signify the Terra Mater, the nurturing mother offering to man the fruit "of every kind of tree enticing to look at and good to eat."

Moreover, the land of Havilah where there are gold and precious stones (bdellium, the most precious stone of the ancient world, and onyx) symbols of spiritualization and sublimation, is certainly symbolically included in the "Garden of Eden"; the presence of the gems stresses that the conquest of the earth which is made possible by the development of the intellect must be linked to the indispensable work of spiritualization-sublimation.

Verses 15 to 17:
"Yahweh God took the man and settled him in the garden of Eden to cultivate and take care of it. Then Yahweh God gave the man this admonition: 'You may eat indeed of all the trees in the garden. Nevertheless, of the tree of the knowledge of good and evil you are not to eat, for on the day you eat of it you shall most surely die.'"

Let us once more reiterate that man means here human being, whether man or woman. Thus does his own superconscious talk to the human being: if you want, man that you have become, to remain in the animal paradise and "eat of all the trees of the garden," that is, in psychological terms, enjoy all the satisfaction it can offer, fulfill in the peace of your heart your biological (material and sexual) desires (life in the Garden of Eden), then do not fall into excessive intellectualization for you will die. God, his own superconscious, warns man of the dangers that he will have to face. It is evident that the myth does not refer to bodily death, an inescapable phenomenon of life to which man, like any animal, is subject but to death of the soul, death of the vital impulse of harmonization to which the senseless multiplication of desires, forgetful of the real conditions for satisfaction, will unavoidably lead him.

Life is harmonious organization, death is disorganization, disharmony. From the first cell to the most evolved animal species, the living being can only survive in a harmonious way (harmonious bond between psyche, soma, and environment).[15] Only human beings can somatically survive in a state of psychic disharmony, of relative death of the essential desire for harmony, which can become quasi total destruction of this desire. Man, who thus believes that he can violate the immutable law of harmony imposed on every form of life, falls into banalization, death of the soul, just punishment for his psychic disharmony. This is why, since the most primitive animistic cultures, the formula "to die in the body rather than in the soul" has been accepted as the only meaning life could have. Only the understanding of true ethics analyzed at length in the first part of this book enables us to measure the loss of satisfaction implied in the symbolic expression "death of the soul."

Verse 18:
"Yahweh God said, 'It is not good that man should be alone. I will make him a helpmate.'"

We will see later on the meaning of this "helpmate." "It is not good that the man should be alone": it would not be good that the human being remain limited to intellectualization, a capacity that is, even when positive, too restrictive for his essential life. Intellectualization without reference to the meaning of life carries the seed of death of the soul; but all of nature aspires to live harmoniously, thus the stage of intellectualization which does not fulfill the essential need, will be overcome by evolution. For this purpose, man must go to the ultimate—therefore perverted—consequences of intellectualization with the help of this new psychic element symbolized by his companion, so that the suffering caused by his excesses can give way to the essential force capable of overcoming them. This will be developed in verses 21 and 22.

Verse 19 and 20:
"So from the soil, Yahweh God fashioned all the wild beasts and all the birds of heaven. These he brought to the man to see what he would call them; each one was to bear the name the man would give it. The man gave names to all the cattle, all the birds of heaven and all the wild beasts. But no helpmate suitable for man was found for him."

Let us reiterate that in the first chapter, the animals were created before man since this vision gave an account of the progressive incarnation of spirit in matter during the course of evolution. In the perspective of the second chapter, the animals acquire a significance with respect to man; they are thus imagined as having appeared after the creation of man. Animals, as the world itself denotes, are mysteriously animated. But they are not conscious of their organization; in this

---

[15]*La Peur et l'Angoisse*, Petite Bibliothèque Payot, 3rd ed., 1973.

sense, they are not animated by "the creative breath" in the same way as man is. This is why the myth underlines that they were fashioned "from the soil." Guided by their instinct in the search for satisfaction, they are not concerned by the fundamental question that man asks: "What is my origin and what must I do with my life?" For the animal, the mystery of its organization is never a concern: "God" does not exist. As is symbolically expressed in verses 19 and 20, God transfers to man all power over the animals. A tight bond is established between the farmer and the animals of which the only ones mentioned here are the "beasts in the fields" and "the birds of heaven" capable of damaging the crops, as well as the "cattle" that he domesticates. However, no fundamental "help" can be given to him by creatures that remain at an evolutionary stage lower than his own.

Verses 21 and 22:
"So Yahweh God made the man fall into a deep sleep. And while he slept, he took one of his ribs and enclosed it in flesh. Yahweh God built the rib he had taken from the man into a woman, and brought her to the man."

Man is still in the innocence of paradisiac life. He has been forbidden to eat of the fruit of the tree of the knowledge but has not yet disobeyed. (As has already been said, evolutionary stages of thousands of years were needed to reach this "disobedience," namely excessive intellectualization.) Most translations stress the lethargic sleep or torpor taking hold of man. Without wishing to enter into a dispute about the usual versions, we must underline the importance of this type of sleep so as to understand the psychological translation of this verse.

Nothing positive can come from a state of lethargy since it is the symbol of the dimming of lucidity, the clouding of foresight. This sleep is lawfully determined ("God" being the symbol of the lawfulness of the psychic functioning) desires ready to be imaginatively exalted. Indeed, coming out of man ("his rib") and thus being the very structure of the thinking being on the way to intellectualization, appears the exaltative imagination of earthly desires. The thinking being, as has already been explained, is able to store the whole world in his psyche in the form of images. Intellect emerges from imagination which is the fundamental function of the human psyche. But exaltative imagination will, in its turn, develop, nurtured by the new possibilities of satisfaction created by intellect. For the perverse temptation to play with the most senseless promises of satisfaction is clearly the consequence of intellectualization by virtue of which man is made master of nature. He fancies himself an omnipotent being, he imagines that he can fulfill his slightest desire. The woman taken out of Adam's structure and who becomes Eve the temptress, *is imagination which can be perverted. It does not characterize woman more than man; it is the exaltative imagination of every member of this thinking species.*

Exalted imagination, dangerous though it be, is inevitably linked to the semiconscious stage. The resulting suffering, in the form of guilty anxiety, will force man—as yet insufficiently lucid—to overcome by evolution this state of half-consciousness which is the species' present level; no evolutionary step is taken without having been imposed by suffering to overcome. Eve is the companion who will walk at the side of intellectualized man, threatened at every moment by the seductions of the imagination. Their children will multiply; men straying in the vain promises of exalted imagination and in the too often senseless achievements of the intellect, they will forget the "call of the spirit," but the ensuing pathological suffering will remind them of the necessity to return to the essential desire of harmonization. Eve, the exaltative imagination, will thus become the necessary help for the pursuit of evolution.

Verse 23:
"The man exclaimed:
        'This is at last bone from my bones,
        and flesh from my flesh!
        This is to be called woman,
        for this was taken from man.' "

In Hebrew, the word for woman "Ishah" is derived from the word "Ish" or man. They have the same linguistic root. Thus does the myth express the biogenetic link between intellect and exaltative imagination; to express this, it also uses reality itself, the bond between husband and wife. In order to better understand this relation between the intellect and exalted imagination, one must know to what extent the conscious being gets lost, at every moment of this inner deliberation, in daydreaming which ceaselessly nurtures exalted material, sexual and pseudospiritual desires; this state of absentmindedness in which the inner dream continues is more or less the constant state of man, who therefore remains a half-conscious being. In this case, the intellect is no longer the "servant of the spirit" but it regresses to a state of exalted imagination. Intellect and exalted imagination cannot be distinguished anymore, exalted imagination perversely structures the intellect ("bone of my bones").

Full consciousness, full knowledge of what motivates man is yet to be acquired, as a new evolutionary step on the way to lucidity.

Verse 24:
"This is why a man leaves his father and mother and joins himself to his wife, and they become one body."

On the plane of reality, this is evident. It is important to realize that there is a great temptation here to see the plane of reality as so eloquent as to believe that the symbolic plane does not exist; but it does exist in this verse and in all those that follow, and in chapter 3, verses

16, 17, 19 in particular. To understand the symbolization, some pre-liminary explanation is necessary. Like all manifestations of life, the human being is an expression of the fundamental spirit-matter pair. His mythical parents, those who essentially begat him, are thus spirit and matter symbolized by the father or fecundating spirit and the mother, fecundable earthly desires. Since the intellect is inescapably tied ("joined") to the possibility of imaginative exaltation, man will leave his mythical father, the spirit, the call for harmony, and consequently, he will also leave his mythical mother, earthly desires in their sensible form, and join the vain promises of exalted imagination which are, at first sight, more attractive than the task of harmonization. Unfortu-nately, he will join himself to this false promise of satisfaction. Exces-sively tied to the flesh, to carnal pleasures, intellect (Adam) and exalta-tive imagination (Eve) will end up forgetting all reference to the spirit. "They will become one body": intellect and imagination will be united perversely.

Verse 25:
"Now both of them were naked, the man and his wife, but they felt no shame in front of each other."

With woman as a negative symbol, with the possibility of exalting the imagination, the danger threatening human life has made appearance. All is ready, but the fall into exaltation of desires has not yet occurred. Man is still as innocent as an animal. He is naked, he can see himself naked, i.e., psychologically speaking, such as he is and he is not ashamed; he does not yet feel guilty because he has not yet fallen into the exaltation of desires.

CHAPTER 3

Verse 1:
"The serpent was the most subtle of all the wild beasts that Yahweh God had made. It asked the woman, 'Did God really say you were not to eat from any of the trees in the garden?' "

The serpent is a mythical symbol, thus it represents just as God, Adam and Eve, a psychic function. On the plane of reality, it is an animal crawling on the earth, hard to grasp, slithering in the grass and its bite is lethal.

On the psychological plane, it symbolizes a psychic function devoid of elevation, more or less impossible to grasp consciously, and whose bite is no longer lethal for the life of the body but for the life of the soul. This psychological function is vanity, the term being used in its strong-est possible meaning: that which is vain, having all the seduction of easy satisfactions. Vanity, being the imaginative seduction leading to the belief that one can be and have everything, is the disharmonizing ele-ment of psychic life because it exalts beyond any real possibility of achievement, both the essential desire or impulse which then becomes an exalted task of perfection and also the material and sexual desires which then become obsessed with pleasure. These propositions, which in themselves are not attainable and contradict each other, split psychic intentionality into two ambivalent poles—exaltation toward the spirit and exaltation toward earthly desires. The immediate consequence is exalted guilt, remorse torturing, biting the soul, the expression of guilty anxiety aroused by the vital error of pretending to the absolute (bite of the serpent). The serpent is therefore the symbol of guilty vanity, of exalted imagination with respect to oneself and ones desires, the justifying principle of imaginative exaltation, the principle of evil, "the Prince of the world" as the New Testament puts it. It is the monster that the hero must fight.

Only a preliminary knowledge of psychic functioning, a preliminary knowledge of the ambivalent relationship between vanity and exalted guilt has enabled the understanding of the symbol of the "serpent," baseness of the spirit whose vain pretensions lead to guilty torment and death of genuine feelings. In the Greek myth, the head of Medusa, the inner monster vanquished by the hero Perseus, is hideously adorned with snakes. Medusa thus appears as the symbol of spiritual perversion, vanity of the spirit. The Judaic myth stresses that "the serpent was the most subtle of the wild beasts that Yahweh God had made." Vanity, the perverted spirit, uses effectively all the subtleties of false justification to achieve its goals, its false promises of satisfaction.

The lawfulness of psychic functioning (symbolized by God) includes the duality on the human level between the principle of harmony or essential desire and the principle of disharmony or guilty vanity. However, the principle of disharmony is also subject to the law of harmony, is included in harmony, since every disharmonious element, no matter what it is, splits into two contradictory poles according to a very precise law, the law of ambivalence;[16] vanity becomes exalted guiltiness; exaltation of the spirit produces inhibition of the spirit. In other words, any exalted desire (even the desire for truth) is by definition unattainable therefore inhibited. The inhibitive punishment which strikes all forms of exaltation is an aspect of the lawfulness inherent in all that exists.

"It (the serpent) asked the woman, 'Did God really say you were not to eat from any of the trees in the garden?' " The woman Eve, symbol of nascent exaltative imagination, asks herself (through the intermediary of the serpent, her own vain temptation) the insidious question: is there anything which is forbidden to me, can I not do whatever I want, can I not multiply my desires to infinity? Since I have become capable of mustering the means of satisfying myself, why should I let anything

---

[16]*Psychologie de la Motivation*, Presses Universitaires de France, Collection de Philosophie Contemporaine, 3rd ed., 1969, Petite Bibliothèque Payot, 4th ed., 1970.

stop me? This is the vain temptation of the intellect to rebel against the law of harmony. It is symbolized in the Greek myth by the rebellion of Prometheus against Zeus. Prometheus brings to his creature made of earth and mud, fire stolen from Olympus; fire thus loses its positive significance. Intellect then deprived of its reference to the evolutionary ideal is reduced, precisely because of this, to being only a perverse form of the spirit, a means of satisfaction of exalted desires.

Verses 2 and 3:
"The woman answered the serpent, 'We may eat of the fruit of the trees in the garden. But of the fruit of the tree in the middle of the garden God said, "You must not eat it, nor touch it, under pain of death." ' "

We do indeed partake of the material and sexual satisfactions offered by life; this is permitted but we are limited by the law of nature itself, by lawfulness (God in the myth). We cannot exalt our desires, eat the fruit of the tree in the middle of the garden, without risking killing our harmonizing spirit, our own capacity for self-limitation. And if we die in the spirit, we leave the evolutionary road.

Verses 4 and 5:
"Then the serpent said to the woman, 'No! You will not die! God knows in fact that on the day you eat it your eyes will be opened and you will be like gods, knowing good and evil.' "

Vanity is falsely justifying. It denies the incontestable fact of the progressive death of the essential desire, of the animating impulse: death of the soul. It pushes man to see himself as an ideal. The farther he is from it, the more he believes himself to be its embodiment. Don't let anything be forbidden to you, whispers man's inherent vanity, justifying his desires, to his exaltative imagination, on the contrary, refuse limitations and you will be equal to God, you will know all aspects of good and evil, you will be master of good and evil. Now, in fact, to really know good and evil would be to know the consequences of what the good man does to himself by self-harmonization and the consequences of the evil he inficts on himself by disharmonization. Such a genuine knowledge would result in acceptance of the law of harmony and not in rebellion. Man would then become not the equal of "God," but a manifestation of "God," i.e., a manifestation of harmony. Such was the man Jesus as he himself expressed it in the New Testament: "The Father and I are one," which means, I am the living expression of the law of harmony.

Verse 6:
"The woman saw that the tree was good to eat and pleasing to the eye, and that it was desirable for the knowledge that it could give. So she took some of its fruit and ate it. She gave some also to her husband who was with her, and he ate it."

Temptation worms its way into the imagination, it blinds the intellect and makes it lose its foresight: the intellect, that is, Adam, also tastes the forbidden fruit, the seduction of false promises of satisfaction.

Imaginative exaltation does not develop intelligence but inflates the intellect, for the latter, excited by exalted imagination, puts itself in its service and becomes extremely ingenious in trying to satisfy the multiplicity of desires. This danger of exaltative imagination of earthly desires is symbolically represented in the Greek myth by Pandora. She is the scourge sent by Zeus (symbol of the lawfulness of psychic functioning) to those who have forgotten the call of the spirit. She marries Epimetheus, the intellect that has lost its foresight and is subjugated by the seduction of exalted imagination. Epimetheus is the brother of Prometheus, the foreseeing intellect. He is therefore Prometheus himself, deprived of his true function, in regression toward affective blindness. Pandora brings him as a wedding gift a box, a symbol of the subconscious, out of which escape all the vices. Exalted imagination, laziness of the mind, is indeed producing all the vices. The Epimetheus-Pandora couple is analogous to the Adam-Eve couple after the "Fall".[17]

Thus enters vain guilt, the original sin of human nature: the repression of vital guilt.[18] Vital guilt, the insufficiency inherent in all that exists, is a condition of life itself, and the evolutionary prime mover is nothing else than the vital necessity to overcome this insufficiency which is the cause of suffering. On the other hand, vain guilt, the denial of this insufficiency, causes the appearance of individual and pathological suffering; in spite of his insufficiency man wants to be and believes himself to be equal to God, i.e., the embodiment of ideal: he thereby enters into stagnating involution, he forgets the call of the spirit which is, above all, knowledge and acceptance of his limitations; he rebels, using the openings afforded by intellectualization and mastery of the outer world, against the law of harmony, against the biological necessity to limit his desires.[19]

Verse 7:
"Then the eyes of both of them were opened and they realized that they were naked. So they sewed fig-leaves together to make themselves loin-clothes."

After man has let himself be tempted by exalted imagination, guilt awakens, a psychological process following every exaltation. Essential guilt is a superconscious manifestation warning man of the loss of satisfaction he prepares for himself when he exalts his desires. It is a foreknowledge of the evolutionary goal, of the harmonization of de-

---

[17]*Symbolism in Greek Mythology*, Shambhala, 1980.
[18]In French: *coulpe vitale*, a key word for Diel, as he defines it here, and in his book: *Psychologie de la Motivation*.
[19]*Psychologie de la Motivation*, Payot.

sires; it is an intuitive orientation toward the meaning of life; every man bears within himself the warning of his vital fault. Without this superconscious feeling, which shows the persistency of instinctive knowledge, human life would not even be possible. Vital energy would be squandered in a multiplicity of desires whose uninterrupted succession would destroy the psychosomatic organization. Yet, essential guilt which is guiding and not constitutive, is repressed most of the time, which however does not still its persistent call. In this verse, the eyes of man are opened to the error he has made, but there does not follow a liberating confession, an understanding of the fault, only shame and the repression of the fault in order to escape from shame. Animals are not ashamed of their desires which are vital needs, imposed on them by nature, by the law of life, and there is no possible transgression on their part; man who has exalted his desires is ashamed of them; shame is repressed, guilt projected onto others, the fault we do not wish to admit but that we imagine to be known by all.

Symbolically speaking, the guilty man covers his nakedness with fig leaves. What he hides is his phallus, the symbol of creative power, of creative power of the spirit. He has been betrayed by it, his ability to distinguish good from evil has been warped; it is marred by the vital error which is why he hides it, represses it. Consequently he hides at the same time his excessive preoccupation with material and sexual satisfactions, the seduction they hold for him, due in fact to the impotence of his spirit. He hides it with fig leaves. The fig tree is a symbol similar to the apple tree of the Greek myth. It symbolizes earthly desires. Exalted intellect and imagination personified by Adam and Eve, hide, justify their impotence of spirit and their fall into exaltation of their desires. In accordance with the law of psychic functioning, man must, in order to repress the call of the spirit and soothe guilty dissatisfaction, indulge in accidental satisfactions (symbolized by the fig tree) which seem to exculpate him from his essential failure or, ambivalently, he must repress his attraction for pleasures (symbolically hide his sexual organ) and thus believe that he fulfills his essential desire. This is nothing but a pseudo-life of the spirit. In both cases, the shame remains.

Verse 8:
"The man and his wife heard the sound of Yahweh God walking in the garden in the cool of the day, and they hid from Yahweh God among the trees of the garden."

In the state of inner confusion the loss of lucidity into which man has been put by his vital error, he hears within himself the essential voice, the divine part of himself, the call to harmonization, the regret of lost innocence. But again, the shame of what he has done makes him incapable of accepting responsibility for his fault. He hides from "God," he represses the call of truth, he represses the warning of essential guilt.

Verses 9 and 10:
"But Yahweh God called to the man. 'Where are you?' he asked. 'I heard the sound of you in the garden;' he replied 'I was afraid because I was naked, so I hid.' "

The dialogue with God symbolizes Adam's inner deliberation. These verses repeat in the form of a dialogue what was already explicit in verse 8. The call of God: "Where are you?" (i.e., in what state of mind are you?) echoes in man.

Verse 11:
" 'Who told you that you were naked?' he asked. 'Have you been eating of the tree I forbade you to eat?' "

Superconscious intention reveals to man that he is naked and ashamed. He knows why since he asks himself the revealing question. The call continues, inculpating him, denoting that even repressed, guilt remains active, showing that the essential desire is not dead.

Verse 12:
"The man replied, 'It was the woman you put with me, she gave me the fruit and I ate it.' "

Which means: I, Adam, intellect forgetful of the spirit, let myself be tempted by imaginative exaltation, symbolized by Eve, the temptress.

Verse 13:
"Then Yahweh God asked the woman, 'What is this you have done?' The woman replied, 'The serpent tempted me and I ate.' "

Imaginative exaltation—the tempting succession of seductive images—is the very manifestation of vanity, of self-overvaluation and overvaluation of one's desires. This is the vain principle of man's quest for satisfaction, the illusion to which he falls prey.

Verses 12 and 13 bring a complementary indication about the psychic functioning: they show how the fault is projected onto others; accusation linked to sentimental self-pity is one of the ways of repressing a fault.

The purpose of projection is to evade one's responsibility by accusing others but with such an escape, any hope of overcoming the fault is lost. The only way out is, on the contrary, to acknowledge the fault. However, the dialogue with God, with the feeling of essential guilt attempting to put the rebellious Adam back on the way to truth, does not achieve release from the fault but, on the contrary, its repression and denial, since it leads to the projection of the fault onto the serpent, vanity.

It is true that vanity is responsible for the errors of man, vanity is his main enemy, depriving him of his lucidity with regard to the meaning of life and it is therefore the source of all his aberrations. Vanity is the fear of man before himself and his abysses, it is the fear of life which is accused of being meaningless. Man must accept his responsibility for the consequences, he must learn to discern the evil he brings upon himself through vanity. This is his only hope of finding the courage to resist vanity's lying promises instead of exculpating himself by the fact that it is the root of all evil, that such is life, that there is nothing to do about it, and further still, that vanity is the very meaning of life.

Verse 14:
"Then Yahweh God said to the serpent, 'Because you have done this,

> Be accursed beyond all cattle,
> all wild beasts.
> You shall crawl on your belly and eat dust
> every day of your life.' "

This is where man is apprised of all the evils that are awaiting him, the consequence of his fall into the seduction of imaginative exaltation. God is the symbol of the immutable law ruling not only the organization of the outer world, but the organization of the inner world, of psychic functioning. He is the immanent justice, the inescapable punishment imposed by life itself; since the finality of life is the search for satisfaction, life punishes all falsely justified errors in this search. The verdict of God (psychologically translated immanent justice) stipulates that the seductive pseudoelevation of vanity is the lowest of all base things: (you shall crawl on your belly). It mistakes itself for the ideal but it is nothing else than inordinate egocentrism and exalted love of pleasures. He who is prey to vanity "eats dust," i.e., nonharmonized earthly desires which become contradictory and produce all resentments, rancors, need to triumph, and hatred pitting man against man, and this, day after day as if under a magic spell.

Verse 15:
> "I will make you enemies of each other:
> you and the woman,
> your offspring and her offspring.
> It will crush your head
> and you will strike its heel."

Conflict enters the human soul; an irreconcilable conflict pitting imaginative exaltation or earthly desires, submission to pleasures (Eve) against imaginative exaltation of the self, the vanity of taking oneself for an ideal (the serpent). This is the irreconcilable conflict between material and spiritual exaltation, characterizing the human species, and which will continue from generation to generation. These two exaltative tensions, through contradictory and ambivalent, nevertheless sustain each other. The exaltation of desires is justified by vanity which is exalted self-love, overvaluation of self. Man believes himself to be an ideal being to whom nothing should be refused. "It will crush your head and you will strike its heel." You will wound each other, each exaltative pole opposing the ambivalent pole.

However, there is already an indication of the positive solution to the conflict. It must be said that symbolization is such a rich means of expression that the facade of the story, while keeping its logical appearance, is able to express not only the punishment, the consequence of the inner conflict, but also the hope that is inevitably linked to the suffering brought about by this very punishment. But before we go any further, a new analysis is necessary for the understanding of verses 15 and 16.

In his positive meaning, man is mythically a symbol of the spirit for he is more inclined than woman to theoretical intellectualization and spiritualization, namely to look for the causes of phenomena and the laws governing them. Woman is the symbol of the earthly desires, the biological basis on which this capacity of the spirit is exerted; biologically she is more closely tied to nature, more alert to the biological needs of life than to the world of ideas; she becomes in her positive meaning the symbol of the earthly desires purified of their affect, of their impatience, symbol of sublimation, the necessary complement to spiritualization. This does not therefore imply any superiority of man over woman, nor of spirit over earthly desires. Earthly desires can be sublimated. Now to say that spirit is incarnate or that matter is spiritualized amounts to the same thing and shows that there is an indissoluble union of spirit and matter in the positive process of evolution. Let us go back to the end of verse 15: "It will crush your head and you will strike its heel." Woman, no longer is the negative meaning of imaginative exaltation of earthly desires (Eve) but in her positive meaning of earthly desires in their harmonious and sublimating force, will triumph over vanity. "It will crush your head," the head is the symbol of the spirit's valuations: the crushed head of the serpent therefore symbolizes the defeat of the valuations of the false spirit, i.e., of vanity. Matter and spirit will be reconciled by evolution, the earthly desires will abandon vanity and return to spirit and harmony, even if vanity never ceases to viciously attack man: "you will strike its heel." The heel is the basis of the foot's strength and the foot symbolizes the soul. The soul will often be stung by vanity, but will ever and again find enough vigor to strike back. The significance is all the clearer that it allows us to understand an image, which though it appears at a later stage, still contains a genuine psychic significance: that of Mary, the Virgin, symbol of the purity of earthly desires, crushing under her heel the serpent, vanity, the rebellion of the intellect. The sane and biologically deep attachment to earthly desires symbolized by Mary, implies their purification and leads to the capacity of enjoying them sublimely since only unexalted desires escape inhibition (law of harmony). Only the combative attitude of purification is able to fight the false promises of vanity for only the real intrapsychic work of self-harmonization enables one to attain the fullness of material and sexual desires.

The exalted pleasures of material and sexual banalization are only a caricature of life, a platitude, a loss of intensity due to the loss of the valuating spirit which is the only force capable of creating vital satisfaction, life's sole value.

Verse 16:
"To the woman he said:

> 'I will multiply your pains in childbearing,
> you shall give birth to your children in pain.
> Your yearning shall be for your husband,
> yet he will lord it over you.' "

On the plane of reality, this seems to be a curse on woman. In fact, it still concerns the human psyche and its conflicts. The human psyche, in a state of exaltation, is pregnant with desires. The exalted desires are contradictory and insatiable. The psyche thus produces only dissatisfaction (pain): moralizing inhibition or amoralizing exhibition in the indulgence of desires. These are lawful consequences of the exaltation of desire, the symbolic "children" of the perverted psyche: pathological suffering.

"Your yearning shall be for your husband, yet he will lord it over you." The woman, representing here the imaginative exaltation of earthly desires, still remains bound to the spirit, symbolized by man, be it only in the form of a feeling of guilt, and the spirit, in spite of its temporary aberrations, will vanquish imaginative exaltation, "will lord it" over it, if not in every man at least through the evolution of mankind. It will tirelessly pursue its task which is to organize and harmonize earthly desires. It is the dissolution of original sin.

Just as the cursing of the serpent (verse 15) leads to the hope of evolutionary triumph over vanity, the cursing of the woman (verse 16) leads to the hope of reconciliation between spirit and matter.

These last verses, whose deep and symbolic meaning have been misunderstood throughout the centuries, are certainly not strangers to the inferiorization of woman in our culture. The vanity of man has used to his advantage the triumphant justification offered to him by the dogmatization of the myth; woman, reacting to triumphant vanity with offended vanity, has developed in her relationship with man insidious and sly defenses; both of them have forgotten their fundamental bond, their essential and biological complementarity.

Verse 17:
"To the man he said, 'Because you listened to the voice of your wife, and ate from the tree of which I had forbidden you to eat,

> Accursed be the soil because of you.
> With suffering shall you get your food from it
> every day of your life.' "

God (lawfulness) predicts that man will be punished for his fault. Because you wanted the unlimited satisfaction of all your desires (because you listened to the seductive promises of exalted imagination without following the warning of your essential feeling of guilt, "the voice of God"), the earth will be accursed by your fault: the earthly desires that you seek excessively will become a source of dissatisfaction. Instead of the satisfaction of harmony, including the material, sexual and spiritual satisfactions, you will have only the satisfaction of material and sexual desires, impoverished by exaltation-inhibition, deprived of the intensity that can only be given to them by right valuation, i.e., by the participation of the spirit and the heart; you will remain bound to the earth, not only to painfully gain your material livelihood, but to get out of earthly desires a meager satisfaction, the only one you will be able to obtain insofar as you betray the spirit.

Verse 18:

> "It shall yield you brambles and thistles
> and you shall eat wild plants."

The exalted quest for earthly satisfaction will be accompanied by the sting of guiltiness (brambles and thistles) and your food shall be meager: it will not be, insofar as you are exalted, the milk of sublimation and the honey of spiritualization (in Greek mythology, nectar and ambrosia).

Verse 19:

> "With sweat on your brow
> shall you eat your bread,
> until you return to the soil,
> as you were taken from it.
> For dust you are
> and to dust you shall return."

However it will still be possible for you to obtain the bread of life if you discipline yourself and till the soil, not only the real soil, but symbolic earth, earthly desires, i.e., if you undertake the intrapsychic work. Besides the danger of multiplication of desires made possible by the sedentary work of the farmer, his work yields an essential profit: the necessity of discipline and acceptance, since atmospheric conditions can in one day of storm or hail, destroy the work of a whole year; the farmer has no choice but to accept and to patiently start all over again. The force of acceptance is psychic energy at its highest degree of intensity. It recuperates the energy of unattainable and unharmonizable desires and rechannels it into sensible projects; acceptance of reality is the indispensable condition for evolution. This verse, like the two preceding ones, includes therefore the hope of a solution. The identical solution to man's problem is also given in the myth of Cain and Abel.

Abel is the shepherd. His heart is pure. His offering is pleasing to God. But he disappears, eliminated by his brother, Cain, the tiller of the soil. (The culture of the shepherds gives way to that of the farmers.) Cain is accursed, pursued by the guiltiness of having killed an innocent man, the innocent culture of the shepherds, and of having replaced it by excessive preoccupation with earthly desires. However, Cain is branded on the forehead by "God" himself, so that he will not be harmed. The farmer, though perverted by his exalted desires "[God] did not look with favor on Cain and his offering," is still the evolutionary element which has led human life toward intellectualization. The latter is both positive (organization of social life, skills and the beneficial improvement they can bring to human life) and negative, which will necessitate a recourse to spiritualization-sublimation, the only remedy for disharmony and its suffering; Cain is, in this meaning, the leaven of evolution because evolution is achieved only through suffering.

> "Until you return to the soil
> as you were taken from it.
> For dust you are
> and to dust you shall return."

On the plane of reality, this is again quite obvious. Man returns to dust because all that which appears is doomed to disappearance. But symbolically, this verse means: from birth to death, you who have been taken out of the soil, i.e., you who have preferred pleasures to the call of the spirit, you will remain exposed to the exclusive call of earthly desires.

Verse 20:
"The man named his wife 'Eve' because she was the mother of all those who live."

Eve is the symbolic mother of all human beings. It is with this fall into the exaltation of desires, the constant and perverse preoccupation of the half-conscious being, that the true history of mankind begins, the history of its fall and possible redemption, the loss of paradisiac rest (free from the torment of guiltiness) and the evolutionary necessity of finding again the joy of harmony, called in the Christian myth "Heaven," in the Hindu myth "Nirvana," in Chinese culture "Tao." If Eve is the mother of all human beings, i.e., if the myth establishes a constant relation between the new evolutionary stage, inseparable from its involutionary dangers, and the whole of mankind, so does the Greek myth, imagining that all the vices escaped from Pandora's box and were scattered over the entire earth.

Verse 21:
"Yahweh God made clothes out of skin for the man and his wife, and they put them on."

Clothes are a disguise, the conventional attitudes that man puts on to repress his guiltiness and justify his faults. They are made of animal skin, a symbol of banalization, of animality, the stage to which man regresses when he is under the sway of his avid desires. Man, having refused to listen to the voice of the spirit, returns to the primitive stage of animality without having retained its masterful instinct. To be animal again means not to accept the responsibility of conscious life, the self-control of desires.

God, the symbol of the lawfulness of psychic functioning, is the one who dresses man in animal skin. In accordance with the immutable law of harmony, any vital fault is punished by a loss in satisfaction. *The punishment is not added to the fault, but fault and punishment are one and the same thing,* or the two aspects of the same phenomenon. Banalization is punished by banalization: for it is the dissolution of vital energy in the excessive multiplication of desires and this loss of essential satisfaction is the unknown punishment of banalization. The banalized man deprives himself of all the satisfactions of harmony; he deviates from the meaning of life, and this is his punishment; could there be a worse one?

Verse 22:
"Then Yahweh God said, 'See, the man has become like one of us, with his knowledge of good and evil. He must not be allowed to stretch his hand out next and pick from the tree of life also, and eat some and live for ever.' "

Man, entering the conscious stage, has become responsible, responsible for the good and the evil he brings upon himself. For man, there is no higher spirituality than this (responsible) knowledge of the conditions for satisfaction. It is the knowledge of the lawfulness of psychic functioning and is, as we have already said, symbolized by God. In this sense, it is possible for man to become like a god; though to do so he should not disobey the superconscious warning of his essential guilt but make it fully conscious.

The tree of knowledge and the tree of life are not radically separated. The tree of knowledge is a branch of the tree of life. Life is constant evolution. Access to knowledge, access to consciousness is an evolutionary stage, but it implies dangers of involution. Should these dangers not be overcome, knowledge that has become involutionary, excessive intellectualization, turns into an obstacle to essential life, to harmony. Thus it is quite clear that man, if he eats the nefarious fruit of the tree of knowledge can no longer eat from the tree of life, i.e., live in the joy of harmony, live in eternal truth. The punishment of death of the soul awaits him. This is the eternal truth that the prophets of the Old Testament proclaim anew when they want to bring back to

God, to harmony, the Hebrew people who have strayed by dancing around the golden calf, the worship of Baal and Moloch, symbols of banalization.

The original sin of human nature, the temptation to excessive multiplication of desires will have to be punished, expiated in order for mankind—through the suffering it endures and for which it is solely responsible—to overcome the temptation of imaginative exaltation and to enter a new evolutionary stage, *full consciousness* (as opposed to the semiconsciousness that mankind has not yet outgrown); this full consciousness has only been experienced by a few exceptional men throughout history. The latter were called sons of God—Jesus Christ and Gautama the Buddha—because God, the eternal law of harmony, was incarnate in them to the extent that all of their activities were dictated by this law.

Verse 23:
"So Yahweh God expelled him from the garden of Eden, to till the soil from which he had been taken."

Man preferred the earth to the call of the spirit; he expelled himself from innocence, and now he must till the soil with all the consequences not only negative but also positive, (as listed above) which are implied in this situation.

Verse 24:
"He banished the man, and in front of the garden of Eden he posted the cherubs, and the flame of a flashing sword, to guard the way to the tree of life."

Man is expelled from the animal paradise, as already explained. Essential guilt, symbolized by the trenchant and flashing sword (the ascending flame is the symbol of the vital impulse), guards the way to the tree of life. It protects life against vital aberration, it guards the evolutionary way leading to harmonization. Thus man has lost the paradise of innocence, but he can find the paradise of truth symbolized by Heaven (Nirvana in the Hindu myth), truth about himself and his psychic functioning, truth about his inner lies, his vital error, certitude of knowing thanks to the intrapsychic work of elucidation, about the good and evil he brings upon himself, certitude of finding the means to overcome evil and acquire good: the return to harmony which is the law ruling the existence of the entire universe.

C. THE BIOGENESIS OF VALUES: THE BIOLOGICAL ROOT OF THE ETHICAL PROBLEM

The ethical problem of values and nonvalues is necessarily included in the universality of symbolic language. This theme has been represented so far by the "elevation-fall" symbol. Mythologies (especially the Judeo-

Christian one) condense the ethical problem in the symbol God-the-Judge, the founder of the guiding values. To grasp the complexity of this God-the-Judge symbol one must understand the psychological significance of values and nonvalues, their psychic immanence and biogenetic origin.

If the myth of the genesis of man contains *an underlying truth symbolically veiled by the mythical "as if,"* we have to admit that this truth must be the actual history of the biogenesis leading to the evolutionary appearance of the thinking being exposed to choice, in other words: *the biogenesis of the conflict* between values and nonvalues.

Symbolic temporalization condenses in seven days the evolutionary epochs from "the creation of the universe" to the emergence of man.

Although the succession of the evolutionary stages is clearly expressed, taking the symbolic "seven days" for a reality induces belief in an intentionally achieved creation that would have taken place in the course of seven days. This spiritualistic doctrine is opposed by the evolutionary doctrines of materialism that see only a mechanism in evolution and reduce the mysterious evolutionary intentionality of nature to chance, completely ignoring the essential problem of the origin of values and nonvalues, prefigured in the myth of Genesis. The myth cannot know the evolution of the somatic morphology of living beings. What it foresees, what it symbolically expresses is the evolution of the psyche from preconscious spirit (animal instinct) to nascent conscious life exposed to choice, and even to permanent choice, i.e., intrapsychic deliberation, which is the most distinctive feature of man. The fall of Adam symbolizes wrong choice; the temptation to confuse the value of life with nonvalue. Symbolic temporalization condenses the essential problem of human life in the story of Adam. However, it indicates through the symbol of "original and hereditary sin" that the temptation to confuse value with nonvalue characterizes all mankind. The myth of the original temptation does not give specific details about the motivations leading to wrong choice. It represents them in general by the symbol of the serpent (vanity), the principle of the multitude of negative motivations.

The God-the-Judge symbol covers the detailed specification of the right and wrong motivations and the cause of their salubrity or noxiousness.

The essential, universal, and therefore biologically profound value is harmony which, through evolution, becomes for man (due to the difficulty of deliberately overcoming vain temptation) the guiding ideal, the ethical value which is superconsciously immanent: harmonization of desires, the condition for joy, which governs the life of every individual. Symbolization stresses this transformation of universal value into individualized value by the fact that God-the-Creator and God-the-Judge are united in one sole person. And this to the extent that in the

Trinity symbol, God-the-Judge does not appear as such. The condensation of the symbols God-the-Creator and God-the-Judge in one sole person is a significant procedure which is in perfect conformity with the means of expression of symbolic language. From the creation of man onwards, the creator becomes judge. This transformation of the God-the-Creator symbol into the symbol of God-the-Judge of fallible man shows, even more clearly than the symbol of the seven days creation that the appearance of man is the product of the evolutionary transformation of previously created animality.

The guiding values of man, diversified yet harmoniously linked, are the evolutionary product of the value of harmony common to all that exists, from the atom to the universe and to all that is in the universe, living beings included.

Theological spiritualism and materialism, as foundations of the sciences of life, are not only metaphysical speculations (absolute spirit-absolute matter); they are also speculations concerning the origin of values. It would even be right to say that their contradictory metaphysics are only the theoretical means of their ill-founded search for a solution to the urgent problem of values: the well-being and salvation of human life depend on the understanding of the biogenetic origin of values, which is transformed on the conscious level into the superconscious immanence of guiding values. For spiritualism, the values are of a transcendental origin; for materialism, the values are, at the very most, social conventions.

The ambiguous valuation—the ambivalence between spiritualism and materialism—thus introduced into the realm of values, is the inescapable consequence of metaphysical ambivalence: absolute spirit (absolutely devoid of matter) and absolute matter (absolutely devoid of spirit). This ambiguity is harmful both for the theoretical procedure of the spirit and for the practical and sensible management of life. Spirit and matter are the most fundamental values of existence. All that has been said so far leads to the observation that the organizing intentionality—no matter how mysterious its origins—also has a phenomenal aspect manifest throughout nature. The phenomenal aspect of intentionality is inseparably linked to soma-matter. Animated matter, the living soma, testifies by its organization to the coexistence of an organizing intention or to put it another way, of a spirit of nature which is finalistic, preconscious and prevoluntary. The common mystery of all that exists does not therefore concern only the preconscious and prevoluntary organizing intentionality but also the organized soma. What is both wholly mysterious and phenomenally manifest is the existence of psychosomatic organisms, among which man is included. In man, the spirit becomes conscious but the soma remains preconsciously organized, partially removed from voluntary control. However, the pre-psychic and preconscious intentionality of the animal gives way to the human psychic functioning characterized by a multiplicity of intentions that have become half-conscious.

Organizing intentionality is the link between all living beings. What separates man from animal is *the scattering of intentionality into multiple intentions, which are the motives of his activity.*

Throughout the whole biogenesis leading to man's appearance, the evolution of intentionality (a psychic phenomenon) and the evolution of soma-matter go together. To overlook the study of the organizing intentionality and to study only the organized soma is to misunderstand the very meaning of evolution. Before going any further, let us look for references and support in linguistic wisdom.

The term "intentionality" has only a global meaning as long as one neglects to explicitly develop the various significances that are implicit in it. Intention is "inner tension," animating energy, vital impulse. Intention or inner tension seeks exteriorization. There is no intension without extension. Psychic intensity and environmental extensity—psyche and world—are complementary.

The point of intersection between psyche and world is the soma. Being living matter, it is at the same time intensively animated and extensively extended. The intentionality of the soma is its appetence that makes it dependent on the favorable or unfavorable conditions of the environment. The environment excites the soma, and through it, the intentionality leading it to actively exteriorize itself. Excitability[20] and intentionality are one and the same thing. Were the soma not intentionalized, it would not be excitable. It would be indifferent to the environment (insofar as it could exist without reference to the latter).

The differentiation (psyche, soma, environment) and the energetic exchange (excitation-reaction) are originally due to the animating intentionality and not to the environment. Excitability, just like intentionality, has a mysterious aspect (the animating impulse) and a phenomenal aspect (the various excitations which set off reactions).

If the energetic exchange (life) is blocked because of an unfavorable environment, the psychosomatic being dies, or else it evolves into a form which is better adapted to the environmental demands.

A living being threatened with premature death could not go through evolutionary change if the organizing intentionality were not able to reorganize the soma. But it is also true that the specific form of the evolutionary reorganization is due to a succession of unfavorable excitations coming from the environment and conditioning little by little the process of somatic readjustment.

There is no conditioning without conditionability, *the transforming dynamism of evolution is the immanent animating intentionality itself.* The environmental conditions have only a triggering influence.

---

[20]In French "excitabilité," a fundamental concept of Diel's which he explains here.

The superconscience and its symbolic language know the conditions of the genesis of the human psyche. How is this possible—even super-consciously—without superconsciously knowing the general conditions of biogenesis, of which the genesis of the human species is only a special instance?

The preceding considerations show that linguistic wisdom implicitly contains in the term "intentionality," if not a detailed knowledge of evolutionary dynamics, at least a foreknowledge of their most fundamental conditions. This being the case, it becomes more easily understandable that mythical wisdom, in its turn, contains a pre-science of the evolutionary birth of the human species and of the inner conflict between its multiple intentions. Would not the apparent unlikelihood of this hypothesis be due to our thinking habits, based on the contradiction of the spiritualistic and materialistic hypotheses?

In fact, unlikelihood is rather to be found in the anathema refusing to see in the intentionality, visibly and uncontestably manifest throughout the whole of nature, the essential problem of existence and consequently, in the multiple and contradictory intentions of man, the essential problem of human existence. All things considered, can there be a hypothesis which would be at the same time more natural and more economical than the one based on organizing intentionality? Of course, it compels us to give up the prejudice—which is perhaps somewhat vain—that spirit is the exclusive property of man. The economy of the hypothesis is to be found precisely in the fact that it eliminates from the study of the evolutionary phenomenon, all metaphysical speculation by acknowledging that there is a mystery and that it proposes on the other hand to accept a preconscious spirit manifestly at work not only in the psychomatic organization of every living being, but also in the evolutionary succession of species that are more and more highly organized.

Economy—a criterion of scientific value—is found moreover in the fact that hypothesis establishes in the clearest possible way both the common feature between animals and human beings and the distinctive feature: the intentionality which in man is scattered into multiple intentions which are often contradictory and thus essentially meaningless.

The hypothesis of dispersal paves the way for the study of the human psyche in all its complexity: its structure (the processes: conscious, unconscious, and extra-conscious) and its functioning (the half-conscious inner deliberation, healthy or unhealthy, depending on its being codetermined by superconscious or by subconscious intentions).

The hypothesis is proved all the more economical in that it can enable us to decipher mythical prescience, the invariable themes of which are the genesis of the human psyche and its deliberating function, at times superconsciously meaningful, and at times subconsciously senseless (the original sin of human nature).

The explanatory spirit of man should knowingly turn to the problem of the biogenesis of human intentionality, not only to find an answer to the totality of the evolutionary problem (from the mono-cellular organism to man) and to all its aspects (psyche, soma, environment), but also to find the answer to the evolutionary problem that has been pre-scientifically discovered by mythical wisdom centered around the image of God-the-Creator, an image that was created by the explanatory effort of the human spirit. The problem of biogenesis in all its vastness would thus stretch from the origins of life to the "God" image created by man.

Chapter VI

The Prologue of John's Gospel: The Myth of the Incarnation

A. Introduction

Among all the texts of the New Testament, the Prologue of John's Gospel is one of the least anecdotal, one of the most purely symbolic. It condenses and generalizes in a striking way the mythical story of the world and of life and shows the eternally exemplary scope and evolutionary significance of the phenomenon of santification which, in the Judeo-Christian cultural cycle to which we belong, is illustrated by the life and heroic death of the man Jesus.

The Gospels (literally the good news) relate the life and words of Jesus. He showed through his life that "original sin" (the exaltation of desires) could be overcome, that the inner conflict could be appeased by a definitive reversal of the calculus of satisfaction, consciously seeking the conservation at all costs of inner harmony, the "life of the soul," be it at the cost of the life of the body. The example becomes for all of mankind a source of hope.

But the Gospels are not only narrative. The Evangelists and especially John (and also the Apostle Paul) grasped the general and even cosmic scope of Jesus' example. They understood that this life was the inimitable but guiding achievement of man's latent possibilities. Thus, with all their emotion, they recognized in Jesus the "Christ," the "Messiah," the one who actually fulfilled the meaning of life, whose symbolic expression was the constant theme of the Old Testament.

Genesis relates how pathological suffering appeared with the conscious being: the Old Testament in its entirety describes the effort, often impotent, of mankind (symbolized by the chosen people) to live in essential satisfaction (symbolically the Covenant) and to escape pathological suffering (symbolically the punishment by Yahweh). The New Testament shows that there is, for the individual, a possibility to find the way to joy, even in the midst of a completely decadent world. The Prologue of John's Gospel shows that this possibility is in conformity with the evolutionary meaning of life, enlightening its past and foreshadowing its future.

This terse digest of the Prologue denotes from the outset that symbolic exegesis is radically different from the literal and dogmatic exegesis. The text of the Prologue of John, taken literally, is the source of the dogma of the Incarnation, a fundamental dogma of the official Christianity which claims to explain God's intentions and nature rationally. Now this text is fundamental when it comes to understanding the *symbolic* meaning of the Christian myth. According to literal exegesis, Jesus is not a man, he is the Word, a real God preexistent from the beginning and deciding at a given moment to take a human form.

For symbolic exegesis, the Prologue of John is the source of the *myth* and not of the *dogma* of the Incarnation. The myth of the Incarnation is the symbolically profound explanation of life in evolution. It was created by the superconscious and veracious imagination to soothe metaphysical anxiety with the certitude that suffering can be overcome and that the mysterious evolutionary intentionality (symbolically "the design of God," the "Word of God") is in itself benevolent and intelligible in its manifestations.

In symbolic exegesis *God-the-Father symbolizes the unfathomable mystery of the origins, the Word symbolizes the manifest appearance,[1] and the Son symbolizes the evolutionary hope of mankind,* meanings which will be explained further on. Thus the Prologue of John is not only the source of the myth of the Incarnation, but also of the myth of the Trinity.[2] The Trinity is the symbolically profound expression of man's religious feeling awakened by the mystery of the origins and the mystery of life in evolution. Dogmatism, confusing in one sole and actual person the two symbolic persons—the Word (second person) and the Son (third person)—makes any understanding impossible. Dogma thus believes itself compelled to add a third person: the Holy Spirit who does not appear at all in the Prologue of John. On the other hand, the symbolic Trinity—Father, Word, and Son—is the central theme of the Prologue. It is the only genuine Trinity and its significance is the same as that of the myth of the Incarnation which it sums up and generalizes. Here is the traditional text of John's Prologue (JB):

1 "In the beginning was the Word:
the Word was with God
and the Word was God.
2 He was with God in the beginning.

---

[1]See note 1 in chapter V.
[2]For further details see *La Divinité,* Payot, Chapter 9.

3 Through him all things came to be,
    not one thing had its being but through him.
4 All that came to be had life in him
    and that life was the light of men,
5 a light that shines in the dark,
    a light that darkness could not overpower.

6 "A man came, sent by God.
    His name was John.
7 He came as a witness,
    as a witness to speak for the light,
    so that everyone might believe through him.
8 He was not the light,
    only a witness to speak for the light.

9 "The Word was the true light
    that enlightens all men;
    and he was coming into the world.
10 He was in the world
    that had its being through him,
    and the world did not know him.
11 He came to his own domain
    and his own people did not accept him.
12 But to all who did accept him
    he gave power to become children of God,
    to all who believe in the name of him
13 who was born not out of human stock
    or urge of flesh
    or will of man
    but of God himself.
14 The Word was made flesh,
    he lived among us,
    and we saw his glory,
    the glory that is his as the only Son of the Father,
    full of grace and truth.

15 "John appears as his witness. He proclaims:
    'This is the one of whom I said:
    He who comes after me
    ranks before me
    because he existed before me.'

16 "Indeed, from his fullness we have, all of us, received—
    yes, grace in return for grace,
17 since, though the Law was given through Moses,
    grace and truth have come through Jesus Christ.
18 No one has ever seen God;
    it is the only Son, who is nearest to the Father's heart,
    who has made him known."

The purpose of this study is not to engage in an argument with dogma. However, dogmatic belief (which is a historical necessity but an involutionary stagnation in the essential history of human thought) is so deeply attached to the superstitious interpretation of the Incarnation that it is necessary to confront dogmatic interpretation more rigorously with symbolic exegesis so as to uncover the deep meaning of the myth of the Incarnation.

The crucial point is this: as far as dogma is concerned, the Word is a truly preexistent deity, entirely identified with Jesus. As far as symbolic exegesis goes, the Word is a symbol while Jesus is a real man. The central affirmation of the Prologue: "the Word was made flesh" is for dogma the account of an actual event, while for symbolic exegesis, it is a symbolic expression endeavoring to show the real scope of Jesus' achievement. Starting from a false premise—namely that the biblical texts have to be understood literally—dogmatic exegesis is compelled, through a *logical* deduction based on an *erroneous* first assumption, to launch a whole series of affirmations, the absurdity of which becomes so patent that the theologians themselves, since they cannot deny it, pretend to use it as a proof: "I believe *because* it is absurd." *Credo quia absurdum.* In the Prologue of John, the misunderstanding of the symbolism in "the Word was made flesh" leads to a total identification between the Word and Jesus. The result is, among others, an interpretation of verse 3 according to which all things "came to be" through Jesus since all things "came to be" through the Word. For dogma, it is all the more difficult to get rid of such an interpretation that verse 10 takes it up again: "the world that had its being through him." *Jesus is the creator of the world.* The logical conclusion of such a conception would be expressed in the final (18th) verse which sums up the dogmatic significance of Christian theology:

> "No one has ever seen God;
> it is the only Son, who is nearest to the Father's heart,
> who has made him known."

Thus, according to dogma, before Jesus (who was erroneously thought of as being only a man by his contemporaries with the exception of a few chosen ones) appeared in Galilee, the world (undoubtedly one must understand by this the cosmos with its billions of galaxies) *knew nothing about the real nature of God. And since then it does!* The Catholic Church would be the depository of this revelation and would transmit it to whoever wishes to incorporate himself into the Church through the rites of baptism and communion.

If the texts can lend themselves to a coherent reading eliminating absurdity, the least one can say is that such a reading deserves to be taken into consideration.

B. PROBLEMS CONCERNING THE TEXT

Before going into the details of symbolic exegesis, certain points concerning the structure of the text must be studied in the light of the preceding observations.

A critical reading of the Prologue and of the first chapter of John's Gospel cannot fail to uncover the heterogeneous nature of the Prologue. It is quite clear that two elements exist side by side and that they are clumsily combined: on the one hand, the symbolic narrative dealing with God, the Word, the Word made flesh, the Only Son and Jesus Christ; on the other hand, an anecdotal narrative in verses 6, 7, 8, 9 and 15, containing the historical witnessing of John the Baptist. The account of this testimony, the annunciation of the preaching of Jesus is, in fact, the largest part of the first chapter, after the Prologue (verses 19 to 38). Since the very purpose of dogmatism is precisely to make of the historical Jesus a supernatural person by identifying him with the Word taken for a reality, one can understand that zealous priests wished to put into the Prologue an element of miraculous prediction, making of John the Baptist—the historical forerunner of Jesus—the annunciator of the miracle. The theologians thus found it opportune to use the testimony of John the Baptist to strengthen the belief in a real Incarnation of the Word, itself a reality. Mixing in this manner history and symbolism, this interpolation (for that is what it is!) manages to induce a belief—in those who are willing—that the Incarnation is a supernatural event, miraculously announced by a prophet who was actually inspired by God himself. Symbolism and history thus confused acquire one from the other the appearance of a supernatural and miraculous meaning.

In verse 6, the appearance of John the Baptist, "A man came, sent by God. . . ," interrupts abruptly the general theme without any transition and without any justification (except the dogmatic ones). The purpose of this interpolation is to have John the Baptist announce the "miracle" of the Incarnation: "The Word was made flesh. . . ." Not only does verse 6 break the continuity, but the latter is reestablished if one removes the sequence of verses 6 to 9 from the Prologue.

Verses 4 and 5 are thus quite naturally continued in verse 10:

4 "All that came to be had life in *him*
   and that life was the light of men
5 a light that shines in the dark,
   a light that darkness could not overpower.
10 *He* was in the world
   that had its being through him,
   and the world did not know him."

It is quite clear that verses 4 and 10 deal with the Word and not Jesus: Jesus is not the creator of the world, but the world is, symbolically speaking, the manifestation of the Word.

The same kind of remark is valid for verse 15, the purpose of which is to confirm that Jesus is indeed he whose supernatural coming has been announced by John the Baptist. As in the case of the previous interpolation, this verse 15 breaks the continuity which is clearly reestablished once we remove the interpolation. Indeed verse 14 talks about "us" (all those who have understood the message of Jesus) and continues quite naturally in verse 16:

14 "The Word was made flesh,
   he lived among *us*,
   and *we* saw his glory,
   the glory that is his as the only Son of the Father,
   full of grace and truth.
16 Indeed, from his fullness, we have, all of us received—yes, grace in return for grace, . . . "

Thus the Prologue recovers its symbolic purity and all its cosmic and metaphysical grandeur embracing the past and future of evolution.

On the other hand, by putting back the verses we have removed from the Prologue to their natural place, i.e., after verse 18 and at the beginning of the evangelical narrative itself, we can see that the historical testimony of John the Baptist is now reconstituted in its integrity.

This testimony continues after verse 15 with the more anecdotal account of John the Baptist's relationship with the traditional ecclesiastic authorities (verse 19 and following). Without any doubt, this simple solution is a shock for those who have a conventional and literal respect for the texts as they stand; our hypothesis is based on the method of symbolic deciphering and a detailed study of the Prologue will only confirm it.

Here is the transcription of the text of the Prologue (as we have reconstituted it), followed by the beginning of the evangelical text:

"In the beginning was the Word:
The Word was with God
and the Word was God.
He was with God in the beginning.
Through him all things came to be,
not one thing had its being but through him.
All that came to be had life in him
and that life was the light of men,
a light that shines in the dark,
a light that darkness could not overpower.
He was in the world
that had its being through him,
and the world did not know him.

He came to his own domain
and his own people did not accept him.
But to all who did accept him
he gave power to become children of God,
to all who believe in the name of him
who was born not out of human stock
or urge of the flesh
or will of man
but of God himself.
The Word was made flesh,
he lived among us,
and we saw his glory,
the glory that is his as the only Son of the Father,
full of grace and truth.
Indeed, from his fullness, we have all of us received—
yes, grace in return for grace,
since, though the Law was given through Moses,
grace and truth have come through Jesus Christ.
No one has ever seen God;
it is the only Son, who is nearest to the Father's heart,
who has made him known.
A man came, sent by God,
His name was John.
He came as a witness,
as a witness to speak for the light,
so that everyone might believe through him.
He was not the light,
only a witness to speak for the light.
The Word was the true light
that enlightens all men;
and he was coming into the world.
John appears as a witness. He proclaims:
'This is the one of whom I said:
He who comes after me
ranks before me
because he existed before me.'
This is how John appeared as a witness, When the Jews sent priests and Levites
from Jerusalem to ask him, etc."

The Prologue thus comprises 13 verses[3] and can be divided into three parts.

The first part (verses 1, 2, and 3) is metaphysical. It deal with the mystery symbolically called God and its relationship with the Word symbolizing the appearance[4] (of the manifest world).

The second part (verses 4, 5, 10, 11, 12, and 13) deals with the

---

[3]For the sake of easy reference, the traditional numbering of the verses has been retained.

[4]See note 1 in chapter V.

relationship between the Word and man who is more or less capable of being moved by the awareness of mystery deeply enough for this to motivate his activity. In this sense, the second part sums up the profound meaning of the Old Testament which is precisely the responsibility of the human being in relation to the meaning of life which is both mysterious and manifest.

The third part (verses 14, 16, 17, and 18) of the Prologue and *only this part* refers to the man Jesus, symbolically called Son of God or Incarnate Word, for he is rightly considered by the Christian myth as the example of the achievement toward which are directed not only mankind since its origins symbolized by the birth of Adam, but also all life in evolution symbolized by the Word of God. This is why he is also called the only Son since he foreshadows the only hope of mankind to overcome by evolution the suffering of Adam's sin.

The Prologue of John has therefore a metaphysical and an ethical significance. In its ethical aspect, it presents Jesus as a victorious hero, he who overcame the sin of Adam. The metaphysical meaning is still more essential: the sanctified man is shown as the clearest, most condensed, most evolved manifestation of the intentionality immanent to nature, intentionality which is just as mysterious as to its origin as it is manifest in the existence of the organized world, and which the myth calls "Word of God." In its deepest meaning, the Prologue of John does not deal mainly with the man Jesus, a historical reality, but with Christ, a symbol and with the only Son, also a symbol. Christ is the eternal truth entirely incarnate in the achievement of Jesus. The only Son is the evolutionary hope actualized by this accomplishment, and which concerns all of mankind.

C. DECIPHERING OF THE VERSES

Verses 1 and 2:
"In the beginning was the Word:
The Word was with God
and the Word was God.
He was with God in the beginning."

The initial verses express in a symbolic and extremely condensed form the epistemological foundation of human thought, the fundamental certitude at which thought necessarily arrives when it pursues right to the end its questioning about existence and its origin.

It is quite significant that the mythical explanation posits as a primary evidence "the Word" and as a secondary evidence indissolubly linked to the first, "God." What is the meaning of this "Word"?

"Verbum" is the translation of the Greek "Logos," which means literally: speech, coherent language, word. The Logos is the Word, the Word of God. It is the manifestation of God's will. It thus symbolizes the fact, evident to the spirit though inaccessible to the intellect, that the existing world can neither be conceived as an effect without a cause (*ex nihilo* creation) nor as the effect of a knowable cause (real God or absolute matter). It can be conceived by man only as the effect of an unknowable cause necessarily imagined as proportionate to the vastness of the effect: this cause can only be imagined in an anthropomorphic manner as if all existing phenomena were the expression of the will of a superhuman being.

The Logos is thus the emergence into appearance of the mystery called God, both the intention and the expression of the mysterious cause: both the creative act and the created world. The existence of the world cannot be separated from its organization. The Logos is thus lawfulness, the basic coherence of the world, the foundation of trust in life (mythical faith) and of the explainability of phenomena (scientific faith). It expresses the fundamental evidence that the world is organized according to laws.

In Greek philosophy, this term is constantly used to denote the intentionality immanent to nature, the intelligible organization, which is manifest in its effects but mysterious as to its origins, and which underlies all existing phenomena. The Word "Logos" is, moreover, akin to "law," "legality," "logics."

Lastly, the image of speech, of a discourse taking place in time is very apt to symbolize the temporal unfolding of evolution, mythically conceived as the progressive explicitation of divine intentionality. It is the world in evolution bearing in itself its own law, its own dynamics, its own mysterious animating impulse through which life creates forms of harmony that are more and more complex and intense.

The Prologue states that "in the beginning," i.e., as far as the human spirit can go back in time, it perceives the Word or Logos, spatio-temporal existence and its organization, without which nothing is given, nothing is conceivable. But it adds immediately that the Word, the Logos is "with God." If one understands symbolism, this way of thinking is coherent. Indeed, for the spirit, the first evidence is the existence of an organized world; but there is a second evidence which is just as fundamental (and which is totally forgotten by materialistic rationalism): *the mysterious aspect of appearance,* the fact that the perceptible and explainable world is necessarily conceived by man as the effect of a cause remaining forever unperceivable and unexplainable for the human mind. The evangelist immediately adds this second evidence, the awareness of the mysterious foundation of existence, to the first evidence of the existence of an organized world. For these two epistemologically profound evidences are connected by the fact that mystery has a twofold aspect: *the mysterious aspect of manifest organization* (the Word of God) and the *unknowable "cause"* (God-the-Creator). The mystery of organization is linked to the mystery of the origins. The last verse of the Prologue will in fact conclude with a new affirmation of the mystery of the origins: "no one has ever seen God" (verse 18).

After having affirmed at the outset the fundamental duality—appearance (Logos) and mystery (God)—after having noted that only appearance, the organized world actually exists (at the beginning) but that it cannot be conceived outside of the mystery of the origins (the Word is with God), the evangelist synthesizes again this duality with the phrase "and the Word was God."

These two concepts of mystery and appearance must be separated but this separation is extremely dangerous: the mystery can be turned into an entity, a mysterious thing or being. The phrase "the Word was God" means that, in fact, for human thought, there exists only one given, which is neither mystery nor appearance (mythically speaking neither God nor Word) but existence under its twofold aspect: its manifest but mysteriously organized aspect (the Word) and its forever incomprehensible aspect: the mystery of its origins (God).

Appearance has thus a mysterious aspect and the mystery is not *mystery in itself* but the *mystery of appearance*. This synthetic complementarity which is a necessary correction to the analytical duality is expressed in the formula "and the Word was God."

The very same epistemological truth is expressed in the Prologue of John, the Hebrew Genesis, the Greek Theogony, and in fact in all mythologies.

Primitive man does not perceive the world as an organized entity, but as a succession of phenomena subject to strange and frightening changes. In the mythical era, fear of the environment is already sublimated: the world is superconsciuosly experienced as being the creation of a benevolent intentionality. Through the evolutionary process of progressive spiritualization, the emotionally compact notion of mystery becomes diversified and enriched by the growing evidence of *the mystery of the organization* of the cosmos (the word "cosmos" means in fact "order"). First the contemplation, and then the methodical study of its mysterious lawfulness become more and more direct sources of emotion, provided that man acknowledges the unfathomable mystery of the origins and gives up any attempt to explain it.

Verse 3:
"Through him all things came to be,
not one thing had its being but through him."

This verse sums up the purely metaphysical part of the Prologue. "Through him all things came to be" means that there is no existing or possible phenomenon, whatever its nature, whatever the time and place of its occurrence which does not have an aspect which is forever unexplainable (its very existence), which is not analogically linked to all other phenomena, and which is not included in the evolutionary dynamics of existence. "Not one thing had its being but through him" is the corollary of the previous statement. This phrase precludes any possibility of metaphysical speculation vainly trying to prove that a supernatural being, thing or event could exist without being bound by natural laws (spiritualism) or that there can be a being, a thing or an event whose existence could be entirely conceivable and explainable without any reference to mystery. The latter approach leads necessarily to the dogmatic materialism which is now in fashion and which, denying the mysterious though manifest intentionality is compelled to bring in the pseudoexplanation by the concept of chance, which is just as unacceptable for the human mind as the pseudoexplanation by the will of an actually existing God.

Thus it is not an exaggeration to say that the first part of the Prologue of John, in its striking brevity and simplicity formulates the epistemological foundation of human thought, the basis of the certitude on which a coherent vision of the world and life can be built.

Verse 4:
"All that came to be had life in him
and that life was the light of men."

This verse constitutes a transition between the first two parts of the Prologue. Since the Prologue is the source of the myth of the Incarnation, it can also be said that the first part deals with the primary incarnation or creation or in other words, with the appearance of organized matter, or materialized organization. The second part deals with the incarnation of the spirit in mankind under the form of reflective consciousness and ethical conscience. (The third part will deal with the complete incarnation of the enlightening spirit in the *sanctified man*). Starting with verse 4, the Word, the manifest and mysterious animating impulse, is no longer considered only as the mysterious aspect of the world in evolution. It becomes specifically the vital force which "kindles," "lights up" life and finally enlightens the human psyche.

"All that came to be had life in him" refers to the mysterious source of life seen as a biological phenomenon, the dynamics through which the inner world seeks a more and more intense union with the outer world.[5]

But the Prologue, unlike Genesis, does not develop the diversification of the animating impulse into the countless species out of which will finally emerge the human one; here, the evangelist almost immediately deals with the human stage of evolution, i.e., "and that life was the light of men." This fourth verse establishes a link between the three words: *Word, life,* and *light.*

In the Christian myth, the "Logos" or "Word" symbol belongs exclu-

[5]*"Psychologie de la Motivation"*, Payot, introduction and chapter 1.

sively to the Prologue of John. On the other hand, "Life" and "Light" are frequent symbolic expressions in all myths, and in the Judeo-Christian one in particular. The word "life" throughout the Bible, and in the Gospels and the Epistles of Paul in particular, is frequently opposed to the word "death," just as the word "light" is opposed to the word "darkness," as is the case in verse 5.

It is therefore indispensable to introduce for the word "life," besides the biological meaning already noted, the psychological significance which is constantly encountered in biblical writings and which alone can explain how "life" can become "the light of men."

In the same way as death appears constantly in Scripture as the symbol of death of the soul, of banalization, so does life constantly appear under its meaning of life of the soul, essential joy, harmonious activation of thoughts and feelings, concord with oneself and the environment and therefore with the meaning of life.

If the Word, is (in this way) considered as source of life, it is because man is essentially alive insofar as he is essentially animated, motivated by the very same vital impulse which is incarnate in the preconscious being under the form of instinct and which becomes on the human level a superconscious and guiding force. "That life was the light of men" because the only criterion man has for truth or essential error about the meaning of life comes from his deeply felt experience of being psychically "alive," of feeling his vital impulse in action.

Man is alone in his quest for essential satisfaction: the harmonization of his desires. No one outside himself dictates to him what he must do with his life in order to attain essential joy. Yet, this very same immanent organizing and harmonizing spirit manifest in the "blind" intentionality of preconscious life, blossoms in the human psyche in the form of an intuitive knowledge—which is more than conscious, superconscious—of the conditions for essential satisfaction, for harmonization. The sureness of the animal's grasping reflex becomes the certitude of man's reflective grasp of life.[6] Mythically expressed, it is the animating Word which becomes, reflected by the conscious psyche, valuating, enlightening, "light of men."

Verse 5:
"a light that shines in the dark,
a light that darkness could not overpower."

This verse sums up all the ethical meaning of the Old Testament. Indeed, the deep meaning of the Judaic myth is that the spirit having organized matter since the beginning, ceases on the human level to be instinctive and constitutive and becomes guiding and superconscious.

---

[6]See *La Peur et l'Angoisse*, Payot.

This is why the call of the spirit can be ignored and repressed. However, it does not cease to be manifested under the form of essential guiltiness symbolized in the Old Testament by the call of Yahweh. The light shining in the dark is the truth "shouting in the market place" as the psalmist says. This eternal truth cannot impose itself since the "darkness" of the subconscious, of the repressing process, continues to rebel generation after generation against the elucidating influence of the superconscious. The light is the light in man and the darkness is the darkness in man, as for instance the following passage from the first epistle of John shows:

"Anyone who claims to be in the light
but hates his brother
is still in the dark" (1 Jn 2:8 JB).

There are many passages of Scripture which oppose the light of superconscious elucidation to the darkness of repression which prevents man, blinded by imaginative exaltation, from grasping the truth about himself and life. Verse 5 is generally believed to be a reference to the incomprehension and hostility encountered by Jesus among his contemporaries. Such an interpretation does not agree, as we have seen, either with the translation of symbolism or even with dogmatic exegesis. It is true that for dogma, Jesus is the Word and the Light but it is only in verse 14 that it is written that the Word was made flesh.

Thus, according to the present explanation, there is absolutely no allusion to the preaching of Jesus before verse 14. Verse 5 therefore deals with light in general, with the truth. It remains true that verses 6, 7, and 8 also deal with light. But it is precisely this fact which permitted the interpolation of these verses in the Prologue. The similarity of the theme (light) was used to slip in three verses after verse 5. However, as we shall see, the light in these verses is the truth *brought by Jesus,* symbolically called Christ.

Jesus, in fact, uses the same image when he talks about himself:

"I, the light, have come into the world,
so that whoever believes in me
need not stay in the dark any more" (Jn 12:46 JB).

Here Jesus talks about truth in general and his preaching in particular. This similarity in images only stresses the depth of analogy linking the Old and New Testaments, the myth of Yahweh whose call is heard but often rejected (Adam's sin) and the myth of Christ whose call remains misunderstood by most people.

Verse 10:
"He [the Word] was in the world
that had its being through him,
and the world did not know him."

This verse is difficult to understand because the term world (cosmos) is used here successively in its two different meanings, both of which are constantly encountered in the New Testament. The world created by the Word is the universe, harmoniously organized existence in its entirety. The world "that did not know him" is the banalized world, the society of men who are too blinded by their affect to be moved by the feeling of mystery, by true religious faith. It is in the latter meaning that Jesus talks about his kingdom "which is not of this world," a phrase generally understood by dogmatism as the promise of a better fate in the beyond, while the belief in an actual beyond is totally alien to Judaic thought and, in fact, unacceptable for human thought in general if the latter is based on a coherent epistemology.

The verse sums up again the fundamental theme which is found throughout the Old Testament. The intentionality immanent to nature is at the same time manifest and mysterious. It is the lawful and evolutionary organization of the outer and inner world, thus also of the human psyche in which the preconscious intentionality of the animal is dispersed into multiple intentions which however still remain under the law of harmony, as does all that exists. *But man, alone among all beings, can survive physically while being subjected to psychic disharmony.* He can let his feeling of being mysteriously animated, his vital impulse die in him. Blinded by the massive affect of his desires, he can let die in him the religious feeling, the emotion awakened in him by the mysterious aspect of what he perceives and of what he is. He can ignore the Word, refuse to know it, refuse to know the essence of life, the meaning of life.

Verse 11:
"He came to his own domain
and his own people did not accept him."

This verse particularizes the meaning of the preceding one. All myths symbolize the intentionality of nature by anthropomorphizing it (it cannot be otherwise). The "will" and "wisdom" of God are imagined by analogy with the will and wisdom of man. Conversely, the myth conceives the half-conscious intentionality of man as a particular case of intentionality in general: "God created man in his image."

The same vision is expressed here in the more impersonal form which is that of the Prologue. "[The Word] came to his own domain" means that the intentionality diffuse in all nature becomes specific, progressively incarnate and, at the most advanced evolutionary stage, becomes human intentionality diversified in multiple intentions. Preconsciously organizing spirit becomes consciously valuating and explanatory. But the conscious psyche (or rather, still half-conscious psyche) of man is not only spirit,[7] it is also intellect.[8] The spirit looks for a

---

[7]See note 1 in chapter I.
[8]See note 2 in chapter I.

sensible orientation, the intellect for a utilitarian adaptation. The intellect by itself is unable to grasp the mysterious aspect of existence and to be moved by it though it is also an evolved function, mythically speaking: a creation of the Word.

The specific danger threatening the evolution of mankind is precisely that intellectualization prevail over spiritualization. It is the danger symbolized in the Judaic myth by Adam's sin and in the Greek myth by Prometheus's punishment. It is the same truth expressed in verse 11: though he is a creation of evolution, "created" by the animating impulse mysteriously immanent to the whole of nature, man when overintellectualized, does not recognize himself as mysteriously animated. Animated beings have become conscious through the progressive incarnation of the spirit, the Word, yet they "do not know him." They forget what is essential in themselves.

Verse 12:
"But to all who did accept him
he gave power to become children of God."

"All who did accept him" (the Word, the Logos) are the men in whom vital impulse is strong and who, throughout the centuries, have been moved by the feeling of mystery symbolically called God and for whom this emotion has become motivating, creative of harmony of thought, feeling and volition; it is the line of essentially animated men whose story is the central theme of the Old Testament.

All these, whether history mentions them or not, are "children of God." Partially animated by essential emotion, they are distinguished by the myth from the "only Son," the sanctified man.

How could we fail to perceive that the phrase "children of God" is just an image and not a reality, a symbol and, moreover, a symbol known to all mythologies? If this is the case, why should the phrase "only Son of God" be of another order and be understood literally? Mere respect for the texts, even regardless of any theoretical consideration, should impose a univocal translation. Either the theme of divine filiation is to be symbolically understood or, if one takes the Prologue literally, one must admit that those who believe in the truly divine filiation of Jesus themselves miraculously receive the same privilege of being actually begotten by a real God.

There is no point giving further proof of what has already been proven. Belief has subconsciously obsessive motivations; its roots are deeply embedded in the magical layer of the psyche as yet insufficiently penetrated, in most men, by progressive intellectualization and spiritualization. The somewhat infantile belief in a providence which actually watches over each one of us remains the surest support of dogmatic belief.

Obsessive belief may well admit the supernatural and transform it

144 / SYMBOLISM IN THE BIBLE

into a dogma; the human spirit which is the most evolved function of nature is such that it cannot, however, do so without falling into the ambivalent anxiety of doubt. Now doubt—like any other anxiety—must seek appeasement by resolving the ambivalent split. Real appeasement can come only from a certainty based on a knowledge that eliminates at the same time the exalted belief and the exalted doubt which is its ambivalent counterpart. And from where could this certainty come if not from the knowledge of psychic functioning extended to the understanding of its symbolizing function?

Verse 12 (second part):
"to all who believe in the name of him."

"The name of God"[9] is a constantly recurring phrase in the Old as well as the New Testament ("hallowed be thy *name*"). "All who believe in his name" (the name of the Word, therefore the name of God) indicates therefore, like "the children of God," all those who are animated by essential trust in life and by emotion in the face of its unfathomable mystery, feeling as they do the danger of transforming it into an entity superstitiously venerated and implored. They are the men of the Old Covenant who understood the essential truth behind biblical symbolism.

Verse 13:
"who was born not out of human stock
or urge of the flesh,
or will of man
but of God himself."

Verse 13 characterizes again this essential humanity previously described as "children of God." It is the symbolism of birth and filiation commonly used by all mythologies. Born of human stock or urge of flesh or will of man describes here human activity as motivated by an excessive attachment to multiple desires. The opposition between the two symbolic modes of filiation is condensed in the juxtaposition of the phrases *born of will of man* and *born of God himself*. What is begotten either by the carnal principle or by the spiritual principle is desire, as is also expressed in a similar formulation "what is born of the flesh is flesh; what is born of the Spirit is spirit" (Jn 3:6 JB). The dual filiation of man is a fundamental mythical theme. It appears in Genesis: Adam is made out of the soil and animated by the breath of God. Here, it is less the intrapsychic conflict of man that is considered than the distinction revealed in the essential history of mankind between men of strong vital impulse and the mass of conventional beings. The men of strong impulse, the "children of God," are not only the exceptional

---

[9]For an explanation of the term see page 28.

men of the Old Testament, the great characters of Genesis or the prophets, but the anonymous men of good sense who are relatively harmonized and able to instinctively resist the temptations and threats of the environment, the very same people Jesus will call "salt of the earth."

One should certainly not confuse mythical images with reality, but it is very important also, once the meaning has been uncovered, to free oneself from the persistent suggestive power of the images. God does not exist; the Word does not exist; the beginning does not exist; Christ is not a person; spirit and flesh are not entities. *All these words are only symbols,* "manners of speech," used to express that which alone exists: the capacity of man to be moved, during his ephemeral life, by the unfathomable mystery of life and death, and the specific danger of letting himself be totally captivated by his multiple desires and anxieties. It is the conflict in the human being, symbolized by the duality of spirit and flesh.

This conflictual duality between spirit and flesh is misunderstood by moralizing dogmatism as well as by banalizing atheism which see in it an invitation to asceticism. The flesh would be guilty and the strength of the spirit would lie in its capacity to suppress the desires: this is a fundamental error. The natural function of the spirit, in fact its only function, is to master and organize the material and sexual desires, the desires of the flesh, with the purpose of harmonizing them. "Born of God" or "born of the spirit" means: animated by an essential desire strong enough to let the ideal of harmonization prevail in the inner deliberation of the individual over the attraction of the multiple desires which, begetting one another without end, end up losing their point of unity and dissolving the essential self, which is *the state of banalization.* Born of human stock and of will of man thus denotes the innate weakness of the vital impulse (original sin) which renders individuals incapable of resisting the imaginative exaltation of the contradictory desires invading their psyche. In this text showing that the *incarnation* of the Word, the spirit, in matter, is the evolutionary process immanent to nature, it is impossible that the ambivalent and ascetic split between exalted spirit and exalted material desires be presented as the ideal goal.

Quite the contrary, complete mastery over earthly desires by the valuating and harmonizing spirit, complete incarnation of the spirit in the flesh, which is the central theme of this text, is condensed and made more specific in the following verse toward which the meaning of the whole Prologue, and beyond this of the whole New Testament, is directed and in which it culminates.

Verse 14:
"The Word was made flesh . . ."

It is now, and only now, in this third part of the Prologue, that the myth refers to the real man Jesus, the sanctified man whose example (as in another culture the example of Buddha) was suggestive enough to inspire those who had understood it with the courage to oppose the decadent world of their time and to become initiators of a new culture.

Jesus is symbolically designated as the one in whom the Word became incarnate. Sanctified man, purified from the sin of Adam, animated only by his essential desire, by emotion inspired by mystery and who attained the imperishable joy that no accident could destroy, he can be called the incarnation of the meaning of life, the incarnation of the Word. The mythical phrase "the Word was made flesh" has a biogenetic meaning and a psychological meaning. Under its biogenetic meaning, it signifies that the sanctified man who was able to totally master (though dynamically so) the blinding affect of the multiple desires and invest all his energy in the essential desire, can be considered as the most evolved form of harmony, as the most perfect achievement of what nature "wants"; the re-creation of more and more complex and intense forms of harmony being the very meaning of evolution.[10]

And indeed, what more perfect image can we find for the meaning of life than that of a human being who has overcome the suffering inherent to life by achieving in himself a complete harmony of thoughts, feelings and will? To such a degree that this harmonious organization resists, even in its final agony, the opposition and hatred of the world? From the psychological viewpoint, the incarnation of the spirit is the total penetration of the flesh, of the carnal desires by the spirit.

For spirit, on the human level, is not only organizing, it has become valuating and explanatory. The spirit which fulfills its function ceases to escape from reality, to play imaginatively with the unachievable and the unprovable, and thus becomes an effective guide of activity. The superconscious spirit, when it is no longer clouded by multiple affects, dictates to man what he must do to achieve essential satisfaction, it becomes *incarnate*. The Son (the sanctified man) obeys in all things his Father (the superconscious spirit, his own spirit) as Jesus talking about himself, does not cease to affirm. Dogmatic exegesis and symbolic exegesis are radically opposed to each other concerning the interpretation of this verse and hence concerning the myth of the Trinity. If one is right, the other is wrong. For *dogmatic exegesis,* the hope of mankind to overcome suffering depends on the good or ill will of a real God who is really concerned with judging men. Those persons named "Word" and "Holy Spirit" have been at his side since the beginning. Tired of punishing mankind in his anger since the disobedience of

---

[10]See *"La Peur et l'Angoisse,"* Payot.

Adam, he sends the Word, a real person, really preexistent, who assumes the human form of Jesus, and thus becomes his Son.

For *symbolic exegesis,* God is not a person, but a symbol, created superconsciously by man in order to express his emotion in the face of the unfathomable mystery of life and death. The hope of mankind does not depend on the decisions of a transcendent being, but on *the immanent vital impulse, the evolutionary drive through which all of nature frees itself from the dissatisfaction of vital anxiety.*

On the human level, this anxious dissatisfaction is the consequence of vanity. The individualized vital impulse is the fight against vanity and this impulse, when it attains ultimate victory and imperishable joy in an individual, becomes for all mankind a source of hope, pointing towards the evolutionary path, and even a source of faith in life itself since life's meaning—that anxiety can be overcome—is most clearly manifested in the achievement of the sanctified man.

To sum up, this verse can be taken in two ways:

- For dogma, *Jesus is the Word* made flesh. The Word conceived from the first verses on as a real person, decides to take on a real body.
- For symbolic exegesis, Jesus is *the Word become flesh.* Jesus is considered by the myth as the incarnation of the meaning of life symbolically called the Word.[11]

Verse 14 (3rd part):
"he lived among us,
and we saw his glory,
the glory that is his as the only Son of the Father,
full of grace and truth."

Here we see the fundamental theme of divine filiation and especially the expression "only Son" of the Father, therefore the third person of the symbolic Trinity (second person of the dogmatic Trinity).

Now there are many passages in the Gospels, as we know, in which Jesus is symbolically called "Son of God." However, there is a very important distinction between the two meanings of this mythical image: either it is used to metaphorically characterize the man Jesus or it is used to denote the third person of the symbolic Trinity as is the case here.

In the Gospels, the man Jesus talks about himself as "Son of God," "sent by the Father," doing the will of the Father and not his own. The

---

[11]On the linguistic plane, the common translation: "The Word was made flesh" which has now been abandoned in some versions, unduly stretches the meaning of the Greek verb which signifies only "became." Verse 14 does not denote any personal intention, it describes the incarnation as an evolutionary stage. Such slipups are not uncommon in biblical translations. Introduced under the influence of dogmatism, often without the translator knowing it since he only followed tradition, they perpetuate belief and hinder symbolic translation.

witnesses address him as "Son of God." In this context, the expression is metaphorical and has above all an ethical meaning; it is in perfect conformity with the flowery language still common nowadays in the Middle East. It means, I behave as if I were the son of God, it is the divine in me that motivates my actions, my thoughts and my will. Jesus is entirely animated by the essential desire (only son) and not only partially so, as are the many "children of God" (verse 12), for whom the ideal is a goal which they cannot fully achieve. Jesus is the achievement of the ethical ideal and this is what his contemporaries (at least a small number of them) understood when they recognized him as the Son of God. None of them mistook him for a miraculously conceived man-god. On the other hand, they often misunderstood the universal scope of his message and saw in him the one who was going to reinstate Israel in its temporal power.

However, it is essential to take into account the fact that the Prologue of John's Gospel is different from the other evangelical texts in that it deals only secondarily with the man Jesus and his accomplishment (which is the theme of the other Gospels) and is mostly concerned with the phenomenon of sanctification[12] considered as an integral part of the evolutionary process of life. Being the conscious achievement of the ideal of harmonization which is immanent to existence, it thereby enlightens the whole meaning and direction of evolution.

Thus the phrase "only Son of the Father," used in the Prologue, goes beyond the solitary achievement of the man Jesus. The only Son,[13] no longer in the metaphorical meaning of the term, but in its deeply significant symbolic content, is the essence of this achievement; victory over suffering brought into this world by "the sin of Adam" having been achieved once in history, its reenactment throughout the ages is for mankind the only hope of satisfaction.

The myth of the Incarnation is not merely a testimony about Jesus, it is a testimony about the fact that a decisive stage of evolution has been reached and that the result is a great hope for all mankind. Moreover, it shows that the achievement of the most evolved man enlightens all men and enables them to grasp the meaning and direction of life, the past and future of evolution. Symbolically speaking, the achievement of the ideal on the human level "reveals" in its entirety the "design of God," the immanent meaning of life, the ignorance of which is a source of disorientation ("wandering in the darkness"). The Trinitarian myth, in its deepest meaning, is summed up in the last verse of the Prologue:

"No one has ever seen God,
it is the only Son, who is nearest to the Father's heart,
who has made him known."

---

[12]The same is true of the Epistles of Paul.

[13]The phrase "only Son" is found (and rarely so) exclusively in John's Gospel.

What we have analyzed is the deepest meaning of the Prologue. It does not prevent this text, as we have said, from having its *raison d'être* in the example of the man Jesus, moreover Jesus in person is present from verse 14 onward.

In fact, there are two fundamental distinctions to be made in order to grasp the real meaning of the Prologue. On the one hand, one must clearly distinguish *Jesus,* the historical person, from the *Word,* a mythical symbol. The central affirmation of the Prologue "the Word was made flesh" is *symbolic* and refers to the existence of the *real* man, emphasizing the evolutionary significance of his achievement. It is not the proclamation of a miraculous event. It adds to the real hero the dimension of a mythical hero, thereby showing that the truth he incarnates is the same that is present in all myths and in the Hebrew myth in particular, from which stems the entire New Testament. On the other hand, one must distinguish the man Jesus from the mythical *Son* of God, or only Son, a symbol of the evolutionary hope included in the achievement of Jesus. This achievement is thus linked to the meaning immanent to life "from the beginning" since it appears as its outcome and its clarification and it is also linked to the future of evolution since it appears as its prefiguration.

Thus in the symbolic Trinity—Father, Word, and Son—the third person is not Jesus, but the symbolic Son, the evolutionary hope of mankind prefigured by the achievement of Jesus.

A similar distinction has to be made between Jesus and *Christ* (a word which does not appear until verse 17) which is, like "Son" a symbolic image. "Christ," the central symbol of the New Testament, is borrowed from the Old Testament. It is the Greek translation of the Hebrew word "Messiah" which means "Anointed."

The Anointed of the Lord or Messiah of the Old Testament is not a present or future person, but the truth superconsciously known by all men and which, through evolutionary necessity, has to become incarnate and motivating in all men, the only condition for justice to rule on earth.

The Christ of the New Testament is the fulfillment of the ancestral hope of seeing the superconsciously known truth verified and actualized. Jesus is symbolically the Christ because he has attained the ideal whose relative achievement is the responsibility of every man. But the existence of Jesus does not *achieve,* contrary to what dogmatism pretends (and history cruelly disproves) the hope of mankind. His achievement, symbolically called *Christ,* shows the *possibility* and thus strengthens the *hope* that the suffering which rules because of the greed of desires can be overcome through evolution. Jesus is the Christ, but he is only, to use the expression of the Apostle Paul, "the first fruits" of the complete incarnation of the truth in the thinking species. In this sense, he is "the Son," the bearer of hope. "Christ" is the ethical achievement, the Son is the evolutionary hope.

Verse 14 continues as follows: "he lived among us, (literally he pitched his tent among us) and we saw his glory." The *tent* is a symbol which appears quite frequently in the Bible. A recollection of ancestral nomadism, it is protection and shelter. Therefore it symbolizes that which essentially protects man, i.e., his values. The "tent" pitched by Christ in the world is a refuge for the disoriented souls who understand his message. Verse 14 can be compared to a passage from Paul's Epistles: ". . . so that the power of Christ may stay [literally pitch his tent] over me." (2 Cor. 12:9 JB). The tent also symbolizes the detachment, the simplicity of Jesus' way of life.

"And we saw his glory" is interpreted by dogmatism as the testimony of eyewitnesses who had seen the supernatural phenomena that would have marked the passage on earth of the man-god: the miracles,[14] the actual resurrection and ascension. Thought, when it loses the methodological certainty which alone can distinguish between the possible and the impossible, can keep a pseudological structure while losing itself in absurdity. The epistemological basis of thought lies in the distinction between mystery and appearance, and the fundamental methodological rule of scientific thought lies in bringing neither existing modalities into mystery nor mystery into modalities.

In keeping with the meaning of the verses that have been deciphered so far, the phrase means that the disciples of Jesus have grasped the scope of his example, the achievement that makes him truly worthy of the title "glory" of mankind. They have, more essentially, seen the "glory," the splendor of the universal and fecundating truth which is symbolically called Christ.

The "only Son" symbol has already been translated; as to "grace" ("full of grace and truth") which is interpreted by theological dogmatism as the miraculous gift bestowed on human beings by a real and transcendent God, it is indeed a gift but the unexplainable and undeserved (gracious) gift of life and of vital impulse that, through its own evolutionary dynamics (to use psychological terms, through the strength of its sublime calculus of satisfaction) can create complete harmony in the human psyche, faith in life, joy in life.

Verse 16:
"Indeed, from his fullness we have, all of us, received—yes, grace in return for grace."

Through our substraction of verse 15, this verse comes quite naturally as a follow-up of verse 14. Grace is most certainly the gift of life, but this gift is lost if one does not have the capacity to receive it, to deserve it. In this sense, grace is the enlightenment of the soul and

---

[14]The Greek word *"semeion"* erroneously translated as miracle, simply means "sign" and has no supernatural connotation. The "miracles," like all illogical mythical episodes must be symbolically interpreted. Their study would go beyond the scope of this book.

spirit, the power of the vital impulse capable of overcoming the torment of anxiety extending over past and future. The soul, shrivelled and blinded by the egocentric affectivity of multiple desires, becomes objective when man experiences himself as mysteriously animated, as an attempt of nature to break through toward essential satisfaction. Grace is the gift of life received and accepted: responsibility fully accepted in the face of the mysteriously immanent meaning of life.

Whoever lives in such a way, without guilty vanity or accusing complaint, entirely animated by the evolutionary impulse which kindles, "lights up" preconscious life and enlightens conscious life, is "full of grace and truth" and becomes for others a vivifying example, a bearer of grace, a source of grace.

Verse 17:
"since, though the Law was given through Moses,
grace and truth have come through Jesus Christ."

This verse unites and at the same time opposes the deep significances of the Old and the New Testament, of the Old Covenant and the New Covenant.[15]

The truth has always been known. It has always been expressed anew by the myths of all peoples, under its two essential aspects: metaphysical truth which is the radical and definitive distinction between the unfathomable mystery of the Origins and manifest appearance; ethical truth which is the immanent call to harmonization whose executive is immanent justice. The life of cultures depends on the importance of the response to this truth in the souls of individuals. Decadence sets in with the growing disorientation bred by oblivion of the essential truth.

Truth cannot be completely incarnate in individuals, it has to be *suggested*. This is the task of the sacerdotal class during the periods when culture is flourishing, when the veracious suggestion based on myth, finds an echo in the souls of individuals.

With the progress of intellectualization, suggestion which is at first magical, then mythical, can become conceptual formulation. This is what happened with the Law of Moses. But truth, as long as it is not incarnate, as long as it is not imposed on the individual by his own superconscious, always runs the risk of being degraded into magical suggestion or verbal impositions, i.e., into moralism which will never cease to be fought by growing immoralism.

The santified man does not obey the law, he obeys his own superconscious. He is a law unto himself, he incarnates the immutable law of harmony ruling all that exists. He does not want to impose a new law—to judge the world—but to free man from the law (though it is a

---

[15]The title of the Greek Bible *Koine diatheke,* usually translated as New Testament, can also be translated as New Covenant.

historical necessity), i.e., to save the world. Neither does he ask man to follow him on the way towards sanctification. He shows that everyone can, according to his own strength, find essential satisfaction if—rejecting all precepts—he listens to the call of his own superconscious, were he the only one to do so in the midst of a disoriented world. His example makes the law, the collective guide of a people, obsolete and brings "grace and truth": the possible awakening in every human psyche of the evolutionary impulse (Word and Light) incarnate in all of nature, but stifled in the human being by the imaginative exaltation of desires and by inhibiting anxiety.

Verse 18:
"No one has ever seen God,
it is the only Son, who is nearest to the Father's heart,
who has made him known."

Thus the mythical tale of the Incarnation goes back to its origin. It strongly reaffirms the mythical foundation of all cultures, more central and more explicit in the Judeo-Christian myth than in all others: God is the forever unfathomable mystery. He makes himself known only through the Word, the evolutionary impulse whose clearest manifestation is the truth incarnate in man, the only Son. The Son "visible image of the invisible God," as the Apostle Paul puts it, the fully accomplished vital impulse, motivated by emotion inspired by mystery, is symbolically speaking, *"near the heart"* of God-mystery. The Son did not make known the real nature of God in the sense of dogma, because nothing can make it known.[16] Who would dare say that he knows God without being struck by the blasphemous absurdity of such an assertion? Yet, this is what people affirm when they claim that Jesus, a god-man, an integral part of the deity, reveals the divine nature to those who are incorporated into the Church by the magic of the rites. How much deeper is the mythical truth. The only Son, transcending the example of the man Jesus, is the evolutionary hope of all mankind, insofar as mankind is heir to the only truth, experienced by one man and thereby become the hope of all men. Through this possibility given to mankind to overcome the suffering due to intellectualization (the sin of Adam), the design of God "is made known": the evolutionary future of the thinking species is clarified, i.e., the incarnation in mankind of the eternal and only truth called Christ.

Here ends our deciphering of the symbolism in the Prologue. It will be followed by a translation of the symbolic meaning of the first verses of the Gospel proper, namely verses 6, 7, 8, 9, and 15 of the traditional text of the Prologue. If the Prologue of the Gospel of John can be called a cosmic vision of evolution and a foreshadowing of the essential

---

[16]The original text reads literally: the only Son was his interpreter, the explainer of his intentions.

future of mankind, the Gospel itself (which starts after verse 18) can be called a testimony for Jesus Christ. That is to say that the evangelist is not so much concerned with an account of the life of Jesus (and still less, with the proof that his origin and destiny were supernatural) than with showing that *Jesus is the Christ,* not in realistic terms, but symbolically so.

Verse 6:
"A man came, sent by God.
His name was John."

The Gospel itself starts with the testimony of John the Baptist. The scope of this testimony of John the Baptist is much greater than that of a historical anecdote, not because—as dogma would have it—John was the predestined annunciator of the miracle, but because he symbolizes and sums up the prophetic spirit of the Old Testament, and at the same time ushers in the New Covenent, i.e., a new expression, fuller and more universal, of the eternal truth.

Verse 7:
"He came as a witness,
as a witness to speak for the light,
so that everyone might believe through him."

John the Baptist is introduced as *a witness for the light.* Now light, as we have seen in analyzing verse 5 ("a light that shines in the dark, a light that darkness could not overpower") is the truth superconsciously known by human beings and that the subconscious cannot entirely repress. All the prophets were witnesses for the light, men of strong vital impulse, lucid as to their own motivations and animated by a desire to enlighten others, to help men tear themselves away from banalization.

John the Baptist is of the same stock as all those who have been "witnesses for the light" throughout history, since he too was symbolically *sent* by God *so that* everyone might believe through him. These seemingly finalistic expressions are used by literal dogmatism to assert that the vocation of John the Baptist, like that of the Old Testament prophets, was actually the result of divine will, that it was an element of a truly preestablished divine plan.

John the Baptist was not *sent by God in order* to testify for Jesus Christ, nor was he sent *so that* everyone might believe through him. He was animated by his own vital impulse.

The finalism of the phrase is symbolic and expresses this inner need driving John to support the preaching of the one with whom he felt a spiritual affinity, while recognizing and publicly affirming the superiority of the sanctified man ("I am not fit to undo his sandal-strap" Jn. 1:27 JB). Finalistic language such as "so that," "in order that" is in perfect conformity with the spirit of mythical symbolism. The "will" of God, the "design" of God, are common symbolic formulations through which the myth expresses the mysterious and lawful intentionality ruling all phenomena of the outer and inner world.

The fact that the history of mankind is periodically punctuated by the appearance of men who are animated by an exceptional vital impulse can be explained without invoking a supernatural predestination. From the dawn of life on earth, the prime mover of evolution has been anxious dissatisfaction seeking its satisfying appeasement.[17]

Eras of decadence, such as the Roman Empire, such as our own, are characterized by an anxious disorientation with respect to ethical values, cynically denied or superstitiously hypostatized. Such an anxious disorientation has always, in the course of history, brought about a renewal of reflection on the meaning of life. In a few rare individuals, suffering gives rise to a renewed upsurge of their strength of soul and spirit, of the evolutionary impulse with which they oppose the prevailing disorientation by reasserting again and again the immanence of values that are symbolically called wisdom and will of God, or Word of God, or Light.

In psychological terms, the phenomenon of prophecy, the theme of the Old Testament, summed up in the first chapter of John's Gospel, and the phenomenon of sanctification, the theme of the New Testament, are evolutionary phenomena which—in line with the constant process of mythical language—appear in the Bible "as if" the transcendental "will" of "God" had brought them about.

Verse 8:
"He was not the light,
only a witness to speak for the light."

As we have already explained, the symbol light has two complementary meanings. The light of verse 5 is truth in general; the light John the Baptist speaks for is still truth in general but it also becomes the truth that Jesus incarnates and proclaims anew.

John the Baptist "is not the light" because he is not Christ: he is not totally motivated by the essential truth or light. But if he had not been "witness for the light" in general, i.e., capable of discerning essential truth from essential error, he could not have been "witness for the light coming into the world": for the truth brought by Jesus, by Christ.

Verse 9:
"The Word was the true light
that enlightens all men;
and he was coming into the world."

---

[17]See *La Peur et l'Angoisse,* Payot.

This light is the new formulation of the truth, which is all the more "enlightening" since it appears in "the dark" of a decadent era. *The light is not Jesus, the light is Christ,* the truth already announced in the Old Testament, incarnate, actualized, made active force and elucidating thought through the personal achievement of the man Jesus, who can therefore be symbolically called Jesus Christ, the man animated by faith in the essence of life, capable of emotion in the face of the mysterious depths of existence and its manifest harmony.

It is certainly impossible to radically separate the living man and his message. Jesus says about himself: "I, the light, have come into the world" (Jn. 12:46 JB). But before this assertion, there comes a fundamental distinction voiced by Jesus himself:

> "Whoever believes in me
> believes *not in me,*
> but in *the one who sent me,*
> and whoever sees me,
> sees the one who sent me" (Jn. 12:44–45 JB).

"The one who sent me" just as the one who "sent" John the Baptist (verse 6) is the superconscious spirit, his own vital impulse compelling him to harmonize himself. In order to become harmonized, enlightened by vivifying faith, man must free himself from the imaginative exaltation of desires and their obsessive avidity. The clarification of the meaning of life proceeds from man's clarification of his own motives: from lucidity with respect to himself. Superconscious light must become conscious enlightment opposed to the darkness of the subconscious. Light is thus above all the truth about man, the veracity of his own self-judgment as it appears in many passages of the New Testament:

> "On these grounds is sentence pronounced:
> that though the light has come into the world
> men have shown they prefer
> darkness to light
> because their deeds were evil.
> And indeed, everybody who does wrong
> hates the light and avoids it,
> for fear his actions should be exposed;
> but the man who lives by the truth
> comes out into the light,
> so that it may be plainly seen that what he does is done in God"
> (Jn. 3:19–21 JB).

This is an affirmation of man's solitary responsibility before the ethical law. In this sense, as it is written in verse 9: "The Word was *the true light that enlightens all men;* and he was coming into the world."

The message of Jesus concerns all men. What is of fundamental importance for mankind is the message itself and not the fact that it was formulated and achieved by the man Jesus. The historical Jesus passed away like all men, but his message and his exemplary achievement remain eternally.

The Apostle Paul was the one who understood best that the truth incarnate in Jesus does not only concern the symbolically chosen people, but all mankind.

Verse 15:
"John appears as his witness [thus as a witness to the Word that is the true light]. He proclaims:
'This is the one of whom I said:
He who comes after me
ranks before me
because he existed before me.' "

"He proclaims" stresses emphatically—as does the original Greek text—the persistency of the prophetic voice. Here it is symbolized by John the Baptist, but it is the same voice that has been heard throughout the ages. He refers here to Isaiah, the voice in the wilderness (of the banalized world) and thus appears as the last prophet of the Old Covenant, summing up the entire prophetic message which bears witness to the light.

The declaration of John the Baptist: "He who comes after me" is used by theological dogmatism to support its assertions on the dual nature of the man Jesus: *divine and human.* "He who comes after me" would be the man-god, Jesus Christ. "He who existed before me" would be the Word, a divine person actually preexistent since the beginning.

In fact, the exclamation of John the Baptist, though rather enigmatic in its form, can be understood if one takes the trouble to clearly distinguish the planes of symbolism and historical reality, which is after all a principle of methodology valid for the deciphering of all biblical texts. "He who comes after" John the Baptist in time is Jesus, whose preaching follows that of John the Baptist. He who "ranks before me" refers to Christ, a symbol, not a reality. The essential truth ranks before all. It is expressed in symbolic terms by the myths of all peoples. It always ranked high in the soul of human beings, in the form of an ethical conscience which turns into guilt when man does not listen to its evolutionary call. But it had never been incarnate, lived to such a degree by a man in whom it became the only motivating force. "He existed before me." This again refers to the symbol Christ. If truth ranks before all in the historical conscience of mankind it is because it *existed*[18] *essentially;* it is not linked to accidental phenomena, it is the manifestation in the human psyche of the law of harmony that mysteriously rules, since the

---

[18]The Greek would be better translated by "was" than by "existed."

beginning, the evolutionary interaction between organizing spirit and organized matter.

Thus John the Baptist appears in the Gospel of John as heir to the Judaic culture, the "just man," to use the words of the Old Testament. He is the man who is sufficiently purified in his motives to recognize in Jesus, *the Christ,* the man freed from "the sin" of Adam, he who achieves the age-old hope of mankind. Therefore John the Baptist ushers in a new culture, a universal culture in which the individual, liberated from the forms that are peculiar to any particular religion, can hope, by developing his own vital impulse, to overcome the anxiety of disorientation.

This hope, stifled since the dawn of Christianity by dogmatizing error, perdures however and finds support and confirmation in the understanding of the true but symbolically veiled significance of the myth of the Incarnation.

In the last analysis, the fulfillment of this hope depends on the introspective method capable of studying the psychic functioning down to the extraconscious depths where symbolic language is elaborated.

CHAPTER VII

THE EPISTLES OF THE APOSTLE PAUL: THE MYTH OF THE RESURRECTION

The epistles of the Apostle Paul, being religious writings, have a symbolically veiled meaning. During his lifetime, there was already a tendency to misinterpret his Epistles. As Peter testifies: ". . . our brother Paul, who is so dear to us, told you this when he wrote to you with the wisdom that is his special gift. He always writes like this when he deals with this sort of subject, and this makes some points in his letter hard to understand; these are the points that uneducated and unbalanced people distort, in the same way as they distort the rest of scripture—a fatal thing for them to do" (2 Pet. 3:15–16 JB). The misunderstanding of symbolic texts, then as now, consists in mistaking the images or metaphors of the façade for reality. Now according to the warning formulated by the Apostle himself: the "letter bring death, [therefore so does the belief in the letter] but the Spirit gives life" (2 Cor. 3:6 JB). We should not take "bring death" literally here since it is clear that the Apostle does not expect physical death to follow literal misunderstanding. This is a metaphor with a very deep symbolic meaning.

Hence the primordial question: in what sense can the letter "bring death" and what is this life-giving spirit, the truth, hidden in the writings of the Apostle? It is the same spirit as that hidden in the biblical texts to which the Apostle refers.

The problem is all the more important that religious feeling (as opposed to dogmatic belief) is the foundation of all cultures and that our Western culture is based on the letter (dogmatically enlarged) of the Judeo-Christian writings, the Old and the New Testaments. The Judaic myth of Genesis gives an account of the creation of the universe and of the fall of the first man. The undefinable "creating cause" is personified by God-the-Father, and the destiny of mankind is foreshadowed by the disobedience of Adam.

The New Testament appears as the completion of this account. It brings the story of forgiveness. The fault of Adam is atoned for by Christ Jesus, the savior of mankind, crucified, buried and risen.

The central theme of Paul's epistles is the resurrection of Christ. The Apostle himself sees a link between this resurrection and the original fall: "Death came through one man and in the same way the resurrection of the dead has come through one man. Just as all men die in Adam, so all men will be brought to life in Christ" (1 Cor. 15:21–23).

Since the Apostle specifically warns against the danger of the letter, this warning concerns primarily the constant theme of all the Epistles: death and resurrection. These words have a veiled, symbolic meaning summing up the content of the Judeo-Christian myth starting with the account of the fall of Adam, the cause of evil, and leading to the myth of Christ, the restorer of good. The Epistles of Paul speak of "the mystery of Christ," i.e., the achievement of the man Jesus who, by restoring good, is mythically transfigured into the messenger of the divine will. The real nature of this good—the symbol of which is "resurrection from death"—becomes comprehensible through a preliminary elucidation of the real nature of evil and its origin, namely the understanding of the myth of Genesis. According to its hidden meaning, the Judaic myth of Genesis and the original fall contains the seed, as has been explained, of all the themes developed in the two Testaments and thus in the Epistles of Paul which can be considered as their summary. The vital error consists therefore in preferring earthly desires to the call of the spirit, in exalting carnal desires at the cost of the spirit. Expelled from the paradise of innocent animality, mankind can find salvation only in seeking the paradise of the spirit, "Heaven," a symbol of the perfect knowledge of the meaning of life and consequently a symbol of joy, which is imperishable because it has been freed from the temptation of error. Adam lost the grace of living essentially, of living in the truth which—symbolically speaking—is the divine essence, and which, because it is immutable, is symbolically called eternal.

Adam personifies mankind, and the latter, through its inclination toward wrong choice, through the exaltation of carnal desires is—symbolically speaking—dead to essential and eternal life.

The conflict between spirit and flesh being the principle of evil, the principle of good is the concord between spirit and flesh: harmony of desires. The spirit must dominate but not suppress the flesh: "For it is not against human enemies that we have to struggle, but against the Sovereignties" (Eph. 6:12 JB). ("Human enemies" personify here flesh and blood, the desires of the flesh and natural instincts; while the word "Sovereignties" is used for the perverse temptations ruling man: the temptation to exalt his desires.)

This understanding disposes of all the enigmas. Man is not condemned because of a fruit that has been eaten but because of his own perverse propensity, the consequence of which is not physical death but "death of the spirit" ("death of the soul"). The justice of God—mythical judge—is perfect. The apparent injustice of the punishment is, in truth, and according to the hidden meaning, the justice immanent to life, because the exaltation of carnal desires—immanent principle of evil—pits man against man and nation against nation. It breeds hatred. Now hatred, according not only to mythical truth but also to linguistic wisdom, ruins the profferred chance which life is (grace); hatred begets the very principle of mischance (disgrace).[1] The whole significance of Scripture is summed up in the vital requirement that hatred be transformed into love, meanness into good will (into a lucid will for good). This fundamental requirement condenses and sums up the enigmatic meaning of the symbols contained in the Bible. As to the Epistles of Paul, they are all built on the same pattern: the Apostle first develops his teaching in symbolic terms "death and resurrection," then adds the key to understanding: exhortations to charity which is neither alms, nor material gifts, but the gift of one's livng soul capable of nourishing and vivifying other souls. "If I give away all that I possess . . . but am without love, it will do me no good whatever" (from 1 Cor. 13:3 JB).

Hatred being the consequence of original sin, of the perverse inclination to exalt desires, does nothing but mortify the soul (*mors facere:* to make dead), whether this be understood in the sense of killing the soul through mutual rancor or in the sense of mortifying oneself as a vain ascetic defense against the intrusion of rancor. Man must be reborn from this death of the soul to the love of life. Since—symbolically speaking—life is a gracious gift from God, man must—on the mythical plane—be reborn to love of God, to obedience and to grace.

The resurrection from death (of the soul) has to take place during life. However, to the "death-resurrection" symbolism referring to the symbol of God-the-Judge is added the symbolism of a resurrection after the death of the body, which refers to the symbol of God-the-Creator. Life, not having come from nothingness cannot end in nothingness. For mythical imagination, life, coming from God, will return to God. The man, who during his life is reborn from the death of the soul will be reborn—according to the mythical image—in God after the death of the body. The mythical reunion with God leads to the symbol of immortality. Related to the "God-the-Creator" image, immortality after death is a symbol of a quite different order than those representing the relationship between living man and the deity-as-judge. Having a metaphysical significance like the symbol of God-the-Creator, the symbol of immortality remains undefinable and inexplicable as to its

---

[1]French has the same word: *chance,* and the feeling of hatred is *méchanceté. Mé-chance* (mis-chance) therefore alludes both to the consequence of hatred and to mischance, disgrace and unhappiness, the contrary of "grace."

mode. Only images dealing with the death of the soul and its rebirth during life are translatable into conceptual language, since these images represent the immanent meaning of life, the actual modalities of life, be it meaningful or senseless.

In order to better understand the meaning of the Epistles, it is necessary to look not only at the essential aspect of the vital problem of life (theme of the myth) but also to give an outline of the historical situation at the time. The myth symbolizes the essential theme of which the historical events are a factual illustration.

The characteristic of the "original sin" in human nature being the transmission of punishment from one generation to the next, this transmission becomes the determinant factor in the destiny of individuals and nations.

The Old Testament, when elaborating the theme of obedience and disobedience, grace and disgrace, Covenant and breach of it, is in the first place concerned with the destiny of the nations in general and of the Jewish people in particular, symbolically called the chosen one, the symbol—just as Adam is—of all mankind. The entire Old Testament is a historical illustration as well as a verification of the meaning symbolically expressed by the myth of Adam: the exaltation of material desires leads to the destruction of strength of soul. Far from leading to the achievement of its false promises, the principle of evil does not even achieve material well-being, but—through essential cowardice—laxity of morals and downfall of an entire people. Rebelling against the call of the spirit (symbolically speaking: the voice of the Almighty), the chosen people, wallowing in luxury, becomes incapable of defending itself against its enemies and falls under the yoke of the conquerors (symbolically speaking: the Almighty punishes the people). The collective and superindividual aspect of the fall and its punishment is symbolized by the myth of the flood, the story of the tower of Babel (the fate of Babylon), the destruction of Sodom, the captivity in Egypt. After Exodus, the hereditary sin of human nature and its punishment are symbolized anew by the dance around the golden calf and exemplified by the history of the Kings up to the destruction of Jerusalem.

During the course of this history, the prophets announce the advent of a Messiah of the spirit who will free the people from death of the soul. But the people are expecting a Messiah of the flesh and its desires, one who will ensure material power and riches. The Roman yoke has finally exacerbated the age-old hope, and the messenger of the spirit, the man in whom the essential truth is incarnate—whose fleshly desires accomplish the works of the spirit, the one who has risen from death of the soul—disappoints the banal expectation fleetingly attached to his message. He will not be forgiven for having detached himself from the common belief, and he will be treated as a renegade to the Law given by Moses. He will be put to death. The man Jesus dies in the flesh. But the truth incarnate in him—the truth symbolically personified and called Christ—will rise from the tomb. Christ being a symbol, the "resurrection of Christ" is also a symbol. It has a quite different meaning from the "resurrection during life" of the man Jesus, and its significance is also different from the metaphysical resurrection symbolized by immortality (the myth of the return, after death, to the creating principle). Christ—the teaching of Jesus—resurrects on the third day, the day of the spirit according to one of the most ancient of numerical symbolisms: the day when the truth embodied in Jesus is understood and experienced by other men (within the limits of their strength) or by all mankind. Christ cannot rise again, truth cannot live again except if it is thus reexperienced—" . . . until Christ is formed in you" (Gal. 4:19 JB). That comprehensive and active reincarnation is the life giving faith. Merit (on the plane of reality) and grace (on the plane of symbolism), active faith is life-giving because it does not content itself with resuscitating from the tomb the teaching, that is: Christ; it also resuscitates from death of the soul the man in whom the truth is reincarnated; his soul is reborn from the tomb of the flesh (of exalted earthly desires). This truth, symbolically personified and called "Christ," i.e., the importance of the life and message of Jesus, appeared to Saul of Tarsus on the way to Damascus and this understanding overwhelmed him to the extent that he became Apostle to the nations. For, through the understanding of this truth he, like Jesus, detached himself from the dead beliefs of his childhood, from the Law of Moses petrified in dogmas and rituals. The revelation of the truth made him understand that the message of salvation, the "mystery of Christ" is not exclusively meant for the Jewish people, but for all mankind. Every man can be " . . . built into a house where God lives, in the spirit" (Eph. 2:22 JB).

The Gospel is the message of joy because, completing the Old Testament, it shows that even in the midst of social decay, every man can, through his own strength—the intensity of his essential desires—cast off the common suffering caused by death of the soul and be reborn to God, to the meaning of life, and to joy. This rebirth, achieved by the Apostle Paul after the example of Jesus, has one condition: freedom from dead beliefs, active understanding of the truth immanent to life but symbolically presented by the myth as a transcendental revelation.

The meaning of the Epistles is finally summed up in the distinction between vivifying faith and mortifying belief.[2] "Faith" according to the

---

[2] The verb *pisteuo*, which recurs quite often in the New Testament, never had in Greek the meaning that the translations give it, i.e., "to believe the unprovable," "to believe blindly," which is set against the supposedly insufficient knowledge of "reasoning reason." This verb always had in Greek the meaning: "to trust," "to rely on." The Greek substantive *pistis* is accurately rendered by the Latin *fides*, from which "faith" is derived. In Latin, the verb corresponding to *fides* is *fidere*: to trust, and not *credere* which becomes in French *croire* which is an ambiguous word meaning both "to be assured" and "to remain hesitant." The same holds true to a certain extent for its English translation "to believe."

New Testament is not the belief in a real God, nor in miracles,[3] but trust that is shaken and destroyed during times of decadence by the anxiety of disorientation and the doubt born out of multiple ideological sophistries.

To believe in a real God and his gratuitous intervention is mortifying (it kills the vital impulse or convulses it into sterile remorse and biting guilt) because it infallibly leads to the erroneous hope of obtaining grace through the magical means of verbal imploration and ceremonial achievement. Genuine religiosity, emotion in the face of mystery, dies out and is replaced by religious traditions and dogmas. Belief, instead of being—like faith—a vital phenomenon of essential importance, becomes nothing more than an accidental adherence to a social institution in which people participate according to the chance of birth which determines which community they will belong to.

Through the Epistles, the Apostle wanted to obtain, in the churches he founded, that the spirit prevail over the letter and that living faith was not overcome by dead belief in the ancient Law entrusted then to the priests of that time, the Levites and Pharisees. To abandon childhood beliefs and their literal understanding and to return to the spirit is *madness for the world,* because unconditional love for the spirit is not without danger for the flesh as history has proven through repeated examples. The Mystery of Christ—seen in this light—is nothing but the perfect exemplification of the overcoming of this danger by the power of the human spirit (outer defeat transformed into inner victory). The holy madness that the Apostle preaches is that of all the prophets preceding Jesus and the very same one animates him. This madness is faith, inspiring the strength to resist the world, its seductions and its threats. It is *glory before God* because, by submitting the flesh to the demands of the spirt, by incarnating the spirit, the madness of faith *glorifies,* sanctifies the flesh, i.e., spiritualizes and sublimates the material and sexual desires and thus achieves the immanent meaning of life whose symbol is God. Active faith *gives thanks to God:* it is grateful to God for the unmerited grace of life, by turning this grace into the merit of an ardent soul. In this vein, the Apostle ceaselessly repeats that he has been called to his ministry by the grace of God. This is the grace that he invites the members of his churches to join in by stimulating their faith through his Epistles and by tirelessly fighting a tendency that was already manifest during his lifetime: the nefarious tendency to replace living faith by dead belief in the letter and in rituals.

Just as the letter expresses and at the same time hides the meaningful message, so ceremonial cult, in its turn, hides and expresses meaningful activity. The suggestive power of the cult resides in its capacity to bring about a feeling of gratitude for the gift of life, felt as a grace

---

[3]See note 12 in chapter VI.

bestowed on man: all peoples' cults contain the symbolic promise to sacrifice to the spirit excessive attachment to carnal desires. But suggestive ceremony remains nothing but a magical spell if the symbolic promise is not followed by the actual achievement of meaningful activity carried on in the midst of life's daily vicissitudes.

According to the old Law and its letter turned into dogma, the posterity of Abraham is chosen and each descendant is in a state of grace if he is circumcised. But according to the hidden spirit, the circumcision of the flesh is a ritual symbolizing the limitation of carnal desires and their domination by the spirit, "the circumcision of the heart," as Paul calls it. The argumentation of the Apostle is based on the understanding of this symbolism which enables him to include polytheistic peoples in the symbolic promise made to Abraham, in the Covenant and in grace. By founding churches, the Apostle obeyed the necessity to assemble converts into communities, for nothing is more difficult for an isolated person than resisting the assaults of threats and temptations. Common convictions stimulate the forces of resistance. But this advantage, which is more or less conventional and required by the weakness of human nature, does present an essential danger: conventions can become stronger than the ardor of faith. In the Christian churches founded by the Apostle, the ritual of circumcision—which had long lost its meaning—was abandoned and replaced by a new ritual: baptism.

Symbolically speaking, such a substitution is perfectly justified because circumcision and baptism are identical in their deepest significance. Man is symbolically reborn from death of the soul through baptism, just as he was symbolically included in God's grace through circumcision. All the Epistles' meaning is summed up in the warning that ceremonial grace and resurrection remain worthless if they are not followed by a real effort to be reborn to a meaningful life. To imagine oneself as being called, without a true resurrection during life and only by virtue of a magical grace, to an eternal happiness starting after the death of the body, is to kill the spirit of the "death-resurrection" symbolism and to degrade, to the extent of entirely falsifying, the meaning of the Epistles.

The degradation comes from misunderstanding the symbol of "original sin." For it is indeed this hereditary propensity at its peak, the love of the flesh at its most exalted degree to put one's hope not in life but in the resurrection of the flesh after the death of the body.

The spirit hidden in the letter and thus deciphered shows a consistency in the message of the Epistles which implicates the whole meaning of life. But is the general meaning analyzed so far effectively found behind the façade of the Epistles of Paul? To answer this question, we must study the texts of the Epistles in greater detail.

"To set the mind on the flesh is death" (Rom. 8:6 RSV). This is the definition of "death" as the Apostle sees it. "To set the mind on the flesh" is to exalt carnal desires, the cause of death of the soul. This symbolic meaning—"death through sin"—is found throughout the Old Testament starting with the myth of Genesis. It reappears in the New Testament: "Let the dead bury their dead." Taken literally, this passage is devoid of meaning. Conversely, it becomes deeply significant if we bring in the symbolic significance of "death through sin": let those who live with their mind on the flesh mutually kill their soul by fighting for material goods. They will bury one another for their bodies are only "sepulchers for dead souls." The symbolism of "death through sin" common to the Old and New Testaments is also used by the other apostles " . . . the desire conceives and gives birth to sin, and when sin is fully grown, it too has child, and the child is death" (Jas. 1:15 JB). ". . . the dead [in the soul] had to be told the Good News as well" (1 Pet. 4:6 JB). No one has ever heard of a miracle enabling the preaching of the Gospel to the dead. On the other hand, the message of joy is not only proclaimed to the members of the churches but also to those who do not want to listen to it: those who are dead in their souls.

> "We have passed out of death and into life,
> and of this we can be sure
> because we love our brothers.
> If you refuse to love, you must remain dead" (1 Jn. 3:14 JB).

The following passage is just as clear:

"And you were dead, through the crimes and the sins in which you used to live. . . . We all were among them [the dead in the soul] too in the past, living sensual lives . . . but he [God] brought us to life" (Eph. 2:1–5 JB).

These passages and many others which are too numerous to quote here show clearly that the "death" in question is the result of the concupiscence of the flesh, that resurrection means rebirth to the life of the soul, and that the "dead" just as the "reborn" are in fact living human beings.[4]

Yet there is an additional difficulty due to the fact that Paul uses the term "death" in another meaning, diametrically opposed to the sense of "death of the soul." The meaning of the Gospels lies in the fact that one must rise from "death *through* sin." Now to rise, to be reborn to essential life, one must—in the language of the Apostle—"die *to* sin," abandon the exalted desires of the flesh, die to the body, an expression that leads to the erroneous belief that resurrection, access to essential life, cannot be achieved before the body dies. (The phrase also leads to the erroneous belief that the apostle proposes the mortification of the body or asceticism.)

---

[4]The Greek word *anastasis* just like the Latin *resurrectio* does not mean at all bodily rebirth after actual death, but straightening up, the action of getting back on one's feet.

How could it happen that the term "death" and consequently the term "resurrection" were understood literally? We must pause a moment here to outline, were it only briefly, the historical progress of this distortion. Dogmatic interpretation which places resurrection exclusively after the death of the body is based not only on the literal understanding of the Epistles but also on the legend, related in the Gospels, according to which the crucified, risen again, would have appeared to the Apostles before ascending into Heaven to sit in flesh and bones at the right of the Father. This naïve and moving legend is a reminiscence of the ancestral hope of the survival after death. The ascension of the victorious hero—half-man, half-god—is a theme common to the mythologies of all peoples. More ancient yet, in the premythical and animistic era, the father-ancestor, the founder of the tribe, a totemic deity, imposes his taboos on the men who are his sons and each man, after his death, having in turn become a father-ancestor, gains immortality and is included in the ritual of worship provided that during his lifetime he was worthy of his ancestors. In the animistic beliefs, the two principal themes of mythical symbolization already appear: the symbol of immortality linked to the symbolism of judgement after death, and the requirement for moral behavior during life. As mythical representation deepens, it frees itself from the superstitious realism of the animistic era. There is a reversal of the importance given to the two complementary themes: the requirement for a meaningful behavior during life (symbolized by the struggles of the heroes with the monsters) becomes more important than the hope of immortality prevailing during the animistic era. This hope, however, remains an underlying factor while being transposed from the plane of reality to that of symbolism. According to the spirit hidden under the façade of the fable, survival no longer concerns man as an individual but the mysteriously inexplicable principle of existence: animation (mythically symbolized by the soul). Due to this evolution within mythical representation itself, the conditions for a meaningful life are no longer only symbolized by heroic struggles with monsters (which express the conflicts of the soul) but are explicitly formulated (commandments of Moses).

At the peak of the mythical era, in the Christian myth, the exemplary hero is no longer, as he was at the outset, an unreal and legendary figure, but a man who actually lived though legend continues to credit him with a divine filiation. The legend links his achievement with the age-old hope, by illustrating the birth of the exemplary man by divinization and his death by immortalization. The exemplary life he led, on the other hand, does not have to be symbolically illustrated: it is actively manifested in his works. However, symbolization does not entirely give up its way of condensing in suggestive images (all too easily misunderstood) the exemplary significance of this unique life: it presents the man who has fulfilled the meaning of life as being the only one who is essentially alive among the multitudes of men who are "dying" since they do not know, as he does, how to vanquish the conflicts of the soul.

If the myth of the divine filiation and the legend of bodily ascension are taken literally, a quasi unavoidable necessity ensues—since the supernatural is thereby accepted—to interpret dogmatically the life and death of Jesus, which infallibly leads to the *credo quia absurdum:* Jesus, being a real God, came down from Heaven and became a real man, he died on the cross "for the sins of the world." The men who crucified the Son of God, instead of being punished for this crime which is far more serious than the sin of Adam, benefit thereby from a superabundant grace, provided they are included by baptism in the community of believers. This common belief is based on the "fact" that the Apostles saw "the Son of God" "risen from the dead," ascend into Heaven.

"Christ died for the sins of the world," "God raised Jesus from the dead," these phrases are indeed frequently found in the Epistles of Paul. It is undoubtedly in the Epistle to the Romans (chapter 6) and in the first Epistle to the Corinthians (chapter 15) that these symbols of "death" and "resurrection" appear in their most condensed, and admittedly, in their most enigmatic form, if they are read without the help of a method based on the knowledge of psychic functioning. As already seen, the term "death" is used by the Apostle with different meanings. These become clear if, following the text, at least in its general lines, one endeavors to elucidate its psychological meaning: "We are dead to sin, so how can we continue to live in it?" (Rom. 6:2 JB). The sin in question is the sin of Adam, the hereditary tendency of human nature to imaginative exaltation of desires. As to the word "dead" it does not mean here "death of the soul" which it usually does in the Epistles of Paul as in all other mythical texts; it means: we, through understanding the example of Jesus, have stopped committing sins, so how could we still find satisfaction in sin?

"You have been taught that when we were baptized in Christ Jesus, we were baptized in his death; in other words, when we were baptized we went into the tomb with him and joined him in death, so that as Christ was raised from the dead by the Father's glory, we too might live a new life" (Rom. 6:3–4 JB).

Again this passage does not deal with Jesus' actual death. To understand these verses, we must refer to the very ancient symbolism of death and resurrection such as it appears for instance in the image of the Phoenix rising from its ashes or in the Mysteries of Eleusis where the buried grain must be reborn. These symbols mean that death of exalted desires, i.e., abandoning excessive attachment to the earth is the necessary condition for a rebirth to the life of the spirit, the essential life ("life eternal" in New Testament terminology). This rebirth is also symbolized in the Gospel of John (12:24) by the image, analogous to that of the Mysteries of Eleusis, of the grain that must die in order to bear fruit. The ritual of baptism contains the same meaning: to baptize signifies etymologically, not to purify, but to immerse, to drown. The ritual of baptism symbolizes the death of the old man, the abandoning of exalted desires, and emerging from the water means being reborn to a new life.

Thus this entire passage means that, just as Jesus caused the old Adam (imaginative exaltation) to die in himself, so as to rise during his lifetime from death of the soul, his disciples symbolically committed themselves through the rite of baptism to die the same death as he did (death of exaltations) and to be buried like him (abandoning sin and preparing for a new life), so as to be reborn to the life of the spirit. This meaning is clearly expressed in Rom. 6:6 (JB) ". . . our former selves have been crucified with him to destroy this sinful body and to free us from the slavery of sin." To this meaning concerning the ethical resurrection during life, such as it was exemplified by the heroic life and death of Jesus, another significance is added.

A distinction must be made, as we have seen, between Jesus, the man who is an example for all mankind and Christ, the eternal truth, already proclaimed by the prophets of the Old Testament, but historically incarnate in the life of Jesus. Christ is the eternal truth about man and life, a truth that had been "buried" throughout the centuries because of Adam's sin, a truth that was "awakened" or resurrected when a man, in this instance Jesus, made it the principle of his life. Thus the resurrection of Christ means: the reemergence of the truth buried by centuries of dogmatism and misunderstanding. This explains, among others, the passage of the First Epistle to the Corinthians in which the Apostle sums up all his teaching (Chapter 15): ". . . I taught you what I had been taught myself, namely that Christ died for our sins, in accordance with the scriptures; that he was buried; and that he was raised to life on the third day, in accordance with the scriptures; that he appeared first to Cephas and secondly to the Twelve . . . and last of all he appeared to me too" (1 Cor. 15:3–8 JB).

The Scriptures to which Paul refers can only be the Old Hebrew Testament. Now the texts of the Old Testament never said anything about the real death and bodily resurrection of a man called Christ. On the other hand, the constant themes of the Old Testament are the death and burial of the truth forgotten and misunderstood by the people (refusal to listen to the voice of God) and the prophetic promise that truth will be reborn. The third day is symbolic, since the figure 3 is a constant symbol of the spirit.

However, this reemergence of the truth called "Christ" is indissociable from the moral resurrection of the man Jesus through which precisely the buried truth was manifested anew. It is thus quite clear that it can in no way concern the real resurrection of the man Jesus.

What was "seen" by Cephas (Peter) during the lifetime of Jesus (Jn.

6:68), by the Apostles at Pentecost shortly after the death of Jesus, and by Paul himself many years later on the road to Damascus, what was understood, is the truth about the meaning of life and the fact that the man Jesus, through his example, was the incarnation of this truth.

Many other passages of the Epistles confirm this significance. For instance: "For if the dead are not raised, Christ has not been raised, and if Christ has not been raised, you are still in your sins" (1 Cor. 15:16–18 JB).

If it is impossible for the dead in the soul to be reborn during their lifetime, if it is impossible for the banalized individual to free himself from excessive and multiple desires and to find the way to essential satisfaction, then it means that the truth (Christ) did not "rise," incarnate and manifested in the life of the exemplary man called Jesus. If the example of Jesus is an imposture, if the truth expressed by his words and actions is not the eternal truth, then there is no hope for mankind, "you are still in your sins."

"But Christ has in fact been raised from the dead, the first-fruits of all who have fallen asleep" (1 Cor. 15: 20 JB).

The awakening of the truth, killed by the banalization of the world, the example of Jesus, is the first hope for those who have fallen asleep (in banalization).

It is false and "unhappy" to hope in Christ, while remaining in *"this life"* in a life haunted by exalted carnal desires (to believe that baptism is enough for salvation) instead of being reborn to the life of the spirit, the vision of the spirit, faith in possible achievement (within the limits of man's strength). Fidelity to prescriptions, without a life-giving faith, makes man unhappy—says the Apostle—because it does not lead man to freedom but, at the most, to a mortification of the flesh. "Christ, as we know, having been raised from the dead will never die again. Death has no power over him any more" (Rom. 6:9). This passage does not mean at all that Jesus lives eternally but that the truth, once it has been manifested, risen from the misunderstanding in which banalized beings had kept it, cannot be forgotten; "it will never die again." It also means that through his achievement Jesus conquered the death of the soul, overcame banalization, showed that the death of the soul could be defeated and robbed of the power it had in the beginning. This is the decisive hope for mankind to vanquish perverse temptation, since it has been proven that death of the soul can be defeated.

"If my motives were only human ones, what good would it do. . . . You say: Let us eat and drink today; tomorrow we shall be dead" (1 Cor. 15:32–33 JB).

If it is not possible to overcome the flesh, why bother to improve? Let us satisfy the desires of the flesh as long as we live on this earth!

In this passage, it is clear that the Apostle has no hope in an individual survival after bodily death. Life cannot go back to nothingness. But the return to the mysterious source of all life, of which the symbol is God-the-Creator, cannot be achieved in the carnal mode. (Though mythical language—through its process of personification—uses the carnal mode as image and symbol.)

"Come to your senses, behave properly, and leave sin alone; there are some of you who seem not to know God at all; you should be ashamed" (1 Cor. 15:34 JB). To know God is "not to sin," it is to die to exalted desires with the help of vivifying faith. To "know God" it is not enough to mortify the flesh, and to believe that a purely ceremonial justification during this life will ensure a personal survival which is more or less imagined in a carnal mode after the death of the body.

The true meaning of the Epistles deciphered so far is summed up as follows: Jesus is a real man, but he is symbolically "God," because during his life, through "death to sin," he has demonstrated the possibility of moral resurrection. The man Jesus was crucified. His death on the cross would have been only an accident if the way he died—without complaints or reproaches—had not imbued his actual death with the essential meaning of a decisive victory of the spirit over the flesh. The real death of Jesus reverses the sin of Adam and thus acquires a mythically deep significance: death accepted without hatred has the meaning of an ultimate sacrifice of the flesh to the spirit; the flesh accepts to die rather than betray the life of the soul. Through this way of dying, achieved by a real man, the "divine mission" is fulfilled: the "redemption" of human nature with its inclination to sin.

In this sense, the Apostle refers several times to the redemptive virtue of shed blood. By dying and shedding his blood (see Romans 6) the crucified man carries the sins of the world. The formula "he carries the sins of the world" has two complementary meanings: he bears the hatred of the world without faltering and, having thus conquered in himself hatred (the principle of evil), he brings his sublimated soul to "the Father," to the divine principle animating every man as long as his soul is alive. The death of a god whose survival is guaranteed would only be a pretense. How could a supernatural grace result from it? The death of "the Son of Man" is a tragic reality, the most tragic reality. From this death, this blood shed, comes, for other men, the grace imparted by the force of his example: the stimulation of their own vital impulse through enhanced faith in the possibility of essential achievement. This is the only vivifying faith. The redemptive value of the example and of faith in the example lie precisely in the fact that the victory over hereditary weakness is accomplished by a man like all the others, albeit endowed with exceptional strength of soul. Through his life resurrected from death of the soul and through his fidelity to his own accomplishment even unto his real death, the man Jesus exemplifies this salutary truth. He has become—symbolically speaking—the immortal Christ, the Messiah of the spirit, the message of God-the-Father, his only Son showing the way of salvation to all mankind: ". . . the good act of one man brings everyone life and makes them justified" (Rom. 5:18 JB).

The understanding of this message and of the example of Jesus is the "Mystery of Christ" which was revealed to the Apostle and which he endeavored to reveal to all men, Jews and Gentiles. (The interpretation of this "Mystery" as given here, may seem strange because it goes against the customary way of thinking. This interpretation based on the texts, proposes an explanation purified from all supernatural elements unbelievable by definition. It is the only explanation which—since it is rid of the supernatural—can reconcile religious feeling and reason. Yet, it is not rationalistic because it takes into account the unfathomable depth of mystery.)

The enigmatic formulation of the Epistles was required by the metaphysical image of "God-the-Creator" and by the ancient symbolism of "death of the soul." In order to remain consistent the Apostle had to use a language which constantly refers to death and resurrection. This symbolizing terminology is in full conformity with the Gospels. In his talk with Nicodemus (see John), Jesus reproaches the Pharisee for not understanding that one must be reborn, even though he is a teacher in Israel. Yet Nicodemus understands quite well that Jesus talks about a rebirth during life; the idea of a resurrection after death does not even occur to him:

"How can a grown man be born?" (Jn. 3:4 JB)
Jesus replies:
"If you do not believe me
when I speak about things in this world,
[rebirth during life]
how are you going to believe me
when I speak to you about heavenly things?" (Jn. 3:12 JB) [return to the creative principle]

The rebirth of the soul during life and resurrection after physical death (a metaphysical symbol) are quite clearly distinguished here.

The symbolic terminology of the Apostle, who explains moral rebirth by contrasting the two phrases of "death through sin" and "death to sin" (death of the Old Adam), is in itself extremely simple and economical. But at the time Paul wrote his letters, Jesus had been dead for many years. This historical fact helped propagate in the barely established churches, the erroneous belief that the symbolic terms "death and resurrection" referred to the crucifixion and a miraculous rebirth. If one does not take into consideration the fact that the Apostle speaks about the exemplary moral resurrection making Jesus, on the symbolic plane, the divine messenger and Son of God, one is compelled to interpret all the passages dealing with the resurrection in the sense of a miraculous carnal rising to life, proof of the real divinity of Jesus. Faith then consists in hoping to be reborn in the same way as Jesus, after the death of the body. In order to shore up this faith, the interpretation of all the Gospels and Epistles had to be adjusted to this version, which did not fail to happen. But is it not obvious that this version is the fundamental error? It lends to the apostle a fallacious argumentation: the physical resurrection of an immortal god brings no hope of resurrection for mortal men. No conclusion, logical or analogical, can lead from the so-called reappearance of Jesus on earth to immortality for men. In order to reach such a conclusion, the modalities would have to be identical: either men would have to return to earth before being admitted to heaven or Jesus, without reappearing on earth should have (as the fate of men after death is generally imagined) ascended into heaven shorn of his physical body (and that would make his ascension unprovable). It is precisely the so-called reappearance of Jesus on earth which makes this so-called proof inadmissible. It is too easy to rely on the unprovable and to believe in the unbelievable bodily resurrection of a man taken for God. Everyone has the right to believe. But no one has the right to make of his belief an irrefutable and allegedly proven argument. The Apostle—as is proved by symbolic exegesis—was careful not to do so. The end of the First Epistle to the Corinthians brings the most enlightening example of the real contents of the teaching: "Someone may ask, 'How are dead people raised, and what sort of body do they have when they come back?' These are stupid questions" (1 Cor. 15:35–36 JB).

This "stupid" is enough in itself to bring down the whole dogmatic structure. It is stupid to ask with what bodily dead people come back, because the question shows that the teaching has not been understood. Those who have risen from death of the soul do not change bodies. In the following verses (37–58), the common theme of all the Epistles is developed in a new way: the Apostle talks about a glorious body for the resurrected. But if it is stupid to believe that the dead come back after their demise with a new body, is it not obvious that the Apostle cannot mean to say—contrary to what literal exegesis claims—that the deceased rise with a glorious body?

Talking to Greeks the Apostle, as we have already said, first uses the image which had already served as a symbol in the mysteries of Eleusis to describe the resurrection of the soul during life:[5] just as the grain must die in order to bear fruit, so man—in order that his life may also bear fruit—must give up the exalted desires of the body. He must sow, as the Apostle says in verses 42–46, the body [which is] perishable, contemptible, weak (the body tempted by sin) in order to rise imperish-

---

[5]*Symbolism in Greek Mythology*, Shambhala, 1980.

able, glorious, powerful . . . embodying the spirit. The error of interpretation is strengthened by the word "perishable" understood as relating to the corruption taking place after bodily death; *the error is definitely eliminated if we understand that here, as everywhere, the Apostle talks
about moral corruption.* The spirit must become incarnate. This incarnation is the glorification of the body. It is clearly shown in Phil. 1:20
(JB): ". . . for Christ to be glorified in my body" which means that the
body will be glorified by Christ: by the incarnation of truth. See also
the following passage: "Christ among you, your hope of glory" (Col.
1:27 JB). This glorification takes place without visible transformation
of the body, for "everything that is flesh is not the same flesh" (1 Cor.
15:39 JB). The Apostle uses (verses 40–41) a comparative image that
can be summed up as follows: in the realm of matter, there are earthly
bodies and celestial bodies, i.e., the stars.

It is not matter which is changed but its radiance. In the same way, in
the human species, it is not the body which will change, but its animation. It must become—in keeping with the image—glory, luminous radiance analogous to the light of the stars: lucidity of spirit and warmth
of soul. This comparison leads the Apostle to say: "The first man,
being from the earth, is earthly by nature; the second man [he who
appears after the moral resurrection] is from heaven" (1 Cor. 15:47
JB). In this connotation, Jesus—called "the last Adam" (verse 45) for
his exemplary resurrection—abolishes in principle the reign of death of
the soul due to the original human weakness and symbolized by the fall
of the first Adam.

Thus does the Apostle come back to the fundamental relationship
between Adam and Christ Jesus, relationship underlying all the Epistles. But by elaborating on it, he widens the significant scope of this
relationship: Adam is the symbol of the birth of mankind and Christ is
the symbol of its rebirth. All mankind will ultimately be reborn.

"Just as all men die in Adam, so all men will be brought to life in
Christ" (1 Cor. 15:22 JB). This is the myth of the Parousia. In the
future, through the exemplary truth experienced by Jesus—the
Christ—all mankind will be reborn and not only, as in the present case,
those few men who are capable of being inspired by the example. The
Apostles did not believe in an early Parousia since ". . . with the Lord a
'day' can mean a thousand years" (2 Pet. 3:8 JB). Hope for the Parousia
is the completion of the mythical cycle, going from the emergence of
death of the soul to the moral rebirth achieved by Jesus, and from
there to the final resurrection of Christ: the incarnation of the truth in
all men. If one man was able to be reborn from death of the soul, the
hope for rebirth is in principle valid for all men. However, speaking
about the hope for the Parousia, Paul says: ". . . we are not all going to
die, but we shall all be changed" (1 Cor. 15:51 JB).

It is worthwhile insisting on this quotation because it underlines at the same time truth and error. If, as dogmatism claims, to die and to change means "to die and rise again with a glorious body," one would, according to this passage, be compelled to believe that on the day of Parousia those who would be changed without dying, would go about the earth endowed with glorious bodies. In the light of symbolic understanding, the passage means even on the day of the Parousia not all will die to sin, but all will be influenced by truth when it becomes the ruling convention.

The day when all men will be changed by the radiance of the glory of Christ, the day when all will conform to the life of the last Adam will be the last day of a world subject to the temptation of "dying in the soul," of exalting without limits the earthly desires. On that day, as it is said, Christ, the truth, will come again, he will clear up the darkness and Heaven will come down to earth: imperishable truth and joy will reign. The world will be under the rule of Christ (1 Cor. 15:24–26 JB) ". . . having done away with every sovereignty [perverse sovereignties] authority and power [proceeding from the mortifying temptation of exalted desires]. For he must be king *until he has put all his enemies under his feet* and the last of the enemies to be destroyed is death." "The sting of death is sin" (1 Cor. 15:56 JB).

On the day of the Parousia, on the last day of the reign of "death of the soul," sin, the sting of death, will vanish; its deathly power over souls will be destroyed. The signal will be given (the trumpets will sound) and all souls will rise again: they will come out of the sepulcher which is the body insofar as it is the seat of exalted desires, the cause of moral corruption.

"Because our present perishable nature must put on imperishability and this mortal nature must put on immortality" (1 Cor. 15:53 JB). This is one of the passages which—when taken literally—have been the most responsible for causing misunderstanding. In the terminology of the Apostle, the body during life is symbolically immortalized when its animating principle is moral imperishability. The body is imagined as being the envelope of the soul. Thus it is called "the sepulcher of the dead soul" or "the tent that we live in on earth" (2 Cor. 5:1 JB). And since the body should shelter an imperishable soul, freed from death whose sting is sin, it is necessary—says the Apostle—that already during life this perishable and mortal body put on imperishability and immortality (that it become the garment, that it shelter an imperishable soul freed from the death that is sin). All the meaning of the Epistles is to be found in this demand that the body (earthly desires) be glorified. From the symbol of the "death through sin" of Adam up to the symbol of the resurrection of Christ through "death to sin," the Epistles—like the Gospels—are concerned, according to their deepest meaning, with man's immanent responsibility for his behavior whether negative or positive. The images of transcendence are only a symbolic wrapping.

What matters is to see through this wrapping since the confusion that mistakes symbol for concept and image for reality can only satisfy the most primitive and animistic layers of the human soul.

A comparative study of the texts is certainly useful. But most important is to understand the symbolism. The latter remains detectable in spite of the unconscious tendency of the translators to alter the meaning in order to fit the doctrine.

The symbolic significance has been illustrated in this book through a few examples only. Let those—believers or atheists—who prefer lucidity to blinding bias read the texts with the guidelines we suggest. Confronted with the many significant passages, it will be difficult for them not to perceive the truth.

Literal exegesis was a historical necessity, since there was no method for true understanding and only centuries of effort have succeeded in bringing it forth. Symbolic exegesis shocks pious tradition. But piety, in order to be genuine and valid, must keep to the sources of tradition, to the texts and to the restoration of their deep significance.

The present work should be proof that the central theme of symbolization is concerned with the death and life of "the soul," from the fall of Adam into banalization (death of the soul) to the resurrection of the man Jesus during his earthly life.

The truth about the meaning of life present in all myths can, through its psychological translation, emerge from the "tomb" where religious dogmatism has buried it. The hope of a renewal of essential life and of culture, outside the beaten paths of moralizing and amoralizing conventions, can thus be found in an understanding of symbolization and above all of the central symbol of "divinity." Only the elucidation of the "divinity" symbol can bring about a methodical and effective attack against vanity by offering to the human spirit the knowledge of the limits of its competence. For it is vanity to believe that only matter exists, just as it is vanity to believe that a real God exists. In both cases, man thinks that he is exempt from undertaking the essential work of harmonization even though the latter has always been proposed by the symbolic ethics of myths. Vanity can be vanquished, this is the message of joy expressed by all symbolization, and victory over vanity is the condition for essential rebirth. This message is all the more convincing if it is placed in the evolutionary perspective of the biological quest for satisfaction: progressive ascension towards greater consciousness and lucidity.